retrⓄHOME

retrOHOME

SUZANNE TROCME
PHOTOGRAPHY BY NEIL MERSH

WITHDRAWN

MITCHELL BEAZLEY

Previous page: A room by Danish architect–designer Verner Panton, who in the 1960s sought to promote the redemptive power of synthetic materials

This page: At Ivy Rosequist's nature-inspired California home, a Roman stone basin set upon a fir-wood plinth forms a sculpture

Following page: In Paris, decorative objects by Serge Roche are grouped in front of a mirror, whose frame encases butterflies by Bolette Natanson (c. 1934)

First published in Great Britain in 2000
by Mitchell Beazley, an imprint of Octopus Publishing Group
Limited, 2–4 Heron Quays, London E14 4JP

Executive Editor: **Judith More**
Executive Art Editor: **Janis Utton**
Project Manager: **Jo Richardson**
Project Editor: **Emily Asquith**
Layout Design: **Tony Spalding**
Special Photography: **Neil Mersh**
Picture Research: **Clare Gouldstone**
Production: **Catherine Lay**
Proof reading and indexing: **Kathleen M. Gill**

ISBN 1 84000 265 4

A CIP catalogue record for this book is available from the
British Library

Typeset in Gill Sans
Printed and bound by Toppan Printing Co. (HK) Ltd.
Produced in China

Contents

Foreword

Susan Crewe, Editor-in-Chief of British *House & Garden* (who has a talent for nutshell commentary), once said to me that if you want to have your hair cut you should seek a good hairstylist, not attempt it yourself, and if you want to re-design or decorate your home, you should follow the same advice – consult a professional. My, less weighty, experience tells me to agree with this view, except that there seems to be a certain amount of room for scope with residential interior spaces, even if a professional has not been consulted, by way of "dressing" or personalizing – as you might dress your hair, wear a braid, or put on a hat or scarf, making the look complementary to the person you are.

The interiors covered in *Retro Home* are not professionally interior-designed nor architecturally altered or built spaces – with the exception of two: the 1990s case study, where it seemed relevant to accept the role of the architect in "normal" people's lives, which occurred with the advent of the "loft" as a feasible home; and the 1970s case study, a rooftop penthouse built by the father of the current owner. Instead, we reveal the homes of people from many walks of life who, through passion and dedication, have formed environments for their own comfortable living.

The intention has been to highlight those people who feel at home in a particular period from the 20th century, who can talk knowledgeably and lucidly about their collections, and who understand the development of ideas and the importance of new skills and the new materials that became available during their preferred era. The main players, whose homes have been selected to become the "case studies", have varied careers, ranging from architectural salvage specialists to an art consultant and a film professional, and are generally extremely occupied with other aspects of their lives but maintain a standard at home, in every nook, to be admired by even the most stringent interior designer.

The objective of the book is to open the doors of the 20th-century home and unfold the "looks" of each successive decade through the rooms of people living now, rather than to explore a chronology of the century's furniture and developments in design. Every interior in this book, whether designed by a professional or its occupant, is situated in design history and is, moreover, appropriate to the inhabitant. Archive shots and accounts of historical fact support this trail through the decades, providing inspiration for those who want to fall in line. Selection, or collecting, it seems, is really what this is all about. As the prescient Andrew Jackson Downing (1815–52), the American pundit on architecture and landscape gardening, remarked way back in the 19th century: "As a smile or a glance, in familiar conversation, often reveals to us more of the real character of a professional man than a long study of him at the pulpit or the bar, so a table or a chair will sometimes give us the intimate details of those who might be inscrutable in the hieroglyphics of white walls and plain ceilings."

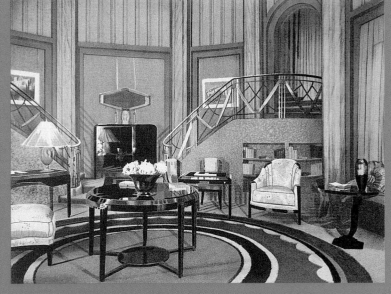

The death of Queen Victoria in 1901 not only marked the end of a long reign spanning 64 years, during which the power of the British Empire found its apogee and industry took its first great strides, but conveniently coincided with the beginning of a new century. This was a century in which developments in science, the arts, and technology would grow exponentially in comparison to previous centuries. As far as the home was concerned, Victorian England saw a period of boosted self-confidence for the self-made man, who used his house as a vehicle to exhibit his new-found prosperity gained through his industry. It was the family that was paramount in the scale of values of the time, and the home represented its haven.

Aesthetically speaking, the Victorian period was a confused time for styles – more retrospective than visionary. Although this mélange is often referred to as being "eclectic" – a word which today not only translates as "diverse" but "liberal" – Victorian style could be considered more as "motley", heterogeneous in nature, and certainly derivative, where a number of unrelated styles were simultaneously popular. A deep sense of nostalgia and continuity with tradition meant a resurgence in Elizabethan and Gothic architecture and interiors, as well as a strong representation of foreign styles, including Rococo, the florid Louis XV, and other historic styles that were not indigenous to England.

A typical Victorian interior could be crammed with overbearing wooden furniture and deep-buttoned, well-sprung upholstery. The prophetic John Ruskin, the leading writer on art and design in the 19th century and inspirer of the Arts

Opposite: Vanessa Bell and Duncan Grant resided at Charleston, a farmhouse in Sussex, England, from 1916 until the end of their lives. The drawing-room walls were originally stencilled by Bell in the late 1920s. The over-mantel painting and log box are by Grant, who also designed many of the rugs for the house.

Above: A studio in Macassar ebony, created for the 1925 "*Exposition des Arts Décoratifs et Industriels Modernes*", exemplifies Art Deco in its purest form, although the term was not coined until a decade later. The general effect of Art Deco was luxuriant elegance, clean lines, and a delight in ornament for its own sake.

1910s & 1920s

and Crafts Movement who sadly just missed the dawning of the new era, took issue with the Victorian habit of packing too much into a room. "I know what it is," he wrote, "to live in a cottage with a deal floor and roof and a hearth of mica slate; and I know it to be in many respects healthier and happier than living between a Turkey carpet and gilded ceiling, beside a steel grate and a polished fender." R. W. Edis, one of the key architect-designers of the Aesthetic Movement, in his book *Healthy Furniture and Decoration*, sensibly advised against the use of "jarring colours and patterns", particularly in the bedroom, as they would cause "nervous irritability". Nevertheless, against such advice from the health-conscious few, every inch of space was filled: walls were heavy with gilt-framed pictures and paltry miniatures; every surface supported trophies and souvenirs, pottery figures, shell-covered boxes, and other bric-a-brac; and trailing plants and aspidistras added a glimmer of life to what many might term an unimaginative hotchpotch of disarray, an audible conundrum. As one of the 20th-century's most prominent and far-seeking architects, Le Corbusier was quick to point out that "around 1900, a magnificent gesture – we shed the tatters of an old culture".

When Edward took the throne of England, the Golden Age was upon us and controversy was about to rear its head. The Glasgow School, which worked toward a statement of design in favour of modern, clean lines and which appeared new and unnostalgic, was initially considered "revolting", "hooliganistic", and "*avant-garde*". Developed by a group of artists and craftsmen who were based in Glasgow in Scotland on the cusp of the 20th century, the school's foremost designer was Charles Rennie Mackintosh, although there were other designers, such as Herbert MacNair and George Walton, who worked for commercial furniture manufacturers, as well as interior designers and architects. The school's original style used organic form, more likened to the work of the Austrian Vienna Secession, being less curvilinear than that of the Art Nouveau protagonists who worked in France and Belgium at the same time.

The Glasgow School despised clutter and appreciated the Japanese concern for simple boxed forms. Using this particular design vocabulary, they produced items for the entire home, including wall decorations, lighting, flatware, rugs, and stained-glass panels. Although

Below: A suburban terraced house in Bristol, England, built in 1937 and preserved in its original state, contains many features with roots in the 1910s and 1920s. The oak fire-surround was found in a local showroom. Such details as the picture rails, dados, and the stain-and-grain woodwork are typical of the period between the wars.

some of the manufacturers, such as Wylie and Lochhead, had outlets in London, the Glasgow style was not widely adopted in England. It appealed instead to the affluent sections of the community in its birthplace, which at the turn of the century was one of the most prosperous cities in the world. Glasgow was the first city in the United Kingdom in which both wife and husband held professions of near equal standing and where the standard of living was increased due to the prosperity of dual-income couples. The first Scottish boarding schools for ladies were founded in Glasgow, and the university was one of the first in Britain to admit women.

In England, a less structured *avant-garde* expression came about by way of the Bloomsbury set, which was made up of literary figures Virginia Woolf, Lytton Strachey, and E. M. Forster, and their painter friends Roger Fry, Vanessa Bell, and Duncan Grant. The painter and art critic Roger Fry believed that young artists should be able to earn a living not merely by the chancey sales of canvases but by the stimulating effect of creating a whole interior, including the design and decoration of tables, chairs, vases, bowls, jugs, and boxes to harmonize with wall-treatments and soft furnishings. Fry had begun to develop a coherent theory of aesthetics and was prepared to risk his reputation by passionately championing an art expressing freedom. In November 1910 Fry organized an exhibition at the Grafton Galleries in London, entitled "Manet and the Post-Impressionists". The reaction in the art world was one of outrage: "the crude efforts of children", "pavement pastellists", or simply "a jest". As a result, Fry forfeited the respect of the art establishment but found many new allies excited by Post-Impressionism.

In 1911 Fry enlisted the help of Duncan Grant, Macdonald Gill, Bernard Adeney, and others in executing a commission to decorate a hall for students at Borough Polytechnic. Following ideas Fry had conceived while witnessing mosaic artists in Constantinople, the group experimented with a new technique in laying on the paint. Fry felt that the delineation of colour and form in mosaic was allied to Cézanne's use of colour blocks in his paintings.

The project Fry set up in London, called the Omega Workshops, began in the summer of 1913 and was patronized by enthusiastic Bloomsbury followers as well as society figures and hostesses of influence. The artists decorated objects to

Above: A bedroom at Castle Drogo in Devon, England, presented in its original state, is clad in wooden panelling. Pre-war home-owners were not afraid to use muted tones, murky colours, and various combinations of wood tones, which gave natural warmth to a room. By contrast, warmth in Victorian interiors was achieved by using fabrics and rich colours.

1922

be sold from Omega's premises in Fitzroy Square, which gave them a small but regular income. Although it began well, Omega ran for a mere six years, in part due to World War I, which began a year after Omega's inception, and through the eventual dissension among its members. In its brief moment, Omega managed to achieve an explosion in the decorative arts unseen in England since William Morris led his movement in the previous century. The Omega Workshops, like the Glasgow School, were not allied to the Arts and Crafts Movement. Their closest model was possibly the Wiener Werkstätte, the decorative arts workshop started in 1903 by the artists of the Vienna Secession. Some of the main inspiration for the Secession's work also came from the French Post-Impressionists.

From the 1890s to the 1900s, Paris had clearly been the artistic capital of the world, with sculptors and painters converging on the city from every quarter. The hierarchy's stranglehold had been boldy broken by the French Impressionists, and talented painters and their bohemian friends challenged artistic barriers and current fashions. Paris's 1890s had been nicknamed "the naughty nineties", and the elegant and chic *beau monde* led a hectic life. The advent of the art poster alone – a new form of advertising made possible by the use of colour lithography – brought bustling life, excitement, and colour to the city in the early part of the century. Entertainments were accessible to all who could afford a drink, and the poster, advertising dancehalls and theatres, became a vehicle for the mixing of social classes.

By 1900 the population of Paris had grown to a total of 3.6 million – an increase of 3 million over a mere 100 years. The Industrial Revolution had created increased material wealth for society's middle classes, and appropriately, in 1889, Paris celebrated the centenary of the French Revolution with the World Fair, giving France the opportunity to display its increased financial status and achievements. The Eiffel Tower was the main attraction, built by Alexandre Gustave Eiffel, since, apart from being the tallest construction in the world at

Below: Irish furniture designer Eileen Gray, resident of Paris, designed a Monte Carlo room – a bedroom-cum-boudoir – that was exhibited in the *Salon des Artistes Décorateurs* in 1923. Monte Carlo was all the rage at the time, and the room was accented by a fur-covered sofa, used as a bed, with a black lacquer frame and plaster legs, and red and white lacquer panels on the walls.

that time, it was a monument to the engineering challenges of the late 19th century.

Freedom of expression was all the rage and materials were being challenged. In Paris of the 1910s, on a typical tree-lined boulevard an Art Nouveau house would boast a wrought-iron or bronze banister to a magnificent staircase. The banister would be cast with climbing tendrils, flower heads, and auricular motifs – a style that drew from nature and attempted to bring about the feeling of movement by the elegant, sinuous, and twisting use of line. Emile Gallé, or Louis Majorelle, another leading furniture designer, might have made the carved furniture, inlaid with floral marquetry, or the glass with all its opacity, iridescence, and saturated colour.

Continuity was an important aspect to Art Nouveau and a sense of stylistic unity would prevail throughout the home, with the same motifs appearing again and again – lilies here, dragonflies there. Most popular among aesthetes, Art Nouveau became the dominant style in France from the 1890s until the outbreak of war, its exponents succeeding in creating an entirely new decorative language.

Following the success of the Universal Exhibition in Paris in 1900, which confirmed France's pre-eminence in the creation of Art Nouveau, the *Société des Artistes Décorateurs* in 1901 planned an exhibition to improve the standards of French design and link France to the rest of the globe. It was also poised to challenge exhibitions held by the German Deutscher Werkbund. Because of World War I, the exhibition, called the "*Exposition des Arts Décoratifs et Industriels Modernes*", was postponed from 1915 until 1925. Although this marked the zenith of Art Deco (the style's name is a shortened form of the exhibition's name), the effect this moment had on the design world was not wholly felt until the 1930s, when it streamlined into Odeon and Moderne styles and hit the movie screens. Functionalism and "fitness for purpose" became the watchwords of Modernists springing from the exhibition, who influenced every aspect of design from entire housing projects to easy chairs (see pp. 31–33).

Above: This young girl's bedroom is by French designer Emile Jacques Ruhlmann, whose work flourished following his exhibit at Paris's *Salon d'Automne* in 1913. At the 1925 Exposition, his work, which used precious veneers, shagreen, and the finest of leathers, was considered a summing-up of the new style. He favoured the *gondôle* form, as exemplified here in the *chaise longue*.

Left: At Charleston, Grant
and Bell painted figurative
and abstract images on
screens, table-tops, metal
trays, vases, mantelpieces,
and doors, as well as creating
fabrics and carpets.

Below: A door painted by
Duncan Grant in a book-lined
study. Freedom of expression
and experimentation led to
hand-painted walls with
intricate detailing and motifs
in casual and flowing strokes.

Creating the Look

During the early 1910s, French fashion designer Paul Poiret decided to encourage the free creativity he so admired in the works of Josef Hoffmann, Koloman Moser, and Gustav Klimt. He took 15 working-class schoolgirls, with no formal art training, and urged them to open their eyes to the scenes around them, from the market-places to Paris's hothouses. He subsequently left them to transcribe their impressions into designs for fabrics, painted pottery, murals, and painted furniture. This instinctive and accessible approach to art is one of the hallmarks of the era. The free hand, a pair of open eyes, and an understanding of colour and form is all that is needed to create interiors reminiscent of the heady, bohemian 1910s and 1920s.

To re-create the atmosphere of the period, consider the colours characteristic of the Post-Impressionists – a harmony of grey-greens, blue, ochre, and Indian red with accents of black – and the way in which colour was organized. Marbling, stippling, and stencilling, or simple painted abstracts, can decorate walls, floors, doors, and furniture in the manner of Vanessa Bell and Duncan Grant. A rustic elegance and comfort can be attained by adding hand-dyed

Right: In the 1920s, fringing and beading for the skirts of tables and consuls became a flippant, more flirtatious, alternative to plain fabric. In the Victorian era, coverings were used to obscure table legs, which were considered too erotic to be seen.

Left: Free-standing chests, stools, screens, and bath panelling have been decorated to add charm to an otherwise plain Charleston bathroom, with its stained and waxed floors and treated walls.

Right: Mme Lafort's Paris bedroom was decorated by Jacques Grange in an *egyptianate* manner. Topical issues and foreign travel have long been inspiration for decorating ideas. Egypt was a relevant theme in the 1920s due to the discovery of Tutankhamun's tomb in 1922.

curtains, cushions, bedcovers, and chair-covers, or painted silk shawls. Collage hangings, embroidered panels, and batiks, like those produced by Omega, will create a lively backdrop in studies or bedrooms.

Glamour was a key watchword in the newly decadent 1910s and 1920s for urbanites desiring to reflect an opulent lifestyle; a "look" to precede the more stylized Hollywood glamour. Decoratively framed mirrors and mirrored-glass details instantly add glitz to any room, as can the addition of crystal chandeliers, as seen in antiquarian Louis Bofferding's townhouse (see p. 25). Bofferding also fabricated a mirrored wall frieze using antiqued mirrored tiles with uniformly spaced bronze bosses, framing the outer edges with gilt-wood objects. Lacquer, ivory, bronze, and gilt- and blonde-wood furniture exude richness, and every piece should speak for itself.

For putting on the ritz, paper taffeta silks in fuschia pinks, together with teal and midnight blue or silver and gold tones as curtaining and cushions, serve to invoke the atmosphere of the Jazz Age salon of the 1920s. A cocktail cabinet is simply vital for existence. The flapper's late 1920s boudoir, always light and airy, included the new fashionable dressing table.

Left: Louis Bofferding's Manhattan home conjures the spirit of the truly eclectic 1920s in a masculine bedroom laden with many rare books. The 1930s rock crystal chandelier balances the austerity of the French Empire bed. The white candlestick is early 20th-century Indian.

Below: Artifacts on display in this Harlem bedroom are *objets trouvés* from thrift and junk shops. The American horn bedside lamps add a touch of the surreal. The bedhead, in front of a contemporary canvas, is a pair of wrought-iron gates with oak beads. The bed drapes allude to Poiret.

Below: French high-back fireside chairs have painted frames and gold detailing, and a pair of commodes of unknown origin flank the fireplace. Collections include George Briard glass plates and Vienna Secession vases.

Right: A zebra-patterned rug suggests further eccentricities in this palazzo apartment. Wild animal rugs came into vogue in the early 1900s. The Rococo Revival furniture alludes to Elsie de Wolfe's Old French Look.

Harlem Palazzo

Between 1901 and 1908, William Waldorf Astor, who built the Waldorf Astoria Hotel and the Hotel Astor, took advantage of the new land laws in New York City facilitating building on larger plots. For the first time, buildings could span the length and breadth of a city block. Astor commissioned three enormous apartment buildings: one on the East Side; a second on the West Side; and Graham Court, which stretches from 116th to 117th Streets on Seventh Avenue in Harlem. Built by architects Clinton and Russell and designed around a courtyard to emulate a Florentine palazzo, Graham Court became home to the wealthiest of Harlem families.

Clair Watson, a British conceptual designer and stylist, and her Chicago-born husband moved their family into a fourth-floor apartment in Graham Court because it displayed the florid characteristics of European Beaux-Arts architecture and contained palatial rooms of perfect classical proportion with intricate cornicing, panelling, and mosaic floor designs. It epitomized the new clarity that arose as a reaction against the Victorian confusion prevalent at the turn of the century. Having previously worked as a fashion director for an Italian clothing company and later for

charity organizations in the vanguard of taking thrift stores into a stylish and accepted realm, Watson has developed special skills in collating colourful fabrics, second-hand furniture, and *objets trouvés*. Although her furnishings are collected from disparate origins, they maintain a look that is relevant to the period of the apartment. "The building has such a history it makes sense to evoke the opulence of the era – to have rich and plentiful things around, to exhibit the cornucopia of the early part of the Golden Age, before the austerity of the wars struck the world."

Draped silks, velvets, animal skins, beaded lampshades, tassels, leather-bound books, needlepoint or embroidered cushions, and elegant carved wood and inlay furniture help to create the prettiness and legerity of a time of prosperity. "I particularly enjoy the fluidity of the art of the early century: the flora and fauna depicted with lightness of stroke, and figurative paintings in which colours seem quite bright and womenfolk unrestricted," says Watson, who has taken this to a further dimension by adding her own fluid strokes of turquoise paint around her drawing-room walls. "The period I feel at home in is one without restriction, where expression is everything."

Left: In a niche of the dining room, an American daybed is draped in pashminas and cashmere blankets. The needlepoint on the wall is a recent homage to artist Frank Stella. The pedestal dish is Lalique and the sequinned fruits were hand-made for the war effort.

Below: In the master bedroom, the Art Deco dressing table with brocade panels is German and a 1960s Gucci belt hangs to the left of the mirror. Watson's clothing and shoe collection includes colourful designs by major fashion houses from the entire century.

Left: The drinks trolley by Jacques Adnet (1946) is brass, mirror, and fruitwood. The armchair is upholstered in azure blue 18th-century document cut velvet.

Opposite: Shards of rock crystal sit on the Beistegui table. The mahogany screen is covered in a Directoire *toile de jouy*. The walnut chair is by Lelarge.

Below: A 19th-century English porter's chair is flanked by 1950s chairs. The Jazz Age porcelain bust is by Richard Janori (1925), with a 1930s reclining lady.

East Side Townhouse

Having devoted his home on New York's elegant East Side to a "by appointment only" gallery, antiquarian Louis Bofferding literally lives with and loves the collections he sells. His collections range from 17th-century Italian to 1960s French furniture, but the spirit, he says, typifies that of the 1920s when colour was myriad and strong, almost vibrant, mirrors were in abundance, fabrics mattered, and where eccentrically diverse objects cohabited. "I recently acquired a circular table from the Beistegui collection in Paris," he says. Carlos de Beistegui, deemed a true arbiter of taste, was an ardent art and furniture collector whose contributions to interior design spanned a half-century until his death in 1970. "The table is nothing underneath, but the history is there and the fabric and trimmings are exquisite," Bofferding says of the blue, heavily skirted table.

"Frivolity and fun with underlying integrity is really what interests me – quality, fineness, grace, and romance," further claims Bofferding. "The 19th-century Venetian mirror valances [atop his drawing-room windows] used to belong to Rose Cumming," he says. The intricately detailed mirrors, featuring a lion motif, held pride of place for over 25 years in the interior

Left: A silk ikat (*c.* 1900) on a hyacinth-coloured velvet 19th-century Irish sofa is framed by a Belle Epoque mirrored screen by Bernados (it has movable ormolu candle branches). The cabriolet-legged table by Jansen (*c.* 1940s) came from Elsie de Wolfe's suite at New York's St. Regis Hotel.

Below: Bofferding created the wall frieze using antiqued mirrors and bronze bosses, framed by a pair of Belle Epoque gilt-wood palm trees. The black lacquer commode is by Jansen (*c.* 1950) and the chairs are by Moreux. The commode holds a Louis XVI urn and a pair of gigantic rook chess pieces (*c.* 1700).

designer's New York townhouse. Bofferding found them in Dallas, Texas, and brought them to New York, "although they are off to Palm Beach now," he admits.

Having previously sold contemporary art, Bofferding became a decorative arts dealer in 1994 because "clients always wanted to buy the chair they were sitting on rather than the painting". He handles a multitude of pieces designed by 20th-century *haute-couture* decorators, including Jean-Michel Frank, Georges Geoffroy, Elsie de Wolfe, Syrie Maugham, and Stéphane Boudin – all designers who embraced and re-interpreted the past instead of rejecting it. "It is the eclecticism, the mix, that entices me to collate these pieces together. I do not specialize but haplessly fall in love," says Bofferding. He not only knows the provenance of the pieces he collects but their relevance to the time. "Chairs are my favourite forms of furniture," Bofferding says, citing his gilt-iron chairs by Jean-Charles Moreux as superlative examples of sculpture, comfort, and elegance. "Many of these pieces come from a later period than the 1920s, are all glamorous, but are all objects that referenced the past and helped people feel grounded in wildly changing times. After all, style is about artifice, not authenticity."

The 1930s and 1940s were periods of extremes. On one hand, the world suffered the most dire Depression imaginable; on the other, it had never seen so many new millionaires. Newspaper magnate William Randolph Hearst, immortalized in the 1941 film *Citizen Kane*, had set the pace for such wealth when, in 1925, he sent his famous cablegram beginning: "Want buy castle in England…." Many of the new millionaires had made their fortunes in the United States and Canada, like Lord Beaverbrook (William Maxwell Aitken), who, having benefited financially from Canadian cement mills, arrived in London to take over half of Fleet Street. Lord Beaverbrook was eventually appointed by Prime Minister Winston Churchill to become a member of the war cabinet. Many bought their way into English society, favouring social events such as Ascot, Henley, and Cowes. Not all rich *arrivistes* wanted a castle like Hearst, but many bought traditional country seats and breathed new life into crusty old buildings. Nancy Astor, born into the respectable American Langhorne family, created an updated but classic interior in the stately home of Cliveden, which she and Waldorf Astor had been given as a wedding gift in 1906. At the time considered the foremost social and political centre in the country, it is today hallowed as one of the most influential interiors in England between the wars. At Cliveden Nancy Astor maintained a salon that exercised influence in many fields, notably foreign affairs. Lady Astor also broke new political ground by being, until her retirement in 1945, Britain's first female Member of Parliament. Her vitality, gaiety, trenchancy, and courage made her one of her generation's most noteworthy public figures.

Opposite: By 1932 European immigrants, including Viennese architects Rudolph Schindler and Richard Neutra, had brought Modern Movement design to the United States. After working for Frank Lloyd Wright in Los Angeles, Schindler built his own European Modernist house in West Hollywood.

Above: American Donald Deskey came to prominence when he won a competition for his New York City Music Hall furniture and furnishings in 1932–3. The powder room, shown here, contains typical Streamlined Moderne mirrors and a table. The contrasting florid wall decorations are by Yasuo Kuniyoshi.

1930s & 1940s

For many others, there was the stock market crash. From the moment the New York Stock Exchange closed its doors on Thursday 24 October 1929, the onset of the Depression had a massive impact in every major trading city, resonating to a worldwide financial slump. Unemployment peaked and the global economy would take a long time to recover. France, however, had a somewhat better time in the arts and fashion industries, although luxury fabrics were in short supply. The arts continued, as they always do, though in a reduced manner. For both decorative arts and fashion, the toll was far greater in other countries. Well-seasoned timber for fine furniture was scarce and exports to the United States were important to countries with colossal war debts. Paris, the epicentre of style and acknowledged leader of fashion, still attracted the rich and discriminating from other countries, which meant that a vast number of skilled artists could continue to divert and astonish clients with their masterpieces. The furniture, film set, and jewellery designer Paul Iribe, who was also a political critic, illustrator, and founder of *Le Mot* and *Le Témoin*, remained in the vanguard of keeping French things French and the "machine" away from man.

The debate on ornament, *Pour ou contre ornament*, had been ongoing since 1908, when Moravian architect Adolf Loos suggested that ornament was as attractive and necessary as graffiti and tattoos on prisoners' arms. Paul Iribe joined the battle to preserve ornamentation and in 1930 published a luxuriant volume *Choix*, which applauded the awakening of the "French genius". He considered the years following World War I to be a time of "mourning", which resulted primarily from mass production and the standardization of furniture. In its place he advocated French furniture, "because it is at the same time luxuriant and feminine, conceived for women, and we are the sole race to be able to create it". He commented "the machine has killed luxury" and he sought "the arabesque that is a bird, a woman, a flower, a song, a perfume…that is the word, the dream; that is French thought, because we don't think in cubes, nor in machines".

The complexity and the diversity of Iribe – his talent, his passion, his nationalistic tendencies, and his political motivation – reflects the tenor of the early part of the 20th century in France.

Below: The infiltration of Art Deco into ordinary homes was less pervasive in Britain than in France and America. It did, however, prevail in public auditoriums, cinemas, and theatres under the guise of the distinctive Odeon style.

Many theories advanced by the Bauhaus movement were entirely abhorrent to the French decorative artist or designer who prided himself on his inherent "good taste" during the 1930s. Not all French decorative artists were as adamant or nationalistic about the future of fine furniture as Iribe, but the debate was widening.

The Paris 1925 Exposition had existed to challenge exhibitions held by German designers associated with the Deutscher Werkbund, which had been founded in 1908 by architect and artist Peter Behrens, supported by Hermann Muthesius and Henry van der Veld, with the intention of improving German design by bringing together manufacturers and artists. Walter Gropius, endorsing a Modernist aesthetic, found favour with the Deutscher Werkbund, and from 1919 went ahead to set up the Bauhaus. The Paris Expo, in turn, aimed to improve standards of French design and created a platform for both the decorative artist possessing fine skills and the modern architect with neoteric vision. If the exhibition had been staged on time, between 1907 and 1912 as originally planned, architects such as the Swiss-born Le Corbusier would not have developed such a clear modernistic vision and the results would have been vastly different. As it turned out, the "*Exposition Internationale des Arts Décoratifs et Industriels Modernes*" became the seminal moment in 20th-century design history, exposing both Modernism and high decorative style to the delegates who flocked from all countries. Both styles had enormous impact on the decades to follow, the stricter Modernism witnessed in the 1930s later appearing as the new Contemporary aesthetic in the 1950s, and high decorative style becoming the popular vision of Art Deco in the 1930s and 1940s, which saw a resurgence as late as the 1970s.

Le Corbusier, born Charles-Edouard Jeanneret, moved from Switzerland to Paris in 1920 and was one who represented the Modernists at the 1925 Paris exhibition. Having worked under Peter Behrens in Berlin before dedicating his efforts to perfecting architectural theory in the 1920s, he was a link between the Germans and the French. His "engineer's aesthetic" was clearly evident in his Esprit Nouveau pavilion at the exhibition. Le Corbusier continued his German associations in 1927 when he took part in a Deutscher Werkbund project in Stuttgart, Germany, with Ludwig Mies van der Rohe and Walter Gropius. Mies van

Above: Lloyd Loom chairs are here seen in a conservatory in the hotel on Burgh Island, off England's Devon coast. The exterior of the building has remained unchanged since the 1930s. Mainly mass-produced period furniture decorates the interior.

Below: The American Institute of Interior Decorators, now the American Society of Interior Designers, was established in 1931. Trade magazines were also founded at the time, including *The Decorators' Digest*, renamed *Interior Design* in the 1950s, and *Home Furnishings*. This interior was featured in the popular *House & Garden*.

der Rohe took over the Bauhaus in 1930. Architect Hannes Meyer had taken charge from 1928–30, but was considered a communist sympathizer, and Gropius had retired in 1928. When the Bauhaus was closed by the Nazis in 1932, the United States became the focus for Modern architecture and design, with most of the staff emigrating, some via London, including Gropius, Mies van der Rohe, Hungarian constructivist László Moholy-Nagy, Marcel Breuer, and Erich Mendlesohn. In 1937 the New Bauhaus was formed in Chicago. Following the 1932 "Modern Architecture: International Exhibition" at New York's Museum of Modern Art in connection with Philip Johnson and Henry-Russell Hitchcock, the Modernists' American work was also coined the International Style, from the exhibition's accompanying catalogue entitled *International Style: Architecture since 1922*. The movement was characterized by internal spaces that could be altered and a lack of applied decoration.

Considered the Parisian equivalent of the Deutscher Werkbund, the *Union des Artistes Modernes* was founded in 1929 by furniture designers and architects who had contributed to the Paris Expo, including Pierre Chareau, Robert Mallet-Stevens, Eileen Gray, and others, who cared little for their political theorizing but embraced the industrial materials favoured by the Modern movement, such as glass bricks, iron beams, and concrete. All styles popular in the 1930s and 1940s had been represented in some way at the Paris exhibition, not least Art Deco. Travel abroad often inspired designers of Art Deco interiors and furniture. The Swiss artisan Jean Dunand designed a smoking room for "A French Embassy Abroad" for his pavilion at the Expo, which included Cubist-inspired chairs and lacquered walls. Many public buildings in Britain and the United States adopted the Art Deco theme. In Britain a look termed Odeon developed, since a quantity of cinemas (two per week by 1935) were being built in the style.

The flamboyant but stylized Art Deco combined with Modernism in America to form Moderne, a popular translation of Deco for public and private buildings. Some mavericks took what they had seen in Paris and made it wholly theirs, like

Minnesota-born Donald Deskey, whose Streamlined Moderne became a distinctly American style. Due to its exposure on film sets, Streamlined Moderne largely encapsulates what is understood today to be Art Deco. The furniture is based on fundamental shapes – the circle, the square, and the triangle. Lines are sleek and curves free-form yet simple. Furniture was low and horizontal. Wood, which featured highly in French Art Deco, was less popular in the United States than brass, chrome, aluminium, and glass. A new kind of contemporary decoration explored the use of exposed neon and strip lighting.

Apart from the glamour of Hollywood, interior design began making real headway as a profession. Former actress Elsie de Wolfe followed the teachings of architect Ogden Codman and the novelist Edith Wharton, who together wrote the book *The Decoration of Houses* (1897). De Wolfe decorated her own home before going on to design the interior of Madison Avenue's Colony Club in 1905. She was the first professional to call herself an Interior Decorator on her business card. De Wolfe preferred a look that became known as the "Old French Look", an Americanized version of the amalgamated later Louis XV, Louis XVI, and Directoire periods, and other decorators soon followed suit. The look found its heyday in the 1930s and early 1940s through her interiors and the work of Francis Elkins in California and Syrie Maugham in England and America.

In England, Lady Sibyl Colefax had developed her own elegant version of the "English Country House" look when she turned from society hostess to decorating in 1933, having lost her fortune in the Wall Street crash. She took on John Fowler as a partner in 1938, and in doing so, forged one of the most important decorating firms of the 20th century, still active today. Surprisingly, many interior design companies survived World War II. Colefax and Fowler used mattress ticking to economize and the American Eleanor Brown, founder of the design firm McMillen Inc., designed miniature room sets rather than rooms for photographic purposes. When Colefax retired in 1946, the business was bought by another society hostess, the American Nancy Lancaster, a niece of Nancy Astor, who had been inspired to become a decorator when visiting Cliveden.

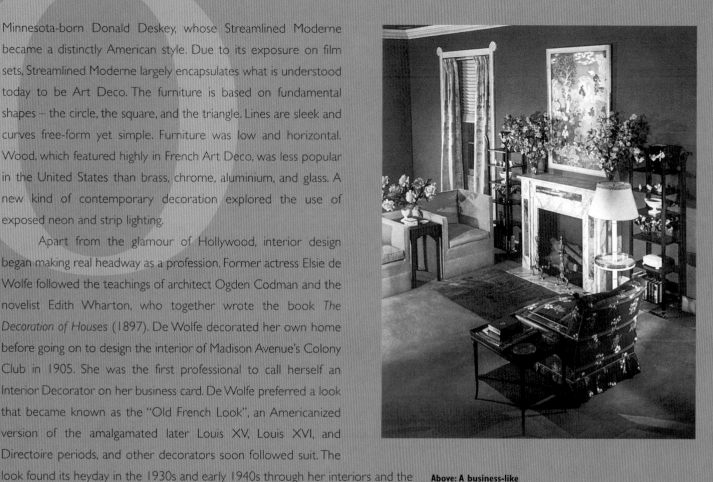

Above: A business-like approach and more extensive formal training aided the rise in status of the interior decorator, as did the improvement in shelter magazine quality, exemplified by this photograph from a 1940s issue of *House & Garden*. Many decorators owned stores, like T. H. Robsjohn-Gibbings, who had architectural training.

Creating the Look

When Elsie de Wolfe heard that Syrie Maugham intended to go into interior decorating, she allegedly commented that with six professional decorators in the world, there were quite enough already! During the first half of the century, professional decorating was considered only for the powerful, rich, and well-connected.

Even Cecil Beaton, who counted the few top decorators of the 1930s and 1940s as his friends, believed that anyone with flair could dress their own interiors. As he explained in *The Glass of Fashion*, first published in 1954, "Interior decorators have come into their own during the past 30 years. Their purpose, like that of the couturier, has been to anticipate taste, to run before it, and often create it…. Whereas a dressmaker can create a dress that the woman, unless she is unusually skilled, is unlikely to produce herself, the interior decorator has invaded a field that any person of taste should be able to cope with."

Interior decorators of the time found inspiration abroad and in fantasy. Elsie de Wolfe translated French style into American homes, which she had interpreted in her own home – the Villa Trianon – in the grounds of the Palace of Versailles. De Wolfe was

particularly fond of walls painted a refreshing white, bold stripes, and the delicate white-painted French furniture of Louis XV or XVI style. When forced to move back to America with the onset of World War II, the transformation of the "ugliest house" in Beverly Hills included the addition of green and white stripes to her rooms. *Parquet de Versailles* or black lacquered flooring formed a chic backdrop for unusual interjections, such as leopardskin-covered banquettes and bamboo bars with high stools. Her style was comfortable and traditional to a point, but lively, light-hearted, and elegant. One of her own inventions, popular in conservatories and appearing in The Colony Club on Madison Avenue, was to use trellises as an indoor device, bringing the garden indoors. An exponent of high style, her Paris bathroom could have been a film set. The size of a bedroom, it featured a sofa covered in zebraskin, a mirrored cocktail cabinet, a white velvet rug, silver curtains, and mother-of-pearl light fittings.

Syrie Maugham produced her own ranges of painted furniture. She developed a distressed finish called craquelure, where paint, many layers of varnish, and a secret technique gave a crackled texture to wood surfaces. Although known for her all-white

Left: Von Hulle, the designer for Scooter jewellery, re-creates Tangiers in the 1940s by enhancing the archways in her Paris apartment. Fabric-draped French club chairs form an arrangement around a table by Isamu Noguchi (1944).

Below: The bathroom and dressing room show a linking floor treatment, though here the tiles are smaller in scale. Plain walls, symmetrical archways, and an eclectic mix of patterned fabrics and robes, found on travels, are dominant features.

Left: Russell Bush's exquisite Park Avenue apartment is full to the brim with Cecil Beaton memorabilia. Beaton's own bed takes up most of the bedroom. A table supports work by Beaton, one showing the British model Twiggy hanging from the same bed in the 1960s.

Right: Interior designer Bush has acquired some of the rarest Beaton images, including Beaton's self-portrait sketch of his legs with the inscription "Finis". The oil portrait of Stephen Tennent, based on a photograph by Beaton, is by Lawrence Mynott.

Below: A beige and black drawing room, designed by Harry Schule, includes rare pieces: a 1930s sofa designed by architect Albert Mayer and a pair of Arteluce lamps (1957), which blend with the overall Deco-luxe style. Curtain trim complements the zebraskin rug.

schemes in the early 1930s, Maugham had passions for different colours at different moments, although always used in a single block for boldness.

Aim for an international flavour and sense of glamour when drawing from the styles of the great decorators. Alternatively, put together rooms to reflect the heady days of British colonial living. The club was a popular meeting place for ex-patriots on foreign soil and reflected a combination of local details and British features. On returning home, the interiors of ex-pats often reflected the life they had adjusted to elsewhere. For those who did not travel, the cinema provided, and can still provide, a source of inspiration for styles with their roots in Art Deco.

An entire scheme can be created to identify with a particular country, as Zaza von Hulle achieved in her Paris apartment. Solid blocks of wall colour, North African rugs and floor cushions, and brass trays and urns mesh with 1940s French club chairs to express her version of 1940s Tangiers. One or two pieces from far-away travels could be used to subtly evoke a theme – by adding a Chinese commode, or by using oriental fabric to rejuvenate a chair or as a tablecloth, to suggest a life abroad.

Right: A portrait photograph of Lady Hazel Lavery, a great 1930s beauty and socialite, and wife of painter John Lavery, was taken in the late 1920s. Books, including Beaton's *India Album* about distant travels, are delightful mementos of the era.

Left: The jammed credenza in Bush's sitting room is American (*c.* 1815). Books from his Cecil Beaton collection include *Face of the World* and *The Glass of Fashion* in which illustrious personalities of Beaton's era are characterized, including Diana Vreeland, Lady Diana Cooper, and Elsa Schiaparelli.

Right: At the far end of Clive Kandel's Manhattan drawing room, books are encased behind chicken wire so they can "breathe". A collection of furniture by Syrie Maugham includes an ivory leather stool and a sofa covered in raspberry moiré silk. The circular buttoned stool is Napoleon III.

Below left: A Venetian
blackamoor and miniature
Regency *récamier* sit in the
corner of the apartment.
"The console behind was
formerly in a Rothschilds'
Fifth Avenue apartment."

Right: The grey striped
Lenygon-style armchairs, grey
console table against the
wall, and a pair of occasional
tables were designed for the
De Witt Wallace house in
Mount Kisco, New York.

Upper East Side Apartment

Collector and advisor Clive Kandel is president of his eponymous firm, which specializes in custom design and the re-creation of the finest jewellery in the world. His clients are prominent individuals and prestigious department stores, including New York's Bergdorf Goodman and London's Harrods. He handles and designs both precious and costume pieces, preferring not to distinguish between the two and avoiding the words "real" or "fake". To Kandel, all of his creations are "real". It is only that the majority of his most commercially viable pieces have synthetic stones, which, with the use of modern technology, can replicate the real stones. "You just have to turn a piece over to see the level of workmanship involved to see it is the same."

Along with a shrewd eye and an outstanding knowledge of the history of jewellery, Kandel has a passion for all the decorative arts, expressing most interest in the halcyon days preceding World War II when "some women had the luxury of time". Admitting to having led a life of serendipity, he says "I am a collector of many fine things for my own home, which I find mainly at auction. The sofa in the drawing room came from a remarkable Park Lane penthouse

Left: The sconces and ceiling light are by Baguès Frères. The dining suite with ivory leather-seated chairs is by Syrie Maugham. The silverware is 18th-century English and the china, a white and gilt chinoiserie pattern by Rouard, is from 1928.

Below: The 1930s palm tree lamp, made from glass and corrugated aluminium, has completely unknown origins. The grey console is by 1930s designer Syrie Maugham and the painted panelled screen "in Rex Whistler-style" is 1930s English.

apartment, from Lady Edwina Mountbatten's former bedroom, for which architect Ogden Codman made the furniture," explains the British-born collector. Other extraordinary finds include a pair of chairs in their original fabric, partners of which are at Monkton, Edward James's semi-surreal home in rural England. "James's were re-covered in a green and white bold undulating design in the 1970s; these are part of the set, from his Viennese actress wife, Tilly Losch."

Admiring interior decorators of the pre-war years, such as Elsie de Wolfe, Syrie Maugham, and Rose Cumming, Clive Kandel appreciates the relevance of French Baroque to an elegant interior. His seating arrangement includes cabriole-legged armchairs and stools that have been painted or limed. Elsie de Wolfe called the limed furniture, *de rigueur* in the early 20th century, the Old French Look.

Through Cartier, Kandel understands France; through Fabergé, he knows Russia. Although a resident of New York since the early 1980s, his home reflects his unerring ability to pull together beautiful objects from diverse origins, usually as a result of his wide travelling excursions. "I have an association with India too," says Kandel, "hence the name Clive."

Left Bank Apartment

Laurent and Aline Maréchal are experts in French 20th-century furniture and artifacts. Unlike other young gallery owners and furniture dealers, they usually keep the pick of the crop for their own collection. "It is so rare to find some of these, like the mirror by Max Ingrand, one of the finest we have ever seen, the only one of its kind produced specifically for an exhibition in the 1940s. We dare not let them go, and we like to keep them as references for other objects we find later. We are trying to preserve as much knowledge as possible about this period, which 10 or 15 years ago was shrouded in mystery." Some of the pieces, like the pair of mirror-legged stools or *tabourets* in mint-green satin, were found at auction in California, but many objects are discovered by luck in *brocantes* and flea markets.

During the 1930s and 1940s in France, many forward-thinking *ensembliers* and cabinetmakers produced furniture in rare and precious materials, but with simplicity of style in mind. The two button-backed walnut chairs in the window of the salon, with their low backs, slub-weave fabric, and deep-seat proportions, look as if they might originate from the 1950s but were produced as early as 1925 by Marc

Right: In the dining corner, shells and vases, a mirrored urn, and a cabinet are all by Serge Roche. The wall mirror is by Bolette Natanson (*c.* 1934). Dining chairs are by Emile Jacques Ruhlmann, a 1950s lamp is by Michel Bufet, and the 1940s ceiling light is by Gilbert Poillerat.

du Plantier. The other four chairs, also by du Plantier, are of a later period. Two have been re-upholstered in coral velvet while the other pair are still covered in their original fabric, a chunkier and more modern-looking textile than might have been expected.

The backdrop for the collection has been carefully considered. Interior doors have been sanded and limed. The *parquet de Versailles* is perfect and needed only finishing. The walls are mottled, having been painted in a neutral matte sand colour to contrast with the gilded metal and ironwork of some of the furniture. "We have added some lamps from later decades because their design is so strong and the materials right," says Aline. "The dining chairs are much earlier, from the late 1910s to the early 1920s, and are by Emile Ruhlmann, who used costly and warm woods incorporated into simple and elegant forms." Ruhlmann was also inspired by an earlier time – the Vienna Secession from the turn of the century.

In choosing to collect such incredibly rare pieces, the Maréchals prove they understand the quality of design from the glorious French period at a time when the rest of the world was looking at the machine. "We collect sentimentally," says Aline.

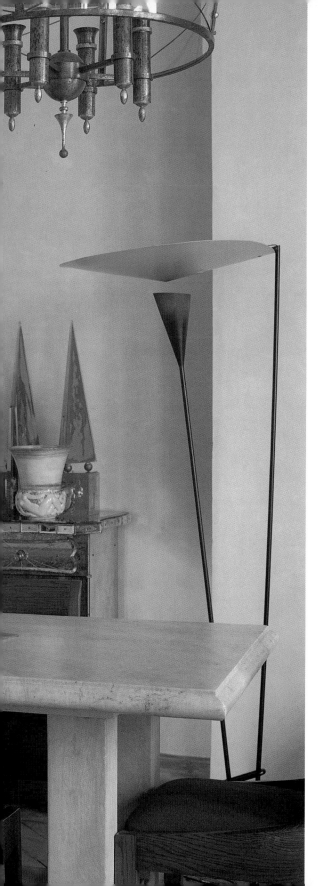

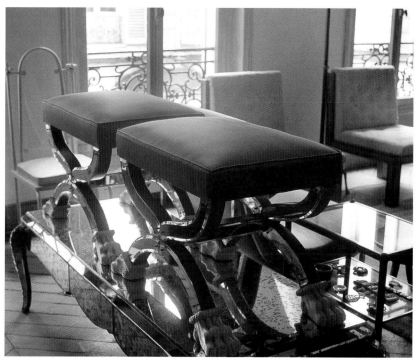

Above: A pair of mirror-legged *tabourets* by Serge Roche for Elsie de Wolfe are covered with green satin fabric, which is of the period but not original. A glass case displays jewellery by Line Vautrin, including a bracelet depicting the seven deadly sins. The coffee table is by Dolt.

Left: The marble fireplace with its shell motif is original to the rue Dauphine apartment. A black ceramic figure is attributed to André Arbus, the mirrored urns are by Serge Roche, and the chair is by Marc du Plantier.

Early in the 1950s, Italian magazine director, architect, and designer Gio Ponti commented: "Everything is going from the heavy to the light, from the gross to the subtle, from the opaque to the transparent, from dark to light, from colourless to colourful, from the fragmentary to the unitary, from the complicated to the linear. Anyone who is going in the opposite direction is in error." Ponti was remarking on the concurrent contrasting tendencies: the popularity of classicism, coupled with a passion for rampant decoration (as expressed by the Novocento and the decorative work of designer Piero Fornasetti, in collaboration with Ponti), and the strictness of Modernism, which had its beginnings 25 years earlier.

Economic growth in Continental Europe and the United States in the 1950s led to a surge in housebuilding, which became increasingly industrialized and mechanized. The housing boom was matched by a rise in interest in goods made from modern materials, ownership of which was perceived as a sign of a new, more affluent lifestyle. In this period of high ideals and mass-market production, the Modern eventually became mainstream and the style known as "Contemporary" emerged. Contemporary design began to influence not only luxurious household items, such as silverware and fine glassware, but practical goods, such as curtain fabric,

Opposite: The Parco dei Principi hotel, close to Sorrento on Italy's Amalfi coast, designed by Gio Ponti in 1959, features ceramic wall plaques, tapered-leg chairs, and mosaic flooring.

Above: Comfort was the major tenet of the 1950s "lounge"; the unified seating suggested a new relaxed attitude toward living. With lower seating, the coffee table became a primary addition.

1950s

earthenware crockery, light fittings, refrigerators, and linoleum. It was accessible to all, even those not fortunate enough to live in a newly built home. But for those with architect-built housing, modern design was fully embraced, and represented newness in a world that had been disrupted by war. Whereas "modern" in the 1930s represented functionalism and austerity, in the 1950s it was identified with independent spirit, liberation, and playfulness.

After the poverty of the Depression, Americans embraced consumerism and aspired to the American Dream, and the nuclear family was born. The vinyl-floored fitted kitchen became an anchor for the home, a "workstation" for the modern housewife. Furniture utilized new technologies alongside new materials. The influence of Good Design was evident in mass-produced and utilitarian objects. Easy chairs, for example, were composed of three singular elements: the supporting structure, padding, and cover. Storage pieces could be easily assembled and disassembled. In Ponti's words, this new approach was "beautiful, pure, simple, and without excess".

Immediately following World War II, stacking and mounting became valued considerations in furniture design. Flat-packing kept export costs down, which was imperative when dealing with low-cost goods. Stackable furniture also translated well into such public spaces as conference halls and schools.

Experiments in the properties of new materials meant forms could defy previously imagined limitations: they could become bulbous or be stretched. This encouraged designers to find inspiration in organic and amoeboid forms. Charles Eames and Eero Saarinen investigated the artistic possibilities of new materials. Charles and Ray Eames experimented with bending plywood, making great strides in aluminium and plastic. Their "Shell" armchair (1949), with single moulded seat-and-back unit, was made of fibreglass-reinforced polyester resin and appeared in homes, schools, and auditoriums across America. Its popularity was due, in part, to its lightness of weight, durability, and ease of storage. Eero Saarinen's collaborations with Eames – his designs usually consisting of an ergonomically formed single-unit seat supported by tapered metal legs – were mass-produced by

Below: Designers produced abstract wallpapers and fabrics with a strong sense of modernity for department stores, including Lucienne Day for Heals from 1954.

America's leading manufacturers, the Knoll Furniture Company and Herman Miller. The latter manufactured innovative storage units, such as George Nelson's "Basic Storage Components" (1949), featuring open shelves, a cupboard, desk, and drawers, whose main attraction was in its ability to replace a non-supporting wall.

Interior designer Russell Wright experimented with melamine, vinyl-spun aluminium, and other metals in creating functional objects, including a chair with a concealed writing table and oven-to-tableware. Wright's highly popular "American Modern" dinnerware design (1937) remained in production until 1957.

The one key element that set the 1950s apart from previous decades was the organization of forms within space, which stemmed from the architect's desire to create, in its purest sense, the "open plan" environment. It was the relationship between the objects, not just the objects themselves, that often helped create the modern interior. One of the new postwar designer–architects to specialize in such interiors was European-born Alexander Girard, whose homes incorporated built-in furniture, screens, and ramps that linked rooms. An atmosphere of spaciousness also characterized the work of William Lescaze. The living room he created for the Norman House in New York (1941) indicated the movement toward plain carpets and furnishing fabrics with floor-to-ceiling windows. Chairs by Alvar Aalto set off the interior and exemplified the continuing spirit of Scandinavian Modern.

In Britain, the spirit of the 1950s began back in 1937, when the Council for Art and Industry filed a report deploring period revival and surface ornamentation, seeking "items in which the design was simple, of good proportions, and without dust-collecting features". The government officially adopted Modernism during World War II with the Utility scheme, under which not only prices but materials and styles of goods were fixed. After the 1951 Festival of Britain, Britain took a lighter approach. "Festival style" applied to both architecture and design, and the Royal Festival Hall today provides a lasting reminder, as do Ernest Race's Antelope chairs, designed as the public seating. Many "Festival" designs are characterized by a playful, whimsical nature, including the works of Robin and Lucienne Day.

Above: Interest in new Modernism encouraged designers to evolve more choice for the marketplace, and to provide a greater variety of standardized goods to respond to the demands of the market.

Below left: A 1950s ceramic
vase by André Borderie sits
on top of a wardrobe in a
Paris bedroom. The 1948
gilded sun-ray mirror by
Gilbert Poillerat was widely
copied by other designers
throughout the 1950s.

Right: An original Verner
Panton "Heart" chair (1959)
and a Serge Mouille ceiling
light set the 1950s tone
with their curved arching
forms. The illustration on
the wall is by René Gruau
for Christian Dior.

Creating the Look

When planning to re-create an interior from a 1950s perspective, elements to consider include its basic layout and structure, and the use of specific materials. Being informed about postwar and "contemporary" objects and furniture, as well as collecting wisely, is also vital.

The re-apportioning of space to open up an interior, by using an open-plan scheme where divisions in living areas are made with freestanding units, is a good place to start. Open-plan is an interior space with minimal interior walls in which temporary walls or flexible systems can be altered to change the shape of the space. A mezzanine, a mid-level between two floors within a room of double height, popular as an interior feature during the period, augments the feeling of continual flow within the environment. Lower ceilings contribute to this effect.

From an architectural standpoint, cladding was a popular device for reapportioning the interior structure of the 1950s home. A thin layer of material was used as surface infill between the main structural post-and-beam supports. Typical cladding materials, including wood, sheet metal, and glass, to form all-glass "curtain walls", can be used.

Left: A room with all British-designed furniture includes a white vinyl chair by Andrew Milne. The cabinet by Robert Heritage features a decorative panel by his wife, Dorothy Heritage. The portraits are by Catherine Goodman and Zara Chancellor.

Opposite: "Recliner" and "High Wide and Handsome" chairs by Robin Day for Hille in collector Andrew Jones's Islington bedroom. The cabinet on the left is by Frank Guille for Kandya, and the one on the right is by John and Sylvia Reid for Stag.

Right: Jones has filled his entire townhouse with period pieces that reveal his fascination with British post-war furniture: a "Recliner" by Robin Day; a "Cloud" table by Neil Morris for Morris of Glasgow; and ceramics by John and Sylvia Reid.

Later in the decade, prefabricated concrete panels were employed. Brutalism, a term coined in the late 1950s to describe the use of exposed concrete, was a trend that continued into the 1960s. Architects Le Corbusier and Kenzo Tange left concrete exposed on both the insides and outsides of buildings without concealing the marks made in the casting process.

New materials, such as fibreglass, Formica, foam rubber, vinyl, and other man-made products, became extensively exploited in mid-century furniture production. Fibreglass was widely used in moulded plastic seating and in woven textiles to give substance and support. Foam rubber, pioneered by the furniture company Arflex, revolutionized the upholstery of chairs and sofas by replacing springs and horsehair.

Formica, and the British counterpart Warerite, is a plastic laminate which came on the market soon after the war. Available in a wide range of colours and patterns, it was used on tabletops and other kitchen furniture. Vinyl, too, was a plastic exploited in the 1950s. In the form of PVC, it became an attractive alternative to linoleum for flooring. Vinyl also appeared as a coating on wipe-clean fabric for kitchen furniture and on wallpaper, making it washable and

Below: The vinyl easy chair is by Peter Hoyte for Hoyte Furniture and the dining chair, part of a set of six, is by John and Sylvia Reid for Stag. The rare "Rotoflex" light, also by the Reids, has a perforated mesh shade. The painting is by British artist Frank Fidler.

Right: The dining room suite, including the sideboard, is by John and Sylvia Reid. The white curved-base lamp is by Phillips and the settee by Ernest Race. The slatted back "Utility" chair, an early version of "flat-pack", is by Eric Lyons for the Packet Furniture Company.

greaseproof. Formica tabletops and vinyl chair covers or flooring can give an instant 1950s look to a room.

Synthetic fabrics, such as rayon, which were durable and cheap to produce, replaced natural linens and cottons in home furnishings. Lucienne Day, wife of designer Robin Day, created colourful geometric textile designs for curtains and upholstery, examples of which, along with other designers' work of the time, can still be found in flea markets and junk shops today.

Mix-and-match schemes, in which colour combinations are drawn from a range of complementary colours, can become a jazzy alternative to matching sets (Harlequin plates, for example, were so-called because each plate in the service was glazed in a different colour). This concept was also applied to glass and plastic tableware. Both Harlequin and the similar Fiesta products remain highly collectible.

Starbursts, abstract geometric patterns, and structures that combine acute angles with curves are indicative of 1950s design. The "ball-and-spoke" configuration, loosely based around models of molecular structures, was incorporated into the design of furniture legs and the frameworks of home accessories, such as coat- and plant-stands and magazine racks.

Below left: A Scandinavian teak dining table is matched with hide-and-chrome tubular steel chairs ("T Chair", 1952) from Laverne International in Michael Wolfson's home. The gilded deconstructed "Box" is his own design.

Right: A pine installation wall incorporates a fireplace, shelf recess, and terrazzo hearth. The low table is by Isamu Noguchi, the circular table is by Warren Platner for Knoll, and the white relief, kaolin on canvas, is by Paul Verburg.

Kensington Apartment

The shell of architect and designer Michael Wolfson's second floor London apartment was a 1950s insertion within a Victorian townhouse. "With that kind of time gap, it seemed a good idea to develop it into an interesting testing zone to see how postwar pieces could work with contemporary pieces – or not, as some people were more than willing to remark."

American-born Michael Wolfson came to London to study at the Architectural Association in Bloomsbury in the late 1970s. Following his studies, he headed the office of world-renowned architect Zaha Hadid, his ex-professor, before setting up independently to design architectural projects, interiors, and furniture. Of his work, he reveals: "The preference for my own design is what may be termed a 'deconstructed modernism', but it is really a continuation of the theories and ideals modernism sprang from.

"I am interested in form, line, and texture, which is very much a part of my work, and also what I look for when collecting postwar objects and furniture," remarks Wolfson, who sources material from galleries, auctions, flea markets, and junk shops on his travels around the world. Speaking of the work that

attracts him, he asserts: "These things are timeless in design and eternal in quality. I am not interested in the kitsch or pastiche of any design.

"The Italian roll-top cocktail cabinet, by Franco Albini from the mid-1950s, is one of my favourites [see p. 67]. What I like is the strength and simplicity of the profile; it is quite striking."

Wolfson takes pleasure from continuously moving smaller objects around the apartment to see them in a different light. "I have a lot of stuff. People are always coming into the flat and saying, 'Is that new?' when in fact it has just been placed in a different context. There are pieces that might get lost as a part of a collection and they take on a new life when they are estranged – arranged on a table or on the hearth to become a more dramatic display. It gives movement to a roomscape; it keeps it changing visually.

"I see myself as a member of the 21st century, and do not consider myself as living in a time-warp. …I am sure I will always have postwar design in my vocabulary and will live with it in a context other than in the time in which it was born. These pieces should be part of the fabric of what makes a truly contemporary space."

Left: The African-style rug is woven with amoeboid patterns in varying textures and piles. Wolfson's collections of period Italian glass, and ceramics by Vallauris including the *faux-bois* design, are on display beside a vinyl 1959 Pierre Paulin chair, "Model No. 437".

Below: For formal dining, the Scandinavian table is moved toward the centre of the living room. The patterned Homemaker dinner service, produced by Ridgway potteries, sits on black Basalt Wedgwood plates. The Scandinavian glasses are by Tapio Wirkkala.

Left: A prototype Michael Wolfson screen in mahogany serves as a bedhead in the bedroom. The acrylic-based lamp, from the 1960s, and the vintage "Ericofon" telephone by Ericsson adorn the bedside table. The small decorative 1950s bowls are by Piero Fornasetti.

Right: The wenge wood pedestals are part of the 1993 "Golden Distortions" collection by Wolfson. Their clean, strict geometric lines complement the curvilinear qualities of such earlier-period furniture as the floor-standing cocktail cabinet on the left by Franco Albini.

A
t a symposium on Pop Art held at the Museum of Modern Art in New York City in 1962, the critic Henry Geldzahler commented: "The popular press, especially and most typically *Life* magazine; the movie close-up, black and white, Technicolor, and wide screen; the billboard extravaganzas; and finally, through television, of this blatant appeal to our eye into the home – all this has made available to our society, and thus to the artist, an imagery so pervasive, persistent, and compulsive that it had to be noticed." In the light of this observation that close media scrutiny of home life contributed to the innovation of Pop Art, it is ironic that Pop Art is now considered to have influenced the house style we currently regard as quintessentially of the era.

Pop Art appeared at the very beginning of the decade and was acknowledged as a movement in the United States by 1962 when a common sensibility was identifiable among a number of artists, notably Claes Oldenburg, Tom Wesselmann, Roy Lichtenstein, Andy Warhol, and James Rosenquist, all using subject matter drawn from the banality of ordinary urban America. Departing from the emotionally charged styles of the Abstract Expressionists, their work also appeared dependent upon the techniques of mass visual culture. Lichtenstein selected individual frames from cartoon strips which he altered before painting, in dot form, onto large canvases, such as his *I know how you must feel, Brad* (1963). Warhol took a similar approach with film stills, studying many celebrities, including Jackie Kennedy in her bereavement and Elizabeth Taylor when the media was convinced of her ill-health.

Opposite: A home with the characteristic 1960s wood-panelled ceiling exhibits open-plan and split-level spaces, which were recurring themes for the period.

Above: Verner Panton's wife is seated here in his "Panton" stacking chair, designed in 1959–60, the first single-material, single-form, injection-moulded chair.

1960s

Pop culture dealt with disposability and egalitarianism. In one of Andy Warhol's famous statements he stressed that we all drink Coke and that no amount of money will give the President of the United States a better bottle than a man on the street. But it was the increased level of communication and consumerism in everyday lives that heralded the acceptance of these ordinary, already familiar images within the home as art. At Warhol's first exhibition in 1962 at the Ferus Gallery, Los Angeles, 32 paintings of Campbell's soup cans were propped on a ledge, as if in homage. This led to subsequent paintings of multiple images of Coke bottles, savings stamps, Brillo pad boxes, and even dollar bills, which served to underscore the notion of art as a commodity.

Some artworks by Pop exponents actually took the form of room sets, where art, sculpture, furniture, and household sounds would merge to replicate the expansiveness of "happenings", as in Claes Oldenburg's *The Store* (1961) and Tom Wesselmann's *Great American Nude No. 54* (1964). These installations were not entirely new, having a precedent in 1956 with British artist Richard Hamilton's emblematic collage *Just What Is It That Makes Today's Homes So Different, So Appealing*. The correlation between home and art was never so prevalent than in the early part of the decade. Ideas on colour, contrast, pattern, and motif were liberally exchanged between artists from every discipline. Apart from Pop and the Modernist continuum, the mid- to late 1960s had another issue to address: the Space Age.

The NASA programme suddenly made science fiction less fictional and technological progress offered prospects of enhanced lifestyles, leading to a newfound belief in a "Brave New World", where global resources still seemed infinite, as did man's ability to create a better environment. Some of the decade's architectural projects envisioning a utopian existence would, in hindsight, have been better left to the drawing-board. Architects' urban dreams rarely translate into satisfactory solutions and Oscar Niemeyer's ambitious early 1960s project for the capital city of Brasília, as beautiful as it is, epitomizes this shortsightedness.

The ensuing Space Race had great impact on many facets of fashion and design. In 1965, couturier André Courrèges launched a collection that changed the ground rules of fashion: all

Below: A cosy cottage scene from Terence Conran's *House Book* of the period shows the use of bold colour and pattern in soft furnishings and the advent of shag-pile carpeting for the floor. The diagonal cladding is a twist on 1950s vertical cladding.

white, with the occasional black stripe, short skirts, "kinky" boots, and slit-aperture sunglasses. A year later, Spanish-born couturier Paco Rabanne, who dressed Jane Fonda in Roger Vadim's cult movie *Barbarella*, proposed a chain-mail dress made from lightweight metal discs or plastic, which was quickly adopted as a uniform for Space-Age amazons. Futuristic interior design was inspired by Stanley Kubrick's 1967 film *2001: A Space Odyssey*, featuring the very sophisticated work of French furniture designer Olivier Mourgue, who won the International Design Award for the "Djinn" *chaise longue*.

The 1960s also saw a revival of interest in turn-of-the-century decorative arts. Major retrospectives of the works of Alphonse Mucha occurred in London and Paris in 1963 and 1966 respectively. The Victoria & Albert Museum in London hosted a retrospective of the drawings of Aubrey Beardsley in 1966. Features of the Art Nouveau style became recurring ingredients in the mélange of design sources, as did Pop and Op Art references. Referring to "optical" art and conveniently abbreviated to have at least a semantic proximity to Pop Art, Op Art explored the use of pattern and colour to create the illusion of movement, as exemplified in the striped canvases of Bridget Riley. Pop and Op merged in the phenomenon of Psychedelia, with an extreme example being the 1967 album cover for *Disraeli Gears* by the group Cream. Considered a psychedelic masterpiece, the cover was designed by Martin Sharp with a photograph by Bob Whitaker. Less radical examples include the gold and black logo for Barbara Hulanicki's London fashion emporium, Biba, which was designed by John McConnell in 1968.

The more dramatic designs for 1960s interiors appear to have been drug-induced, even if they were not. Experimental hallucinogenic drugs, such as LSD, served to either enhance or warp the mind's perception of space, form, colour, and movement. Although taken by only a small percentage of the population, LSD's mind-bending influence in America contributed to the use of psychedelic colour and organic form in 1960s art and design.

Above: A late 1960s interior with soft-sculpture jigsaw furniture in the foreground of a simple dining room. The "Universale" stacking chairs, originally for manufacture in aluminium, were made from ABS injection-moulded plastic by Milanese designer Joe Colombo in 1967. The detachable legs were available in two heights.

Creating the Look

Not all lovers of 1960s design would find it appropriate to turn their home into a wild, bohemian cacophony of colour, inspired by Pop and Op Art influences, or restyle it as a pure and pristine Space Age lunar module. But there are simpler, more practical ways of achieving a convincing 1960s look. The sharpest white room can be transformed with a few easy ideas, such as the addition of orange, red, or purple (or a mixture of all three) shag-pile rugs, 1960s art – even just in poster form, since this decade was its heyday – and swirling, bold, patterned fabric in the same violent hues.

If period collectibles and modular furniture of the era are inaccessible, clever use of simple furniture covered in the right fabrics can create the desired effect. Seating should be low and uncomplicated to mimic the "conversation pit" – a floor recess with a comfortable seating system around a low coffee table, Conversation pits were popular in the 1960s and seen in the film sets of such movies as *Barbarella* and *Help!* Cushions in vibrant colours, blow-up furniture, and bean-bags are still available and newly produced. Soft sculpture of any kind can allude to the art of Claes Oldenburg. Coloured moulded plastic tables

and chairs can make reference to the stackable designs created by the British Robin Day, whose work was highly practical, the Italian Joe Colombo, who was more extreme and flamboyant in his designs, or the American Wendell Castle, whose furniture curiously took on the forms of teeth as well as – but perhaps not so strangely – castles.

To transform a room more permanently, wall-papering is an obvious solution, particularly as it is still possible to buy unused 1960s wallpaper or to find current designs that incorporate bold strokes. Vintage flocked wallpaper can be found intact, and some wall-paper companies are even reproducing this textured wall-covering again, which simulates the look and feel of cut velvet, although perhaps not in authentic period designs. While having been an object of mirth from the late 1970s to the 1990s, its history is grand, mak-ing its appearance in Europe in 1620 and becoming so popular with the ladies of the French court, such as Madame de Pompadour, that many sent their Gobelin tapestries into storage in order to install it.

Panelling, greatly admired since the days of the feudal castle, became affordable to the average home-owner in the 1960s with the availability of ready-cut

Left: The work of Pop artists injected colour, humour, and irreverence for the art industry into the world. Andy Warhol's fascination for Marilyn Monroe began in the month following her death in 1962. This altered image was one of many he created and was originally sourced from a still of Monroe from the film *Niagara*, made in 1952.

Opposite: A lavishly furnished late 1960s to early 1970s interior-designed room. "Ponyskin" flooring adds to the sense of luxuriousness. The mirroring of panels and walls not only ensured the illusion of spaciousness but also added glamour.

Right: Collector Tiffany Dubin found her ideal wallpaper, an original "very graphic" 1960s black and metallic flock, from eBay, the internet auction company. Sadly, she says, "there was only enough for the small bathroom" of her Madison Avenue apartment.

Left: California was the home of the hippy and San Francisco's Haight Street, the epicentre of the cult. West Coast interior decorator Sandra Sakata reflects the 1960s ethnic style in souk-like rooms hung with richly coloured Asian and Middle-Eastern textiles and objects.

Below: In Jimi Hendrix's former top-floor London flat, art and film director Nigel Talamo sets up his own psychodrama of kitsch religious artifacts and 1960s glass, presided over by a kitchen hatch decorated with Vladimir Tretchikoff's *Green Lady* – an icon of the era.

and -finished panels of plywood simulating knotty pine, wormy chestnut, and weathered cyprus, waxed to give a patina. Today's plywood panelling, which can effectively imitate many different types of woods and finishes, can be bought in standard and random widths and is easy to install over plaster or plaster-board walls. Panelling a room or single wall for a 1960s look almost constitutes a do-it-yourself project not dissimilar in level of skill to hanging wallpaper.

For those wanting to go for an all-out 1960s look, authentic panelling and wallpapering can provide strong backdrops for the bold, brash drama of the period inspired by Pop and Op Art, yet equally offer an appropriate setting for the futuristic designs of the Space Age. Alternative 1960s backdrops can be more readily achieved by applying rich dark paint to the walls – deep reds, greens, and burnt oranges – then draping or tenting rooms in layer upon layer of ethnic fabrics, beads, and tassels to create a hippy extravaganza. San Franciscan interior decorator Sandra Sakata's rooms contain lavish pelmets and wall hangings of rare and not-so-rare textiles to achieve the desired effect. Lanterns or candles can be added to contribute mysterious, atmospheric lighting.

Madison Avenue Apartment

Fashion fanatic, businesswoman, and author Tiffany Dubin lives with her husband and daughter "just a breath above Midtown" on New York's Madison Avenue. An elevator opens directly into her apartment to reveal a colourful abstract brick pattern painted by contemporary artist Lulu Kwiatkowski. "We used to live in a really traditional apartment but moved here in 1999 and had the greatest excuse to begin to create a home to suit our passions, our needs, lifestyles, and generation – and the collection is evolving nicely," says Dubin of the classic contemporary pieces she has gathered. "I am not so interested in small pieces and bric-a-brac. More sturdy and substantial items of furniture against interesting wall finishes, typical of my favourite era, the 1960s, is what I had in mind. Next it will be rugs and more art, but my home will never look cluttered."

Although a lover of the Pop period, Tiffany Dubin amalgamates pieces from other, particularly earlier, decades into her living environment. "If you lived in the 1960s, you wouldn't just live with highly contemporary things, but favourites from a decade or so earlier. We are all creatures of habit and sentimental, and some things just don't die so easily." Some of her

Left: Stepping from the elevator, the green and blue wall pattern is by Lulu Kwiatkowski. The ceiling lamp "which looks '60s" is by Gio Ponti for Fontana Arte . (1931). The children's mesh chairs by Harry Bertoia are nylon-coated cast aluminium and retain their original orange vinyl cushions.

Right: Lulu Kwiatkowski's entrance hall walls, the white patent leather fabric panels in an adjoining corridor, and the silver tile paper in the living room act as textured backdrops to furniture by Pierre Paulin and Marc Newson. The striped sofa is from Eero Saarinen's "Womb" collection for Knoll.

Left: In Tiffany Dubin's dressing room, a bench covered in pink velvet acts as a daybed. The "Cone" chair (1958) and the patterned "Ribbon" chair (*c.* 1965) are by Verner Panton. The circular bookcase is perspex and the red cross medicine cabinet is from Cappellini/Modern Age.

Below right: In Dubin's daughter's playroom, a red "Globe" chair by Eero Aarnio, one of a pair, is a "re-edition from the 1990s of the mid-1960s classic". A Marc Newson chair unit is in the foreground, and the side-board was designed by Raymond Loewy (*c.* 1967).

furniture, the Eero Saarinen sofa for example, comes from the 1940s or 1950s but influenced the shape of later years. "In a century's time," Dubin predicts, "it will be difficult to automatically distinguish between late 1950s and early 1960s designs, since the forms they take – mainly biomorphic – have a similar visual persona." Dubin feels that to attempt to live in a truly "retro" home would be a mistake because it would alienate the future and the advances in technology. By way of example, she explains: "The focal point of the living room is the flat-screen television above the fire-place, as opposed to the fire itself."

Having had a change in career direction from Sotheby's New York to Vice President of Marketing for internet company The Auction Channel, Dubin keeps abreast of the latest technological develop-ments: "We do not live in a vacuum. We have to look to the past and the future to see what suits us.

"My love of the last half of the 20th century probably comes from fashion," says Dubin, who has set up seven fashion sales at Sotheby's in the past few years. Colour and fabric are clearly her inspiration: "I particularly like the gloss of the white patent leather walls in the hallway; I found the material downtown."

Early in the 1970s, London fashion designer Barbara Hulanicki, of Biba fame, took over the palatial Derry and Tom's department store, an Art Deco paradise, where she incorporated glamorous retro interiors by film-set designers. The mood was dark, mirrors were tinted, and carpets and wallpapers were sludge brown and beige in colour. Highly polished metals, which alluded to Hollywood, were in abundance. Late 1960s films, such as *Bonnie and Clyde* (1967), had already set the pace for the retro 1920s look, and this theme began to infiltrate decorating schemes, eventually becoming characteristic of the 1970s interior.

Other influences, too, were at work. The hippy look had become mainstream and even drug culture was widely accepted. In 1970 the highly respectable London department store Maples launched an exhibition entitled "Experiments in Living". A project on display, the "Trip Box" by Alex MacIntyre, used music and back-projection to create a hallucinatory environment – not dissimilar to the transcendental experience induced by Martin Dean's "The Retreat Pod" in the late 1960s, which mimicked the effect of a sensory-deprivation tank.

The late 1960s had been characterized by an "alternative" youth culture. Many young people turned against technology and rejected established Western values, including conventional homes and jobs, in favour of a more nomadic lifestyle. As a result, tents, camper vans, and caravans became preferable anti-establishment abodes for many young people. Whereas in the 1960s interior

Opposite: Chocolate brown walls and ecru deep-pile wall-to-wall carpeting line a 1970s studio. The bed and built-in sofa are elevated on platforms and the lighting is a visible feature.

Above: This scheme, by interior designer David Barrett, echoes the 1970s night-club scene with its mirrored ceiling, fox-fur bed covering, and curved steel and velveteen-covered walls.

1970s

design had been fun and revolutionary in style but not in substance, in the 1970s homes became self-conscious political statements, as described in the well-thumbed 1972 almanac *Underground Interiors: Decorating for Alternative Lifestyles*. The West began to be "ethnicized" and artifacts from Third World countries became commonplace in decorating schemes. Natural fibres, patterned textiles, and candlelight were mainstays of the politically aware home. "Organic" now referred to "natural", not to "biomorphic", as it had in the first half of the century.

The mainstream acceptance and success of hippy chic and the return to nature was aided, certainly in London, by one individual, Terence Conran. Having already influenced 1960s interior design by creating Mary Quant's Knightsbridge shop in 1957, which featured bales of fabric as a ceiling treatment and a central staircase where clothes hung underneath, Conran opened his first Habitat store in London in May 1964. His intention was to sell "good" simple design to the mass market at a reasonable cost and to import inexpensive ethnic items.

The plain white painted walls and brown quarry-tiled floor of Conran's store were influential to store and home design, and featured goods with a similar, natural sensibility, such as beech furniture, terracotta, and rush matting. Items were displayed *en masse* to give a warehouse feel. In the 1970s the rest of the world finally caught on, but by then Conran was moving ahead. He had marketed re-edition classic chairs from the Modern Movement in the mid-1960s, and now showed his forward-thinking capabilities by introducing an all-black "Hi-Tech" range, which became more refined in the 1980s and, in turn, the precursor of 1990s minimalism.

With Hi-Tech, the home became more akin to the workplace. Factory kit shelving, metal flooring, and perforated metal staircases and filing cabinets became commonplace in the living environment, indicating changes in attitude toward the office and home. For a woman with a career, the Hi-Tech style suggested a functioning and highly efficient home.

Below: A steel-framed mirrored recess holds a grey sofa which complements the larger built-in sofa opposite. Two independent low seats have the same mix-and-match detailing. The coffee table encases neon.

Not unlike Le Corbusier in 1925, architects celebrated the aesthetic of industry and brought back the "bare bones" once again into interior design. Architects Richard Rogers and Renzo Piano played crucial roles in the formulation of the style when, in partnership, they designed the first public building adhering to Hi-Tech qualities – the Pompidou Centre in Paris (1977). The interior of this national arts museum and cultural centre exists as a vast shed or warehouse. The apparatus for servicing the building is brazenly positioned on the exterior, and at many points is not even visually attached.

One major player in American Hi-Tech was the designer Joseph Paul D'Urso. Apart from his significant contributions to retail and commercial design – he designed showrooms for Calvin Klein in the late 1970s – Joe D'Urso committed his own New York apartment to the treatment. He added hospital doors, steel-mesh fencing for clothes and storage, as well as stainless steel surgeons' sinks. As he remarked in an interview at Parsons School of Design in 1982: "The objects I use are not industrial so much as they are simply designed without arbitrary decoration. They are not trying to be styled elements – just basic straightforward designs."

In France other designers were finding their styles emulated worldwide. Andrée Putman and Ronald Cécil Sportes had a more technical approach, while François Catroux and Alberto Pinto created with luxuriousness in mind. In Italy the focus was on refining a Post-International style using innovative materials. It was the furniture designers that were at the forefront following New York's Museum of Modern Art's exhibition "Italy: The New Domestic Landscape" in 1972, which show-cased micro-environments that had been commissioned by leading *avant-garde* and radical designers Mario Bellini, Joe Colombo, and Ettore Sottsass. Colombo's "Total Furnishing Unit" took the form of a self-contained block comprising four separate units to cater for all needs: eating, sleeping, bathing, and storage. Day and night furniture could be pulled out as desired. Sottsass and Colombo designed highly flexible modules, which connected and disconnected for various functions. Sottsass joined Alessandro Mendini's Studio Alchimia group, formed in 1979, but soon left to set up the Memphis group, which became the lively backbone of residential and commercial design in the 1980s.

Above: The bedroom area continues in the same theme as the living space opposite, where designer Alberto Pinto combines Hi-Tech shelving with luxuriousness. The walls feature Op Art, which was obsessed with retinal sensation and kineticism.

Below left: A curved corridor ceiling with a line of recessed lights is optically altered by a painted striped banner, which sweeps in contradiction to the symmetry of the hallway. The sludge colours serve to break up the cream.

Right: A glossy white floor and white walls in a 1970s bedroom are offset by a painted door surround in this clean-looking environment. The "Elda" chair, a 1970s icon, was designed by Joe Colombo in 1963.

Creating the Look

Modular seating gradually gained in importance and by 1972 designer Eleonore Peduzzi-Riva, with a team comprising Heinz Ulrich, Klaus Vogt, and Veli Berger, produced a potentially endless sofa for Stendig called "Nonstop", where a series of accordian-like modules linked together to form sofas, chairs, or settees in either curved or straight arrangements. Almost a room in itself, there could not have been a more 1970s image.

In America in 1974, designer Don Chadwick produced the "Chadwick Modular Seating" for Herman Miller, where various units linked together in a continuous, undulating row. The characteristic setting it apart from other modular seating is the deep fold where the seat and back meet, which can be bent into a serpent curve or to fit into a curved niche.

Acquiring a "Nonstop" or "Chadwick" system may prove difficult and expensive, and it is unlikely to fit your prescribed space, but it is possible to draw from their design and details. Consider fitting furniture to line walls, and take note of the fabrics and colours used. Brown, tan, red, beige, aubergine, and sometimes dull greens and ochre-based yellows, are characteristic of the 1970s, but only details of black are used.

Left: Carpets such as David Hicks's "multiples" range from the 1960s paved the way for geometric designs that became so popular in the 1970s. The fibre-optic lights are highly appropriate to the 1970s theme. The use of grey walls as a backdrop for brighter colours continued into the 1980s.

Opposite: A laminated cube table matches the futuristic-looking four-poster bed with its white patent leather straps and curved continuous ochre form. Walls are glossy white panels and the artwork is geometric and mirrored – typical of the period.

Right: Red makes a splash of colour against the grey flannel covering on a frameless divan bed. Low ceilings and staggered dais, which shifted floor levels and created platforms, were favoured in 1970s interiors.

Left: This is a more conservative 1970s home: a brown daybed has additions of natural cotton-covered oversized cushions. Traditional paintings co-exist perfectly with the contemporary features of shag rug, glass table, and Miesian ottoman.

Below right: In an Islington warehouse, the 1970s mood is achieved with an original double-seated sofa, although the re-edition white lamp shade on the chest, by Kaare Klint, the Isamu Noguchi table, and the shelf brackets are all from the mid-century.

Walls were plain, either painted ecru or stark white, and often glossy or textured, or partially covered with fabric panels, mirrors, or metallic sheets. Cork, bamboo, and basket were popular for walls in kitchens and less formal areas. Green leafy plants engulfed entire corners. Bathroom furniture, baths, and bidets came in browns and greens, including the ubiquitous avocado suite. The word "fitted" described everything, from carpets and bedlinen to closets.

Open-plan space was still in vogue, affording more light to the home. Mezzanines had become the less-complicated dais or platform, where a simple divan bed or low seating affair re-apportioned the interior space. Conversation pits became less recessed, less secretive, and more at ground level – the accent being on the raised platform.

Geometric pattern as art or textile design accents an otherwise plain interior in the 1970s scheme. Heavy painted wavy stripes can work as permanent art on walls and visually alter a space. Use spot, track, and recessed lights to support minimal floor and table lamps, with fashionable options being neon or fibre-optic. Fur and deep-pile carpets bring a saucier "playboy" or "Hollywood" touch to the scene.

Left: Colombo's "Elda" chair, a rare carpet by Pierre Cardin (1972), and a brown leather tubular settee by British designer William Plunket create an upbeat translation of the era. The "Pantella" lamp (1969–70) and the stretched fabric paintings (1968) are by Verner Panton.

Below: Two sofas – one re-covered in a red slub-weave fabric and the second in its original now worn brown leather – make up the corner of a warehouse. The walls have simply been whitewashed. The natural element of the basket completes the ensemble.

Panelling continued as a popular feature but was often replaced with tiling. In the latter half of the 20th century, the tile rose to prominence yet again, as it did in the 19th century, when home-builders and developers in Florida and the Southwest United States found the tile useful for their hot climates. In more inclement regions, wipe-down tiles are perfect for a patio, a lanai, or an outdoor barbecue, as well as for bathrooms and kitchens. The tiled effect also adds to the geometry of patterned areas.

Although ceramic and vinyl tile dados are commonplace in more functional 1970s rooms, such as hallways and recreation rooms, they can also be effectively employed elsewhere. The designer Ellen Lehman McCluskey, for example, successfully used a dado of grey vinyl tiles in a 1960s dining-room scheme. Ceramic or vinyl tiles laid in a pattern on a floor can be continued up the walls as a dado, or the tiles can be used on just one wall. Even a single wall of tiles gives a great lift to a room. The contrast between a sparkling tiled wall and three painted plaster walls is a superb device for redirecting the focus of the room or for providing an accent of interest. A wall or two of gloss paint in a room can achieve the same effect.

Marylebone Penthouse

Maria Speake and Adam Hills make up the London-based team behind the architectural salvage company Retrouvius. Both are graduates in architecture from the Glasgow School of Art, Scotland, though neither has chosen to practise in the field. Their work, however, requires historical and current-day knowledge of architectural sites, buildings, and detail. They are committed to "salvaging otherwise forgotten or misplaced artifacts from ancient to modern" with a view to selling on for installation "where they might be better appreciated".

Their home, a penthouse in the central London Marylebone area, is atypical of the red-brick Victorian mansion blocks and Georgian houses that are more usual visions on these smart tree-lined streets. Adam's father, architect Nicholas Hills, bought the roof rights to the Edwardian mansion building "in the days when that sort of thing was possible", says Adam. He designed the metal and glass open-plan home for his family. Inspired by a single piece of furniture, a brown leather daybed by Poul Kjaerholm, he incorporated his own fabric, tile, and furnishing designs.

When Maria and Adam moved in, they first installed a more sophisticated heating system because

glass buildings on London roofs can be dauntingly cold in winter. They resolved to resurrect and restore elements that had been lost or damaged throughout the years since the 1970s. "My mother, a successful newspaper journalist, had lived here alone for a time in the 1980s," explains Adam, "and had not really been interested in keeping up the quintessence of the 1970s interior. It is only now we realize the artistic value of something so pure. In the 1980s it probably just looked dated and increasingly shabby."

The single-story structure is an "L" shape of 280sq m (3000sq ft) with windows on all facets. The walk-around kitchen forms the central core of the building accessible from all three areas of the principal living accommodation. The bathroom and dressing room remain at one end of the "L" with a sight-line through to the opposite end, which houses the office.

The south-easterly bedroom, a circular room, is a tower above the red-brick apartment block and forms the outer angle of the "L". The views from the ovoid bedroom windows are stunning. The bedroom boasts a domed ceiling swathed in the original brown and ivory striped fabric used throughout the interior. "The track lights are original – the floor sockets, too," explains Adam; the light switches can be operated by the flick of a foot. "We can't decide if we should apply for a preservation order for the property. On the one hand it will mean this can be preserved forever; on the other it restricts us as owners in case we wish to alter or update the interior in any way." There is still scope for further development. The couple own the rights to the other side of the roof, as yet barren except for a roof garden that functions as storage space for overflow from their larger finds.

Opposite: The space is "L"-shaped around a central kitchen and has clear sight-lines throughout. The table in cherrywood veneer and aluminium is a 1970s copy of Eero Saarinen's "Tulip" table. The black leather chair is by Hans Wegner and the dining chair is by Enzo Mari.

Below: The walk-around kitchen has its own central core. All the rooms in the penthouse open onto the roof terrace. The 1940s lamp was a "lucky find", the kitchen chairs are by Robin Day, and the plastic table is 1970s. The framed cow prints are by Lynne Moore (1971).

Left: Joe Colombo's comfortable white "Elda" chair is positioned near a window in the dining area "for reading". The cushion fabric is true to the period – a shocking pink Emilio Pucci print. "Plia" chairs are stacked against the wall.

Right: The apex of the "L" holds a circular room towering above the Edwardian mansion building supporting the penthouse. The central light in the domed ceiling is by Poul Henningsen, the leather-clad telephone is from the 1970s, and the circular plaster relief is a Michelangelo copy.

The 1980s became a "concept" era, one of consumerism and excess, with the prefix "super" omnipresent. We had "super-efficiency" in every respect — the first supermodels, fashion doyennes whose reputations were hyped by their devoted designers, over-the-top themselves; "super fitness" at the gym; "superstars", whose names only needed to be singular, such as Madonna and Prince; and "super-designers", the extroverts and individualists of design, most of whom possessed an abundant talent for self-promotion. For many, the 1980s was a period of playful vulgarity and excessive fantasy. It became a time when the role of intuition and emotion won over reason, where the artist was better known than the engineer, and where the seemingly beautiful challenged the useful.

French designer Philippe Starck, who enjoys his self-proclaimed bad boy image, became undoubtedly the ultimate "super-designer" or "designer's designer" (to use another overexposed 1980s term) of the latter 20th century. A creative artist who applied his skills to mundane everyday objects, and unique in countless ways, Starck also represented an entire generation of French furniture designers, including Elizabeth Garouste and Mattia Bonetti, Marie-Christine Dorner, and Jean-Michel Wilmotte. Their success was due not only to their rather unorthodox education (Starck, Garouste, and Bonetti all graduated from Paris's forward-thinking *Ecole Camondo*), but also to the support of the

Opposite: In an interior by Laurence and Adrian Mibus, a sculptural floor-standing lamp is a 1960s original by Yonel Lebovici. The clock case, centre, is typical of the bright, brash laminates used by Italy's Memphis design group in the 1980s.

Above: In the 1980s, eclecticism meant combining architecturally altered spaces with classic features. Here, a galleried area, reflected in a mirror, is married with original fireplaces. The tonal grey carpet typifies those popular at the time.

1980s

1908

government-formed *Valorisation de L'Innovation dans l'Ameublement* (VIA). With new design and architecture taking place, President Mitterrand envisaged that France would become renowned once again as a nation committed to high style. In 1983 Mitterrand proved his own commitment by commissioning five leading French designers, including Starck, to create a set of interiors for the Elysée Palace.

Philippe Stark was propelled to fame in 1984 when the VIA commissioned him to design a chair, following a Carte Blanche award for his "Miss Dorn" chair (1982). The new three-legged chair, with a rounded back and a single hole for a finger to lift it at the rear, was spotted by the owners of the planned Café Costes in Paris. Subsequently the owners commissioned Starck to design the entire restaurant. Until its closure in 1990, the restaurant's ultra-designed interior became the focus of pilgrimage for the world's hip and fashionable. The chair itself is still a status symbol in homes, offices, and public interiors everywhere.

Another French superstar designer who came to great fame in the 1980s was Andrée Putman. She was already well known in the 1960s and 1970s for her work on the magazines *L'Oeil* and *Femina* and for developing a budget range of home accessories for the French chain-store Prisunic. In 1985 Putman designed Morgans hotel on New York's Madison Avenue for Ian Schraeger and Steve Rubell. It was considered to be the first "designer" hotel, which in turn spawned many more before the decade came to a close. Apart from numerous hotels, she designed private homes, museums, and night clubs, as well as the interior of Concorde. The "goddess of design" will always be noted for being, as she puts it, an "amateur archeologist of modern times". Through the company Ecart International, which she established in Paris in 1978, Putman single-handedly gave a new lease of life to forgotten furniture designs from the early part of the century. She researched original blueprints, sketches, and plans of pieces by

Below: The Knightsbridge, London, home of fashion impresario Joseph Ettedgui was interior-designed by Eva Jiricna. The re-edition "Transat" chairs, reproduced by Andrée Putman's firm Ecart from 1978, were originally designed by Eileen Gray for the ocean liner *Transatlantique* in 1925–6.

Eileen Gray, Robert Mallet-Stevens, Pierre Chareau, Réne Herbst, and others, and then re-issued the furniture. Hugely different from reproductions, which tend to merely emulate prior styles and forms without the original technical virtuosity, these "re-editions" were staple pieces throughout all fashionable homes. Since Putman recognized its potential, the simple triple-slatted Mallet-Stevens chair (1927) has become virtually impossible to avoid in the most modern cafés on all continents.

Both Putman's and Starck's furniture, lighting, and interior designs, as well as their philosophies, found acclaim on a mass scale, earning them a place in the popular imagination, as did new work by a band of highly talented radicals in Italy, headed by the flamboyant Ettore Sottsass. From the late 1970s, an entirely new vivid, brash look had been heralded by Sottsass's Memphis group of designers.

In a resurgence of the 1920s, the 1980s witnessed matte black and chrome again, although stainless steel became a sturdy replacement at times for the less durable chrome. Films such as *Nine and a Half Weeks* helped affirm the matte black and white minimalist interior; the Mickey Rourke character possesses the ultimate in high-chic with his Le Corbusier *chaise*, minimal bedroom closets, and, memorably, the "designer" kitchen. Retailers Terence Conran, Joseph Ettedgui, and Paul Smith all introduced matte black elements into their stores and newly wealthy bankers fitted their loft spaces with the most masculine sleekness. The decade had become a period for collecting – either re-editions or wholly contemporary pieces of furniture. The work of Israeli-born Ron Arad, whose One-off company produced singularly fascinating sculptural furniture, and the Tunisian-born Tom Dixon are examples of highly collectible furniture, as is that of the Japanese designer Shiro Kuramata. As a foil to this rather more stark approach, the Memphis group was playfully creating Post-Modern designs in bright contrasting laminates. Yet, for many, the new "ethnic", a streamlined translation of the 1960s and 1970s naturalistic style, was still the most comfortable way to live.

Above: The home of hair stylists Irvine and Rita Rusk, in Scotland's Clyde Valley, was built in the early 1980s, when the monochrome interior was at its most masculine and re-issues a popular choice. A pair of Le Corbusier's "Grand Confort" chairs are shown here – Cassina re-issues which were originally produced by Thonet Frères in 1928.

Below: With its oversized furniture in natural fabrics and green leafy plants, Melanie Martin's light and airy living room epitomizes the 1980s California look.

Opposite: The dining area can be seen through an alcove. The wood table and seats have been minimally finished to create comfort, while retaining rusticity.

Right: Melanie Martin's bedroom features a free-form curtain over driftwood branches. An uncut boulder is a bedside sculpture and doors act as a bedhead.

Creating the Look

As early as 1965, Albert Kornfeld, one-time Editor-in-Chief of American *House & Garden*, commented in his book *Interior Decorating and Encyclopedia of Styles*: "Changes in decoration mirror the changing pattern of our daily lives. Less frequent and far less drastic than changes in fashions, they occur often enough to give rise to distinct trends, or 'looks'. Popular among the contemporary looks are the Potpourri Look, the Far East Look, the Provincial Look...." He goes on to say that, as the fashion-conscious look to couturiers in Paris and New York, so the design-conscious look at the current trends in home decoration by leading practitioners. Twenty years later, naturalistic styles remained the most popular choice for home-owners due to their ease, comfort, and adaptability. They mirrored the changing pattern of more ecologically concerned daily lives. The work of top interior designers adopted an almost Zen-like approach. California-based decorator Michael Taylor (dubbed the "James Dean of decorators" by Diana Vreeland) said: "My creed is simplicity." His naturalistic approach made use of fossilized stone, Yosemite slate, logs, and wicker. From 1984, French designer Christian Liaigre took inspiration from the

Below: In David Champion's home, shelves hold objects that are reminiscent of travels to far-away locations. African tusks and statuettes, including Indian Jain effigies, are placed next to highly colourful finds. Natural fibre fabrics cover the seats, suggesting colonial living.

Right: Store owner Champion's North London home is ethnic in sentiment. Rugs are placed beneath Benares tables and cinnamon-coloured walls are textured, although placement of furniture is traditionally Western and table-tops are organized with precision.

East, as did Taylor, and he was also fascinated by African and Polynesian cultures. In the 1980s, London store owner David Champion consciously adopted the Potpourri Look for his own London home, which has retained as much rustic charm today as when it was originally coordinated. His decorating vocabulary – earthy tones, neutral hues, natural materials, and use of colourful patterned fabrics and rugs – can easily be adapted to suit many homes, and with the individualistic approach, can become highly personalized. Many ethnic objects of the greatest aesthetic value prove inexpensive to buy, whether found in import stores locally or sourced abroad. "Found" objects are always the most personal additions, relying purely on opinion.

Ethnic was just one style prevalent in the 1980s. Apart from the minimal monochrome look, a third, brighter force arrived by way of Memphis. Although having first emerged in the 1960s, Pop Art and culture influenced the 1980s, as did classical architecture and 1950s kitsch. Some of designer Ettore Sottsass's early inspirations came from travel to America in the 1960s, which translated through to his later work with the Memphis design group. Formed in 1980, with Sottsass's young friends Michele de Lucchi,

Left: Interior designer Alberto Pinto created an art-lover's paradise in Marbella. Primary colours, a detail in the custom-made bed covering, are a welcome addition to the neutral hues – here used sparingly to keep the feeling of coolness in a warm Mediterranean climate.

Below: The 1980s saw a resurgence in entertaining at home, and the home bar once again became a status symbol. Stools are covered in bright coloured fabrics and have tubular steel legs. The rectilinearity of the bar presages the 1990s minimalism to come.

Left: Nigel Talamo creates a 1980s interior with a rag sofa, the star of the 1981 Milan furniture fair, art by Bruce McLean (1984), and Philippe Starck's "Dr. Sonderbar" chair (1982). The painted chair is by Caroline Greville-Morris.

Below: The tiny bathroom in Talamo's Bloomsbury flat has been completely retiled using ceramic squares in 1980s Post-Modern primary colours. The large figure above the basin was meant to be mirrored, "but I liked it as art", says Talamo.

George Sowden, Nathalie du Pasquier, Marco Zanini, and Aldo Cibic, the Italian Memphis group dictated the new direction in colour. After the browns, plums, sludge tones, mirrored surfaces, and neon that were so pervasive throughout the 1970s, primary colour became an integral element in 1980s interior design.

To achieve the Memphis look, concentrate on using the primary colours – red, blue, and yellow – with interjections of black, white, and grey, applied to create a mottled effect. The playful Post-Modern designs incorporated these bright, bold colours in unconventional large-scale forms, often in decorated plastic laminates, a far cry from the sleek lines of the 1970s. The Memphis message meant that applied art could be industrialized as an intrinsic part of design.

To give a suggestion of the Memphis look, paint walls in a high-gloss primary colour, or use a neutral backdrop for walls to emphasize brightly coloured furniture. In her refurbishment of fashion mogul Karl Lagerfeld's apartment, the designer Andrée Putman followed inspiration from the Milan furniture fair, where Memphis had its first sensational appearance, and achieved an interior of brightly coloured pieces against a grey background.

Below: On the upper floor, a ladder leads to a terrace. The "Le Jour et La Nuit" armchair is by Garouste & Bonetti (1988) and the cushions are by Ulrika Liljedahl.

Opposite: A 1970s sisal rug by Alexander Calder extends through the living room. The 1950s table is by Charlotte Perriand and the *chaise longue* is by Pierre Paulin.

Right: The "Prince Imperial" chair (1985), a painted wood construction with raffia, was designed by Garouste & Bonetti and produced by Néotu in Paris.

Notting Hill Duplex

Tall, effervescent, and highly successful, Jane Barclay lives alone in a duplex apartment with roof garden, which lies on a square in the hub of London's energetic Notting Hill area, famed for its Portobello Road antiques market and fashionable meeting places. Jane does not, however, find herself tripping around the renowned furniture stalls, nor the many burgeoning cutting-edge modern furniture galleries in the locale, for the objects she chooses to live with. Her taste is very specific, she has a good eye, and, true to the essence of her character, seems unafraid of the experimental or outlandish.

The mid- to late 1980s is a favourite era of design for Barclay, particularly the "Barbarian" furniture designs by Elizabeth Garouste and Mattia Bonetti, graduates of Paris's *Ecole Camondo*. Jane collects other late 1980s designers, such as Christian Astuguevieille, famous for his rope furniture, and metalworker André Dubreuil. Both produce work that has been proven to last and looks likely to succeed in the long term.

A busy professional occupied in the film industry as co-Managing Director of Capitol Films, Barclay turned to gallery owner and expert David Gill to help curate her furniture collection. Gill is known to have

From this moment, until next time.

an uncanny skill in predicting the new collectibles. Through his company and gallery, he commissions, produces, and exhibits entire collections by innovative designers he has helped bring to the forefront, and ensures the highest quality. "Jane is a confident and extraordinary woman and knows what she likes. It was wonderful to have collaborated with her," says Gill, who continues to represent the Garouste & Bonetti design team and handles current designers Tom Dixon, Oriel Harwood, and Marc Newson.

Gill commissioned Michael Wolfson to design and install the deconstructed closets in Barclay's master bedroom with gold-leaf motif, which become a sculptural form with a disjointed top edge when the doors are closed. "They are one of a kind," says David. He also suggested that Christian Astuguevieille cut the rope, encasing one of Barclay's chests, into a fringe.

As a keen collector of earlier 20th-century pieces, Gill persuaded Barclay to merge "classics" with later elements – the 1950s bed by Jean Prouvé, storage cabinet by Charlotte Perriand, Escargot sconces by Serge Mouille, and the 1970s sisal rug by Alexander Calder. "It all lives in harmony; after all, the 1980s were about collecting furniture classics," says Gill.

Left: Although most of the rooms are curated, containing select, highly collectible, often museum-quality pieces, the principal bedroom is more relaxed. With its printed cotton bedhead and bed covering, the room retains a feminine quality. The green-shaded lamp, one of a pair, is by Garouste & Bonetti.

Opposite: A shock of colour engulfs the small guest bedroom, creating a simply achieved but stunning room. The naïve art adds an ethnic touch and the striped roller blind diffuses the light. The 1950s bed is a rare collector's item: a coated-steel structure with a wood swing-out tray-table by Jean Prouvé.

Right: In the early 1990s, architect and furniture designer Michael Wolfson (see pp. 62–7) created these built-in deconstructed closets with a layered gold-leaf abstraction.

The 1990s was the one decade of the 20th century which seemed to start resoundingly dead on target, stylistically speaking. The 1910s and 1920s had roots in the latter part of the 19th century; the 1930s and 1940s were interrupted by the war years and meshed into one; the 1950s found inspiration from postwar euphoria and the Modernists of the early 1930s; and the swinging 1960s continued way into the 1970s. But there was something about the end of the 1980s that marked a time of new thought, symbolized quite poignantly by the work produced in fashion, art, and technology. If the 1980s can, retrospectively, be summed up as a period of conspicuous consumption, the 1990s represented a more cerebral vision.

When the Turkish-born fashion designer Rifat Ozbek launched his 1990 Spring collection in the autumn of 1989, his fashion predictions seemed accurate. Far removed from the opulent textiles, sequins, beading, gold-trimmed headwear, and sunshine colour-bursts that epitomized his 1980s designs, he produced a demure collection, still luxurious but all in white. There was not a trace of colour, except for the minutest metallic thread detail. Was this to be the decade to debunk divine opulence for sublime purity? It certainly seemed so.

Emptiness, void, and under-design became reflected in interior spaces. Art, particularly conceptual art, became the new collectible, as it required a different level of understanding. Instead of shopping in flea markets and furniture galleries,

Opposite: Chef and food writer Alastair Hendy's vast London apartment features an elegant antechamber which opens up into a mosaic-tile bathroom.

Above: The ultimate way to stay fit and keep well-informed – a gym provides audio-visual entertainment by way of a flat-screen television and sound system.

1990s

the latest clothing emporiums, and at auction houses, the internet provided a speedy alternative for anyone needing to browse. With the new luxury of more free time, and the creation of more millionaires and billionaires than previously thought imaginable, the opportunity arose to enhance the home environment.

The 1990s also became the architect's decade. Serious home-owners desired to create backdrops for their sculpture and art collections and found that architects' plans saved time, were preferable to briefing construction companies, and avoided "do-it-yourself" – an approach almost at an end. They understood theories concerning the relationship between objects, which is just as relevant as the objects themselves. The new loft dwellers had a better idea of how architecture works thanks to forward-thinking interiors magazines. Tyler Brûlé's *Wallpaper** helped introduce the under-30s to good design and took the fear out of using an architect for home design by covering stories about professionals who were even younger and "hipper" than the readers themselves.

The restaurant industry had an upsurge, introducing celebrity chefs and quality eateries on a large scale, and restaurant designers Philippe Starck, Christian Liaigre, and David Collins found a huge public following. Cooking at home, however, was often a relaxing alternative to finding a table at a fine restaurant, even if entertaining large numbers of guests. For the first time since the 1950s, the kitchen became the core of the home, although merging with the dining area as part of an open-plan space. Alternatively, the kitchen was easily accessible from the other living areas. New York architect Carlos Aparicio created a galley kitchen on a single surface in a tiny corridor linking his bedroom to the living room – the only kitchen in his five-room apartment, positioned near the rooms he most used.

Gym and keep-fit fanatics sought apartments in buildings with their own self-contained pool and work-out room, or would install a gym for personal use. The home gym and office were now major considerations in organizing living space, since the new information age had opened up the potential of "remote access", which facilitated working from home.

Below: Mary Drysdale designed this comfortable 1990s living room for an American home. A serene neutral palette combines with a neatness of line and contemporary furniture.

The interior designer was no longer seen as an interloper among architects. New teams were formed which allowed professionals from both disciplines to work harmoniously together. Interior designers Barbara Barry, Mimi London, Jonathan Reed, and Kelly Hoppen showed home-owners how to combine natural materials with a new, sophisticated clean line. Anouska Hempel took Zen to another extreme with the spartan but elegant interior of her London hotel, the Hempel, the antithesis of her Blakes hotel in which every room was swathed in fabric and extended to a lavish theme.

Advances in new technology, spurred on by the computer industry, allowed the development of fascinating new materials, which possessed properties helping to shape the future of design. Prismex, a transparent material designed by a small Australian company, and further developed by ICI in England, uniformly dissipates light from a single side light source. Light Emitting Diodes, known as LEDs, are minute light sources produced in red, green, or blue light, which together can produce an extraordinary 16.8 million different colours. *New Scientist* magazine paid so much attention to LEDs in 1999 that the publication predicted the demise of the light bulb as we know it and the possibility of producing electro-luminescence from liquid crystal in the near future.

The inception of computer imaging and Computer Aided Design (CAD) has meant that designers and architects no longer have to rely upon flimsy hand-made maquettes when modelling designs. Rapid Prototyping (RP) allows companies to create complex investment casting patterns directly from CAD solid models in a matter of hours in any number of materials – plastic, metal, ceramic, or composites. This not only speeds up the design process, but also accelerates manufacturing, since prototypes can be tested accurately for sound ergonomics, durability, and function. This said, the touch of the hand has not been lost. Artists and craftsmen continue to evolve their skills in the manipulation of the natural materials they sculpt, cast, model, and carve, and like the alchemists of the ancient past, create a different kind of magic.

Above: As in the 1950s, the kitchen became the heart of the home. The open-plan arrangement of this London loft apartment in the Piper building shows the kitchen as an attractive feature of the overall scheme.

Below left: The sandblasted, exposed-brick warehouse of furniture designer Andrew Mortada is home to his own work. A cabinet in MDF and resin provides elegant storage for paperwork and video and CD collections.

Right: Malcolm Temple's work falls between sculpture and furniture. Totemic sculptures, or "love poles", are made from Canadian pitch pine and inspired by Cycladic art. A stereo cabinet features primitive symbols.

Creating the Look

The advent of technology's miniaturization of offices, making them almost bereft of cables and virtually paperless, meant that the new decade witnessed a clean-up campaign in its midst. On the levels of both mind and spirit, this affected the way we chose to live, work, and play. Interior design had a more considered approach, too.

British designer Jonathan Reed has a definite overview of the 1990s, having seen the inception of his firm at the mid-point of the decade, believing that minimalism finally became accepted into the mainstream. In the 1980s, the style-conscious experimented with minimalism – creating it and possessing it as a status symbol. But its exponents in the 1990s, being more familiar with the movement's visual aspects, no longer saw it as an entity and evolved to understand the value of eliminating the excesses with a more humble approach. It had to do with confidence; knowing who you are rather than experimenting with how other people perceive you to be. As the 1980s came to a close, there was a need for more clarity – to create a more contemporary living space, to look at the object, whether it was art or a functional piece, to decide if it is really necessary.

Left: Ivy Rosequist's coastal house is an updated version of elegant rusticity. The lattice-based *equipale* chair, strips of eucalyptus bark over the mantel, sheepskin, brushwood, and raw timber prove nature can supply the best ornament.

Below: A voluminous floating sculptural form, a Haitian fishnet, gives a futuristic edge and alternative focal point. The floors are a continuous run of bleached boards with concrete insets. The spherical cushions are in homage to Michael Taylor.

Right: In New York, the home of the loft apartment, ceilings are rarely altered, except for a fresh coat of paint. This kitchen design, semi-cachéd from the dining area, allows for conversation while avoiding any unsightly debris from entertaining.

Although Reed does not consider himself to be a staunch minimalist, he realizes that the simplification of life has become more dominant. He creates this impression in his uncluttered environments, where the objects speak for themselves against a seamless backdrop. Reed's approach is a good one to follow, utilizing natural materials – honed, battered, and polished stone, slate, bleached and limed woods, and parchment – with neutral hues in textured finishes.

To create a contemporary home is to embrace seamlessness – the fluidity from room to room, the unbroken line, or at best a simplified living space suited to personal requirements. Storage is another feature of the 1990s interior, either cleverly concealed or blending with the scheme so as not to distract from a focal point. Subtlety is achieved by including a few well-chosen objects – vast sculptures, potted trees, or whatever is appropriate to your lifestyle, as long as the relationship between the objects – their spacing – is harmonious. Select what you want with little regard for its value to others. As American naturalist Henry David Thoreau said: "I would rather sit on a pumpkin and have it all to myself than to be crowded on a velvet cushion."

Above: Furniture is personal, and everyone needs storage. The perforated metal-drawered rack in this New York apartment is a former clothing locker from a swimming pool.

Right: In a 1930s office-block conversion, a small *pied-à-terre* required compact thinking. A sleep deck lies above a bathroom with a glass-tiled wall, which allows the flow of light.

Right: A pair of cabinets in Dutch leaf flank a fireplace in the London house of designer Justin Meath Baker. The fire surround is made from rough-cut chunks of wood, shaped to be self-supporting. The ceramic figurine on top is by Oriel Harwood.

Left: Fashion designer Ben de Lisi worked with interior designer Adam Dolle to create storage ideas for his London home. In the rather austere bedroom, a black glass wall partitions off the bathing area. The recessed bed has floor-to-ceiling storage on either side.

Opposite: De Lisi has colour-zoned his apartment in dark and natural hues. Wood finishes with black walls and a putty-coloured carpet set off his collections. An American walnut free-standing wall separates the kitchen from the living area without hindering light flow.

Bermondsey Loft

South of London's Tower Bridge, toward the east, is Bermondsey, a district better known for its fruit, flower, and antiques markets than for its housing potential. In the late 1990s it became, like most areas where warehouses were plentiful, a much sought-after area for those who see potential in off-beat locations, need space, and who are not afraid to be excluded from prestigious residential enclaves. Bermondsey is like New York's TriBeCa used to be. "I have the flat of my dreams, although sometimes it is difficult to find a shop selling basic provisions," says Richard Oyarzabal, a busy arts consultant. He selected his home for its impressive square footage and because many of his artistic friends, including the artist Andrew Logan, found enough space for their creative endeavours nearby. "I enjoy being near others of like mind," says Oyarzabal. One of his recent achievements is helping to coordinate the changing face of London for the Millennium Committee. As an art consultant, his clients include the Cardboard Theatre Company, a theatre group for homeless people.

Bermondsey's buildings are modest, real warehouses and factories, converted by sensitive hands. However, they are in close proximity to chic newly

Left: The colours and sequence of the *White Wall* painting are interpreted on the kitchen wall. Epoxy was poured directly onto the concrete floor throughout the space to re-create the density and consistency of the blue in the paintings.

Right: Oyarzabal is attuned to the need to produce results within a budget. The living area, behind a screen, houses simple cotton-covered sofas. Apart from the horizontal lightbox, all lights, fixtures, and incidentals were sourced from ordinary retail stores.

Below: The bedroom is at one end of the loft, and office space, seen beyond the candy-pink closet/room divider, is at the other end. A double-aspect space, natural light enters from windows at both ends, with the dining area falling between.

developed riverside areas, where penthouses boast rooftop helicopter landing pads and famous British politicians bask in spacious duplexes designed by Britain's great architects. The banks of the Thames on the east side have afforded many developers the opportunity to invest in wasteland space.

If the 1980s were about collecting furniture, the 1990s could be considered a time for looking at art. Although prominent in the 1970s and 1980s, conceptual art found its apogee in the last decade of the century, thanks to patrons such as the Saatchis. Richard Oyarzabal has taken his own interest in art one step further by actually selecting to "live" within a work of art; in this case, a combination of paintings by American artist Ellsworth Kelly.

Oyarzabal collaborated with architectural firm Urban Research Laboratory to create a colourful, sensuous space in which to live and work. "The architects took me literally at my word when I said I wished to live in an Ellsworth Kelly painting, first scanning some of Kelly's paintings into a computer, then, using some 3D CAD [Computer Aided Design] software, built computer models of the loft space and inserted the paintings as objects into the 'virtual' room."

Directory

GALLERIES & STORES

Ace Furniture
269 Elizabeth Street
New York, NY 10012, USA
Tel: + 1 212 226 5123
1950s to 1970s furniture, lights, and objects.

Aero
347–349 King's Road
London SW3 5ES, UK
Tel: + 44 (0)20 7351 0511;
132 Spring Street
New York, NY 10012, USA
Tel: + 1 212 966 1500
www.aero-furniture.com
Retro and contemporary furniture.

Louis Bofferding
New York, NY, USA
Tel: + 1 212 744 6725
Antiquarian, by appointment only.

Boom
53 Chalk Farm Road
London NW1 8AN, UK
Tel: + 44 (0)20 7284 4622
1970s European furniture, including Scandinavian.

Cappellini Modern Age
102 Wooster Street
New York, NY 10002, USA
Tel: + 1 212 966 0669

Century
68 Marylebone High Street
London W1 3AQ, UK
Tel: + 44 (0)20 7487 5100
Mainly American classics from the 1950s.

David Champion
199 Westbourne Grove
London W11 2SB, UK
Tel: + 44 (0)20 7727 6016
Ethnic accessories and contemporary European furniture.

The Conran Shop
Michelin House
81 Fulham Road
London SW3 6RD, UK
Tel: + 44 (0)20 7589 7401;
55 Marylebone High Street
London W1M 3AE, UK
Tel: + 44 (0)20 7723 2223
www.conran.co.uk

The Terence Conran Shop
407 East 59th Street
New York, NY 10022, USA
Tel: + 1 212 755 9079
www.conran.com

Eames Office Gallery and Store
2665 Main Street
Santa Monica, CA 90405, USA
Tel: + 1 310 396 5991
www.eamesoffice.com

Furniture Co
818 Greenwich Street
New York, NY 10011, USA
Tel: + 1 212 352 2010
Furniture, glass, and ceramics by top designers.

Galerie Chastel Maréchal
5 rue Bonaparte
75006 Paris, France
Tel: + 33 1 40 46 82 61

Galerie Yves Gastou
12 rue Bonaparte
75006 Paris, France
Tel: + 33 1 53 73 00 10
French 1930s and 1940s furniture and objects.

David Gill Galleries
60 Fulham Road
London SW3 6HH, UK
Tel: + 44 (0)20 7589 5946;
3 Loughborough Street
London SE11 5RB, UK
Tel: + 44 (0)20 7793 1100
1930s to 1990s furniture and objects, specializing in Garouste & Bonetti.

Harrods
The Contemporary Gallery (3rd Floor)
87–135 Knightsbridge
London, SW1X 7XL, UK
Tel: + 44 (0)20 7730 1234
www.harrods.com
Re-editions of all contemporary classics.

Haus
22–25 Mortimer Street
London W1N 7RJ, UK
Tel: + 44 (0)20 7255 2557
www.haus.co.uk
20th-century furniture classics.

Hemisphere
173 Fulham Road
London SW3 6JW, UK
Tel: + 44 (0)20 7581 9800
French and Italian 1930s to 1960s furniture and objects.

Lobel Modern
207 West 18th Street
New York, NY 10011, USA
Tel: + 1 212 242 9075
1930s to 1970s furniture, lighting, and objects.

Mission
45 Hereford Road
London W2 5AH, UK
Tel: + 44 (0)20 7792 4633
Furniture of contemporary design.

New York City Opera Thrift Store
222 East 23rd Street
New York, NY 10010, USA
Tel: + 1 212 684 5344
Retro thrift furniture.

Liz O'Brien
800A Fifth Avenue
New York, NY 10021, USA
Tel: + 1 212 755 3800
1930s to 1970s American furniture.

Themes and Variations
231 Westbourne Grove
London W11 2SE, UK
Tel: + 44 (0)20 7727 5531
Late 20th-century furniture and objects.

Troy
138 Greene Street
New York, NY 10012, USA
Tel: + 1 212 473 3000
Late 20th-century furniture, lights, and objects.

Twentytwentyone
274 Upper Street
London N1 2UA, UK
Tel: + 44 (0)20 7288 1996
www.twentytwentyone.com
Modern classics, mainly 1950s to 1970s.

Viaduct
1–10 Summer's Street
London EC1R 5BD, UK
Tel: + 44 (0)20 7278 8456
Classic contemporary furniture and lighting.

Gordon Watson Ltd.
50 Fulham Road
London SW3 6HH, UK
Tel: + 44 (0)20 7589 3108
Quality 20th-century furniture.

MANUFACTURERS

Alessi SpA
via Privata Alessi 6
29992 Crusinallo (VB)
Novara, Italy
Tel: + 39 03 23 86 86 11
www.alessi.it
Designs by Marianne Brandt, Ettore Sottsass, Richard Sapper, Michael Graves, and Philippe Starck.

Arflex SpA
via Monte Rosa 27
Limbiate 299951
Milan, Italy
Tel: + 39 02 76 31 81 62
Designs by Marco Zanuso.

Cassina SpA
1, via L. Busnelli
1-20036 Meda
Milan, Italy
Tel: + 39 036 27 03 13
Email: info@cassina.it
Designs by Cassina, Charles Rennie Mackintosh, Frank Lloyd Wright, Gerrit Rietveld, Le Corbusier, Charlotte Perriand, Pierre Jeanneret, Mario Bellini, Vico Magistretti, Gaetano Pesce, and Philippe Starck.

Ecart International
11 rue St. Antoine
75004 Paris, France
Tel: + 33 1 42 78 79 11
Re-editions of 20th-century classics.

Evertaut & Hille (Idem Furniture)
Cross Street
Darwen
Lancashire BB3 2PW, UK
Tel: + 44 (0)1254 778800
Designs by Robin Day.

Formica Ltd.
Coast Road
North Sheilds
Tyne & Weir NE29 8RE, UK
Tel: + 44 (0)191 259 3000;
10155 Reading Road
Cincinnati, OH 45241, USA
Tel: + 1 800 367 6422
www.formica.com

Fritz Hansen A/S
Allerodvej 8
3450 Allerod, Denmark
Tel: + 45 86 55 44 15
Designs by Arne Jacobsen, Vico Magistretti, Hans Wegner, and Verner Panton.

Knoll International Ltd.
1 East Market
Lindsey Street
London EC1A 9PQ, UK
Tel: + 44 (0)20 7236 6655;
105 Wooster Street
New York, NY 10012, USA
Tel: + 1 212 343 4180
www.knoll.com
Designs by Mies van der Rohe, Marcel Breuer, Eero Saarinen, and Ettore Sottsass.

Memphis
via Olivetti 9
20010 Pregnana Milanese (MI)
Italy
Tel: + 39 02 93 29 06 63

Herman Miller Inc.
855 East Main Avenue
P O Box 302
Zeeland, MI 49464, USA
Tel: + 1 800 851 1196
www.hermanmiller.com
Designs by George Nelson and Verner Panton.

Néotu
25 rue du Renard
75004 Paris, France
Tel: + 33 1 42 78 91 83;
409 West 44th Street
New York, NY 10036, USA
Tel: + 1 212 262 9250
www.neotu.com
Contemporary furniture and soft furnishings, such as rugs, in limited editions.

Race Furniture Ltd.
Bourton Industrial Park
Bourton-on-the-Water
Cheltenham
Gloucestershire GL54 28Q, UK
Tel: + 44 (0)1451 821446

Thonet GmbH
P O Box 1520
3558 Frankenberg, Germany
Tel: + 49 64 51 50 80
Designs by Alvar Aalto and Marcel Breuer.

Tupperware
P O Box 2353
Orlando, Florida 32802, USA
Tel: + 1 407 826 5050
www.Tupperware.com

Venini SpA
Fondata Vetrai 50
Murano
Venice 30141, Italy
Tel: + 39 04 15 27 48 32
Designs by Ettore Sottsass.

Vitra AG
13 Grosvenor Street
London W1X 9FB, UK
Tel: + 44 (0)20 7608 6200
Designs by Charles Eames, Verner Panton, Jasper Morrison, Michele de Lucchi, and Ron Arad.

Zanotta SpA
via Vittorio Veneto 57
Nova Milanese 20054
Milan, Italy
Tel: + 39 03 62 49 81
Designs by Achille Castiglioni and Marco Zanuso.

WEBSITE SOURCES

American Decorative Arts
www.decorativearts.com
1925–75 furniture and design resources.

Art Antique Merchants Ebay Auctions
www.artmerch.com
Mid-20th-century vintage.

Century Modern
www.circa50.com
Specializing in 20th-century modern furnishings.

ClassicOnline – Modern Furniture
www.classiconline.com

Collecting the 20th Century
www.collecting20thcentury.com

DMK Online Mainpage
www.dmk.dk
Danish furniture design of the 20th century.

Machine Age – 20th-Century Design, Arts, and Technology
www.machineage.com

Past Present Future Home
pastpresentfuture.net

Postwar Furniture and Design
www.mancha.demon.co.uk

Sourcebook of Modern Furniture
web.wwnorton.com/npba/sourcebk.htm

Swing – 20th Century Design
jgruener.hypermart.net

DESIGNERS & ARCHITECTS

Russell Bush
New York, NY, USA
Tel: + 1 212 829 0771

David Collins Architecture and Design
6 & 7 Chelsea Wharf
Lots Road
London SW10 OQJ, UK
Tel: + 44 (0)20 7349 5900

Oriel Harwood
66 Camberwell Road
London SE5 OEG, UK
Tel: + 44 (0)20 7703 5009

Eva Jiricna
38 Warren Street (3rd Floor)
London W1P 5PD, UK
Tel: + 44 (0)20 7554 2400

Christian Liaigre
42 rue de Bac
75007 Paris, France
Tel: + 33 1 53 63 33 66

Alberto Pinto
61 Quay d'Orsay
75007 Paris, France
Tel: + 33 1 45 51 03 33

Andrée Putman
83 Avenue Denfert Rochereau
75014 Paris, France
Tel: + 33 1 55 42 88 55
www.andreeputman.com

Jonathan Reed/Reed Design
151A Sydney Street
London SW3 6NT, UK
Tel: + 44 (0)20 7565 0066

Retrouvius
32 York House
Upper Montagu Street
London W1H 1FR, UK
Tel: + 44 (0)20 7724 3387
Architectural salvage company, by appointment only.

Philippe Starck
27 rue Pierre Poli
92130 Issy-les-Moulineaux
France
Tel: + 33 1 41 08 82 82

Urban Research Laboratory
Plantain Place
Crosby Row
London SE1 1YN, UK
Tel: + 44 (0)20 7253 6493
www.urbanresearchlab.com

Michael Wolfson
London, UK
Tel: + 44 (0)20 7630 9377

PLACES OF INTEREST

Burgh Island Hotel
Burgh Island
Bigbury-on-Sea
Devon TQ7 4AU, UK
Tel: + 44 (0)1548 810514

Busch-Reisinger Museum
32 Quincy Street
Cambridge, MA 02138, USA
Tel: + 1 617 495 9400

Charleston
Near Firle
Lewes
East Sussex BN8 6LL, UK
Tel: + 44 (0)1323 811265
Open to the public.

Denver Art Museum
100 West 14th Avenue Parkway
Denver, CO 80204-2788, USA
Tel: + 1 303 640 4433

Hill House (Charles Rennie Mackintosh)
Upper Chalhoun Street
Helensburgh G84 9AJ, Scotland
Tel: + 44 (0)1436 673900

Hotel Parco dei Principi (Gio Ponti)
via Rota 1
80067 Sorrento, Italy
Tel: + 39 08 18 78 45 88

Radio City Music Hall
1260 Avenue of the Americas
New York, NY 10020, USA
Tel: + 1 212 247 4777

Vitra Design Museum
Charles-Eames-Strasse 7
D-79576 Weil am Rhein
Germany
Tel: + 49 762 1702 3200

Index

Page numbers in *italics* indicate illustrations.

Acknowledgments

The author and publisher would like to thank:
Simon Alderson, Jane Barclay, Louis Bofferding,
Russell Bush, Tony Cunningham, Tiffany Dubin,
David Gill, Philippe Garner, Adam Hills, Steve
Hudson, Tom and Yvonne Huthert, Andrew
Jones, Clive Kandel, Jeff Kirby at Urban Research
Laboratory, Joanna Luxton, Aline and Laurent
Maréchal, Richard Oyarzabal, Raymond Paynter,
Alberto Pinto, Maria Speake, Nigel Talamo, Paul
Verburg, Clair Watson, and Michael Wolfson.

Picture credits Advertising Archives: **32**, **33**,
53 AKG, London: **52** Arcaid/Richard Bryant:
106 Camera Press: **74**, /Femina: **86** Jean-Loup
Charmet: **9** Elizabeth Whiting Associates: **71**
Philippe Garner: **12**, **13** The Glasgow Picture
Library/Eric Thorburn: **107** Angelo Hornak: **29**
Houses & Interiors: **30** Matthew Hranek: **50**
The Interior Archive/Henry Wilson: **104** Knoll:
51 Octopus Publishing Group Ltd.: **87**,
/Dominic Blackmore: **125**, **131** bottom, **132**
bottom, **133**, /Roger Gain: **70**, **94**, /Ken Hayden:
122, /Peter Marshall: **105**, /James Merrell: **4–5**,
8, **14**, **15**, **16** top, **16** bottom, **17**, **31**, **34**, **35**,
36–37, **37**, **39** bottom, **78**, **108** top, **108**
bottom, **109**, **110** left, **110–111** left, **124**, **127**,
128–129, **129**, /Neil Mersh: **6**, **18–19**, **19** right,
20, **21**, **22–23**, **23**, **24**, **25** top, **25** bottom, **26**,
27, **38**, **39** top, **40** top, **40** bottom, **41**, **42**, **43**,
44, **45**, **46**, **47**, **48–49**, **49** top, **49** bottom, **54**,
55, **56**, **57** top, **57** bottom, **59**, **60**, **61**, **62**, **63**,
64–65, **65**, **66**, **67**, **68**, **72**, **73**, **75**, **77** top, **77**
bottom, **79**, **80**, **81**, **82**, **83**, **84**, **85**, **95**, **96**, **97**,
98, **99**, **101**, **102**, **103**, **114**, **115**, **116** top, **116**
bottom, **117**, **118**, **118–119**, **120** right, **120**
top, **121**, **134**, **135**, **136**, **137** top, **137** bottom,
/Kim Sayer: **28**, /Simon Upton: **58**, **123**, **126**,
130–131, **131** top, **132** top National Trust
Photographic Library/James Mortimer: **11**
Verner Panton: **2**, **69** Alberto Pinto: **76**, **88**,
89, **90**, **91**, **92**, **93**, /Giorgio Baroni: **112–113**,
113 right

MAKING
THE MOST OF
KITCHENS

MAKING
THE MOST OF
KITCHENS

GILLY LOVE

conran
OCTOPUS

For Judith, Charlie, Emily and Georgia and their very happy kitchen

Commissioning Editor   Denny Hemming
Project Editor   Sarah Sears
Designer   Amanda Lerwill
Picture Research   Clare Limpus
Production   Mano Mylvaganam
Illustrator   Sarah John
Editorial Assistant   Paula Hardy

First published in 1997 by
Conran Octopus Limited
37 Shelton Street
London WC2H 9HN

Text © 1997 Gilly Love
Design and layout © 1997 Conran Octopus Limited

British Library Cataloguing-in-Publication Data
A catalogue record for this book is available from the British Library

ISBN 1 85029 861 0

Printed in Hong Kong

CONTENTS

BASIC PRINCIPLES

A kitchen should function smoothly and efficiently, but it should also be a comfortable room where you want to spend time. This is a subtle balance so the more effort you expend planning your kitchen, the less likely you are to waste energy and money trying to make a poor plan work. Be totally honest with yourself and make realistic plans that suit your lifestyle and budget, and the cooking and entertaining styles you enjoy, and you will design a kitchen you will never want to leave.

UPSTAIRS
DOWNSTAIRS

Top priority in this large living space was making the most of the available natural light. A low central partition ensures not only that daylight can illuminate the entire kitchen but also that the dining and preparation spaces can successfully be divided and united at the same time. The cook can also talk to guests sitting at the table rather than working with his or her back turned. Paint colour links the two areas visually: the brick wall, the floor of the dining space, the worktops and unit plinths are all the same blue.

The room seems to exude a feeling of airiness, partly because the tiny but powerful low-voltage halogen lights which illuminate the kitchen at night appear to be suspended unaided, so delicate is the trapeze. Underlining the illusion, the thick glass shelf on the far wall is invisibly fixed and seems to float.

On a more practical note, the low wall provides effective concealment for all the necessary plumbing and electrics so the sink can be situated in the centre of the room, the stove further along the run of units, and several electric sockets fitted into the wall above the worktop. The top of the wall provides additional storage and a serving area too.

ASSESSING YOUR NEEDS

Few people undertake the project of redesigning their kitchen without some expert assistance. Investing in a new kitchen is a major financial commitment and if the project is to be transformed into a successful and painless reality, it will require a multitude of decisions that need careful thought and precise coordination. A stringent budget is sometimes a welcome restraint as it focuses the mind on what your real priorities are and saves you from buying furniture, units or equipment that are superfluous to your needs. As a rule, if you spend more than 10 per cent of a home's resale value on a new kitchen, you are unlikely ever to realize your investment. It is wise to consider, however, that a well-designed and pleasant kitchen is often a major selling point when a house is put up for sale. Equally, you

may decide to recoup some of your investment by choosing items of furniture that are unfitted or freestanding; these, of course, may be picked up and taken with you should you decide to move in the future.

Planning a new kitchen from scratch may involve the services of an architect, particularly if you are dissatisfied with the size or position of the current space. It may be that moving a kitchen from one floor to another, or from the front of the house to the rear, or taking down a wall to create a kitchen and dining space is a better solution than merely refitting an existing room. A good architect will not only tell you what is structurally possible, but will also provide sketches and drawings that will help you to visualize these alternatives. If you are planning a major reorganization of the house, the project management skills of an architect are an invaluable asset; coordinating all the different tradespeople involved, keeping to an overall budget and completing the work to schedule is a difficult task best undertaken by a professional. Even if you are redesigning an existing kitchen, an architect may suggest changing the position of a door or adding an extra window which could make a significant difference to the practicality and atmosphere of the room.

Whether you decide to employ an architect, a kitchen specialist or to do it yourself, you will have to think and plan very carefully before you start if you are to avoid irritating and often expensive mistakes that you will regret later. Kitchen specialists can transform ideas into reality but they do need a great deal of your input if they are to come up with the ideal layout.

It is absolutely not necessary to put the sink in front of a window and yet in so many kitchens that is where you will find it. In this kitchen (left) the sink has been incorporated into the peninsula unit, and in this way it is still possible to access both windows without having to stretch. And anybody washing up has the unusual bonus of being able to face the people sitting in the dining space, rather than presenting them with a back.

Although the room is divided so that the fully equipped and functional kitchen is sited at one end, this merges very comfortably and easily with the dining area. A blue-and-white colour scheme is used rigorously and effectively, from china to fabric, to create a calm but refreshing atmosphere. No other colour is permitted – apart from the neutral tones of the dining chairs, metal pans and the wrought-iron chandelier.

A well-upholstered window seat and thick cushions on the dining chairs (with practical removable covers) ensure comfort. Moreover, both chairs and window seat are exactly the right height for the table so that it is easy for the entire household to relax in front of the inconspicuously positioned television as well as enjoying family meals together.

■ 9

HARD-WORKING SPACE

When space is restricted, compromises need to be carefully considered. While it is more practical in an ideal world to have a work surface between the washing zone and the cooking rings, sometimes it is just not possible.

Hard-working work areas in a limited space need durable surfaces that are easy to maintain. Here a single, seamless stainless-steel worktop incorporates the sink, stove and food preparation areas. Stainless steel can withstand any amount of heat and, as the name implies, is resistant to damaging stains caused by either acid or alkaline foods. Here it is extended over the front of the units below and in this way protects that surface from hot fat and food spills.

Powerful lighting is concealed in the extractor hood which easily covers and extends over the four gas rings, keeping the small area well ventilated. A mobile wooden chopping table with lockable castors provides an extra preparation area, while storage and hanging space is recessed behind the cooking area and open shelves are easily accessible at the end of the draining board. Slimline D-shaped handles on the unit doors and drawers are safer in a narrow galley kitchen than door knobs that may catch.

Much may be achieved by writing down exactly what it is you like and dislike about your current kitchen. For instance, many units are a uniform 90cm (35½in) high which unfairly discriminates against very tall or short people; working at such a height will be uncomfortable for them. Custom-built furniture or units with adjustable plinths can liberate the tall cook previously forced to prepare food hunched over a worktop that is too low.

The requirements of a family kitchen change as the nature of the family evolves. A family with a new baby may need to consider safety elements carefully and might choose childproof catches on cupboard doors, as well as organizing space where a young child can play under the watchful eye of a parent who is working in the kitchen. As children grow up and want to prepare their own meals, however, you will have to take into account that they may need their own space and different equipment.

Sitting down to make a comprehensive checklist of your likes, dislikes, needs and priorities is time well spent and it is worth mentioning even the smallest thing you find irritating at planning stage – however trivial it may seem. If you hate your dishwasher under the worktop, there is no reason why it cannot be positioned at waist level; and if you have a washing machine in the kitchen which seems to be incessantly in use and disturbs the pleasure of your cooking, try to find it a home somewhere else in the house.

FIRST RULES

The best way to begin planning a kitchen is to consider the position of the basic elements: the cooking equipment, the sink and the refrigerator. The formula for a convenient and safe working space between these items can take the form

PLAIN AND SIMPLE

Minimalist interiors, well executed, exude an exquisite simplicity. It is essential that all the materials are of the finest quality and every detail is perfectly constructed. Solid wood such as maple or teak matures and improves with age but needs regular oiling if these surfaces are regularly in contact with water. In this kitchen the work surface is made from a single piece of solid wood, thereby avoiding any joints where water could infiltrate. The sink is inset below the worktop for similar reasons, and sealed around the rim of the sink on the underside of the wood.

The dark richness of the natural timber is given dramatic impact by the white-painted tongue-and-groove cladding on the walls, which contrasts with the black stain that colours the cupboard and drawer fronts.

Above the worktop the simplest wooden brackets support two narrow shelves for plates, utensils and glasses that are regularly used. Yet all the joints are perfectly precise and each fixing point is virtually invisible – concealed with wooden plugs.

BEFORE YOU START

- Decide on a realistic budget that is in keeping with the value of your property, remembering to consider the potential for recouping any major investment – or lack of it.

- If starting from scratch, before you even start to plan the kitchen, decide if the existing room is in the best position. Would another room in the house make a better kitchen?

- Do you have the time or the expertise to embark on the project alone or do you need an architect or a specialist kitchen design company to supervise the installation for you?

- Make a thorough list of your likes and dislikes with reference to your current kitchen and also a list of your needs and preferences.

- Decide which layout you instinctively prefer, and then take into account the ergonomically sound principles of the 'working triangle'.

- Visit showrooms to gather ideas for overall design and appearance. Look at friends' kitchens in a new way and do not be afraid to ask if they 'work'.

- Make a portfolio of cuttings and a list of suppliers for all the elements you want – flooring, furniture, lighting. List prices and delivery times.

of one unbroken line or a closely related 'working triangle'. This work sequence needs to be confined to a distance of 5–7m (approximately 16½–23ft) and remember that you will have to include enough storage space for the materials and utensils you will use to prepare and cook food. Even if you only intend to make tea in your kitchen, you should still examine the relationship in the allotted space between the kettle, water supply, tea and sugar, cups and refrigerator. Ultimately, however, your choice of working triangle is likely to be determined by the size and shape of your current kitchen and whether or not you like that.

The in-line layout, which comprises one wall with a run of at least 3m and no more than 6m (approximately 10-19½ft), where worktops are interspersed with the sink and cooking rings, is probably the only answer for long, narrow rooms. One wall of a studio apartment would also be ideal, as you can hide the kitchen when not using it – behind hinged, fold-away doors or a long, sectioned screen.

With its design origins aboard ships, smaller yachts and aeroplanes, the galley kitchen has since been adopted in domestic interior design because it is ideally suited for small kitchens, where every inch is crucial. Counters run along two parallel walls with the sink and stove on one side, with a worktop between them, and the food preparation area and refrigerator on the other. The sequence is reasonably flexible, of course, even if the space between the elements is restricted. The corridor between the two counters needs to be approximately 1.4m (4ft) wide to provide easy access to under-counter cupboards and drawers.

An island layout is very traditional, reminiscent of huge farmhouse kitchens or the 'below-stairs' basements of grand houses, where the central table is also a serious work surface for rolling pastry, icing scores of freshly made cakes, or shelling peas by the bucketful. It is still the preferred option of many serious cooks who want lots of work surfaces. The additional central work station may even

ISLANDS & OUTCROPS

One end of this basement (far left) has been converted into a small kitchen, with the stove, all the work surfaces and two separate sinks incorporated into a peninsula unit. By positioning the sinks as single bowls on two corners of the unit, they can still be used if the hinged worktop-cum-dining shelf is raised.

If you are going to eat at the island unit on a regular basis, the work surface needs to overhang its base sufficiently to provide comfortable knee room underneath (left). Even if there is a dining table in the room, people love to congregate around the the action, a proposition made even more attractive if there is a glass or mug on the table and a stool on which to perch. An island can also provide a practical serving area, perfect for buffet-style entertaining.

Islands are best in larger rooms (facing page). Some have their own sinks for washing food, and usually groceries and implements are stored in cupboards and drawers in the base of the unit.

As a safety precaution, all island units need to be wired with power points so that small electrical gadgets, such as blenders and juicers, can be plugged in without the cords having to be trailed dangerously from the walls.

incorporate a small sink for vegetable preparation and even cooking rings, though this might necessitate an extractor hood too. It could also include a space that accommodates the more social side of the kitchen's character: everybody is always drawn – as if by magnets – to where the busy cook is working and an island kitchen is an ideal solution if your friends or family like to congregate to talk and eat together.

In L- and U-shaped layouts the working triangle works between two or three walls, an arrangement that works equally well in either a small or large room. Bear in mind, though, that however spacious your room, the triangle still needs to be contained within its optimum span. If you want to combine either alternative with a dining area,

which can often work well, you will have to position the table carefully, in order to give it a feeling of space and ease, whilst ensuring that you do not interrupt or block the working area with unnecessary obstacles.

The cooking zone

Only the cooking rings really need to be part of the working triangle; the oven or ovens and microwave may be built into a tall housing unit quite independently. An oven at eye level can be convenient for the busy cook glancing at what is cooking and it would also be safely out of the reach of young children. Wherever the cooking rings are placed, it is both safer and more practical to have heat-resistant

IN THE CORNER

L-shaped layouts are the best solutions for kitchens that also house a dining table, and in this spacious room (left) the two sides of the L-shape are fitted with work surfaces made of the same wood as the table. With no wall units and simply painted white brick walls, the interior feels more like a dining room even though it incorporates a well-planned working kitchen. There are glass-fronted drawers below the work surfaces; many cooks prefer these to cupboards as all the contents are visible as soon as the drawer is pulled out, even when it is packed to capacity.

A small L-shaped kitchen, or one where working surfaces are restricted, may need a dining table that can be used for preparing food. This table (facing page) has a durable marble top – perfect for rolling pastry, although generally too expensive to use as a work surface throughout the kitchen. Designing a layout that incorporates a variety of materials as work surfaces makes good practical sense, and this kitchen has stainless-steel worktops on one side of the vegetable sink and a solid wooden chopping block on the other.

■ 15

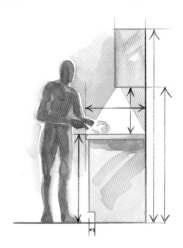

One of the major advantages of a custom-built kitchen (right and facing) over its manufactured counterpart is that all the furniture can be built at a height to suit the particular cook's most comfortable working position.

As a general rule, a work surface needs to be at hip height, so that your arms, even as you work, can be relaxed, although more strenuous tasks like rolling pastry are more comfortably undertaken at a slightly lower level. The depth of all the countertops is generally approximately 61cm (24in), as this is the standard depth of most appliances. Wall units are best hung with the bottom of the unit some 46-51cm (18-20in) above the worktop, so that the middle shelf is sitting just above eye level.

work surfaces either side. Another modern 'must' is an extractor hood above the stove. The most efficient models remove smoke and steam through a pipe vented to the outside while alternatives recycle the air above the cooking zone through a renewable charcoal filter.

The washing zone

Although the space and style of a kitchen will obviously be determining factors in your choice, a double sink is always the most practical solution because it offers you the most freedom. Dishes may be washed in one basin and rinsed in another; vegetables may be soaking on one side while you can be cleaning fish in the other bowl.

Traditionally, the sink would be positioned in front of a window. This may have been so that it could be as close as possible to the outside drain. But it would also have meant that the task of washing up – in the past probably the most time-consuming kitchen task – would at least have been sweetened by having something to look at. The recent advent and popularization of the dishwasher, however, has decreased considerably the scale of this chore so that you should no longer feel obliged to ensure a view from the sink; and if you do have natural daylight in the kitchen, you should use it instead to light the area where you are most likely to spend the greatest time. The dishwasher, meanwhile, although it should be close to the sink, can be at any level; whether you load and unload at floor or waist level is a matter of personal preference.

When you are deciding where you want to position the sink, do remember to give yourself enough storage and draining space for everyday china and utensils and cleaning materials. You might want to consider incorporating a

waste-disposal system into the sink and you will definitely need a refuse area, possibly with separate sections for cans, paper and biodegradable waste.

Washing machines have generally been accommodated in the kitchen as well, except in houses with a separate utility room or laundry, where the washing, drying, airing and ironing of clothes can be contained together. From a purely hygienic point of view, it is obviously more pleasant to keep dirty clothes away from food preparation. You may like to consider the cupboard under the stairs or even the bathroom as alternative sites as this would also free up space in the kitchen to allow you the convenience of that most liberating machine: a dishwasher.

HINTS ON PROFESSIONAL HELP

- Check out companies before you commit yourself – get references, see if you can visit some of their recently installed kitchens, and make sure you look at the quality of the materials and the standard of workmanship. Are the owners happy with the result; have they needed any after-sales service and if so, did they receive it?
- If you put a deposit on a kitchen, make sure that it would be protected if the company went out of business.
- Make sure you ask for itemized quotations for any work, materials or equipment, and check carefully to make sure that the specifications are exactly what you want.
- Be willing to be advised by an architect or kitchen design company but avoid being talked into designs either that you do not like or that you know you will not feel comfortable with, or even appliances and units that you do not need.
- Work out your own realistic time schedule and then add some more for unforeseen and unavoidable events, like incorrect measurements and late deliveries. You might be able to negotiate financial penalty clauses.

■ 17

The cooling zone

Modern technology has given us three types of cool space: the larder, the refrigerator and the freezer. Fresh foods, such as fruit and vegetables, are best kept at a cool (larder) temperature; meat and dairy products require a cooler refrigeration. The deepfreeze is used for longer-term storage of fresh and prepared foods. It is possible to buy one appliance that incorporates all three zones, so once again it is up to you – what you would prefer, or what is most suitable for the space you have available – whether you end up with the deepfreeze as a separate unit. As this appliance has to run continuously it is worth spending some time looking for an energy-efficient model; it should be well designed as well, of course, allowing you the use of every inch of space.

When you install your cooling appliances, you must remember that if they are going to be built in under a work surface, they must be adequately ventilated – either from behind or on top – to operate safely and economically.

IDEAS INTO PRACTICE

Having worked through all these practicalities in theory, you may feel confident enough to design and organize your new kitchen yourself. You may, on the other hand, feel even more in need of the expertise of a professional company; you will find that many kitchen design specialists offer a free design service, although some will charge a fee if you use the design and buy your kitchen elsewhere.

It is definitely a good idea to visit as wide a range of showrooms as possible: consciously pick up tips and ideas; start to accumulate a portfolio of designs, materials and colours which appeal to you. You should also cut pages out of brochures and magazines and start to put together a blueprint of your ideal kitchen.

Never order a kitchen from a brochure without first inspecting the showroom and examining the quality of the units and their finish. If you are unsure about a company and you do not know anyone who can personally recommend their work, make a point of asking to visit previous customers in your area. Smaller local companies are usually responsible enough to want to maintain a good reputation but it is worth checking that they can provide an efficient after-sales service. Do not be rash when it comes to settling your account either. Do not pay in full before your kitchen is installed to your satisfaction. And it is wise to check on whether your deposit is covered by an insurance scheme: you need to know that if your supplier goes out of business before your kitchen is delivered, your deposit will be fully protected.

If you are installing the kitchen yourself, make sure you can organize the electricians and plumbers to coordinate with your schedule. Bear in mind that fitting a new kitchen will probably take longer than you imagine and that it is often more convenient – and more comfortable – to work during the summer months when cooking can be reduced to a minimum. Make sure, if you are working, that the building work does not coincide with a particularly busy time in the office as it can add unwanted stress. And try to avoid clashes with important family events when you will need the full use of the room.

■ 19

PLAIN PLANS

A kitchen inspired by the sea in a house which stands on a clifftop overlooking the Atlantic Ocean. Sea blues contrast with brushed metal, limestone and pale wood fitted with ring-pull handles, the streamlined appearance of these latter creating a further nautical echo.

Every aspect of the kitchen has been considered with meticulous detail. As you enter the room you are struck by a collection of fine china displayed on glass shelves in a cupboard invisibly illuminated and recessed into a wall alongside a pair of raised draining racks, next to double butler's sinks. Built into one of the adjacent cupboards is the refuse bin which can be accessed both from the front and from above – via a round lid which lies flush to the worktop. Next door again is the dishwasher and beyond that a capacious full-height double fridge–freezer. The elliptical island unit not only has a built-in fan-assisted oven and lots of storage; hidden beneath its cool metal top are gas rings, which can be used at the same time as – or as an alternative to – the Aga on the opposite side of the room. The food preparation area, with another sink and a raised glass top, stands within easy reach of both cooking appliances.

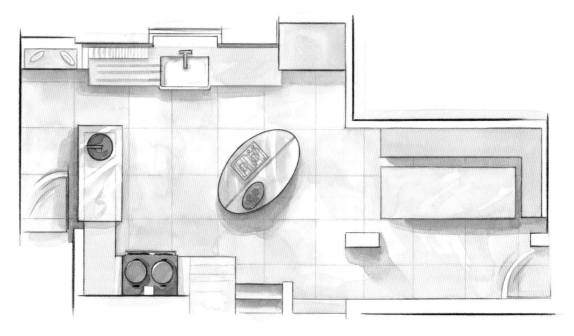

KITCHEN CHECKLIST:

What do you like about your current kitchen? What do you dislike about it? Which members of your family use the kitchen? How old are they? Is the main user right- or left-handed? Are there pets to consider? How frequently are meals prepared in your current kitchen, by whom and for how many people? Do you eat in the kitchen? If not, would you like to? Do you prefer a table or a bar? Once you have answers to these questions, you will find it easier to plan your new kitchen with a degree of focus, but this checklist will ensure that you do not forget to consider a vital element.

■ COOKING: Is electric, gas, or a combination of gas and electric your preferred option? Do you want a single or double oven, a microwave or combination oven, rings or ceramic cooktop? Will the cooker be built-in or slip-in or will it be a traditional cooker? Do you want a charcoal grill, or deep-fat fryer? Will you have an extractor fan, or filter and recycling hood?

■ KITCHEN EQUIPMENT: What equipment do you have, and what must you acquire? For cooling: refrigerator/deepfreeze, larder fridge, separate fridge and deepfreeze. For washing: single or double sink, separate extra sink, dishwasher, washing machine and tumble dryer, combined washer/drier.

■ SMALL GADGETS: Kettle, toaster, food processor, coffee maker, coffee grinder, electric can-opener – are they all essential? Plan where you will keep them before you rewire.

■ STORAGE: What can you accommodate in the available space and what must go elsewhere: china and glass, saucepans and cookware, fresh vegetables and fruit, canned and boxed food, wine and other bottles, small jars of spices and herbs, and heavy-duty objects – broom, mop or vacuum cleaner, plus the cleaning materials, and a waste bin (separated for recycling?).

■ LIGHTING: Well-lit worktops and ambience are both crucial.

STYLE

The one compliment guaranteed to make
you glow with pride and satisfaction is
being told that your kitchen has style!
Defining exactly what having style
means or how you achieve this desirable
quality is open to debate; it is probably
easier to define what it is not. Spending
masses of money does not necessarily
create a stylish kitchen, nor does
slavishly adopting someone else's taste.
And though you may be inspired by one
look and copy aspects of many others,
your own style will be totally personal.

AWAY FROM IT ALL

The kitchen in this beach house in Western Australia (right) opens onto the sand and the ocean beyond. You can almost feel the warmth of the sun and the cooling breeze as it moves through the wall of louvred window doors. Comprising two island units with a hob set into one and a sink in the other, it is simply furnished; meals are probably cooked on the barbecue and eaten outside on the deck.

Echoes of the sea abound: from the bright turquoise paint which reflects the colour of the sea, to the seaweed-shaped cutouts and the furniture, which has been distressed with a wash of soft colour to resemble sea-tossed driftwood. Maintaining the natural theme, the floor is simple wood.

This country kitchen in the northern hemisphere (facing page) is cool too – like a larder – but you can imagine how warm and cosy it would be during the winter. Eau-de-nil walls and cupboards contrast with the warm tones of the scrubbed pine of the table. One wall is lined with shelves filled with rustic bowls and china, creating a traditional dresser effect, while a collection of hand-woven baskets is stored and displayed on the corridor wall outside.

COOL & COSY

The weather has a major influence on the way we live. Homes in climates that are constantly hot are constructed in a completely different manner to those that have to withstand dramatic changes from one season to another. In a country where for most of the year food is cooked on an outside barbecue and meals are eaten al fresco the kitchen design may reflect this lifestyle. It may be that ensuring that you have good ventilation to maintain a cool atmosphere inside becomes your primary concern, and of course efficient refrigeration will be vital if perishable foods are to be stored safely. Choosing lightweight furniture that can easily be moved into the garden, or onto the verandah, patio or terrace is another practical aspect to consider; it is usually made of woven cane or pale timber.

If it is continually hot outside, you may prefer to create a kitchen that will also be visually cool – by devising a pale, soothing colour scheme. Use flat matt shades of blue and grey with pale painted walls and try to avoid complicated patterns that would upset the sense of calm. It is worth remembering, however, that these decorative schemes need lots of bright clear light, or their coolness tends to become clinical and unwelcoming.

The enduring appeal of the white villages of rural southern Spain, Provence and Tuscany is due in part to the other colours – drawn from the surrounding countryside – that are combined with that white. These baked terracotta, natural sandstone and dusty pink tones also provide warmth in the winters, which are often harshly cold. Of course you can glean inspiration and decorative ideas from holidays abroad, but to transport the style of one country

to another may be completely disastrous: colours that look sensational in sunshine can feel oppressive unless you can reproduce a similar light, by natural or artificial means.

Thick wooden shutters on the windows, or canvas canopies, function not only to provide shade in summer but protection from freezing winds too. Stone or tiled floors are pleasantly cool in the summer and may be warmed up by mats or rugs if necessary. And you may have a door opening directly from the kitchen onto the garden that can be left open permanently when the weather is fine

to allow a cooling breeze to refresh the kitchen. But cool breezes become icy draughts in winter so this will probably need weatherproofing – with a warm and colourful curtain perhaps. And flexible but reliable heating that can respond quickly to changes in the weather is a modern convenience that nearly everyone would consider essential.

It is obviously sensible to wait for a year before you make any major design decisions, unless you are really confident that you can anticipate any seasonal weather changes. Real style is definitely more than surface deep.

CONTEMPORARY

While so many apparently modern kitchens are in concept deeply rooted in history, or at least have some nostalgic reference point, real contemporary style is always original. To be successful this very individual approach takes a good deal of expertise and experience and, of course, supreme confidence. These kitchen interiors are unforgiving and exacting, devoid of clutter and superfluous decoration. If necessary, in order to achieve what is considered correct proportion, form and an appropriate quality of light, rooms are dramatically restructured: ceilings are raised, windows replaced and doors moved from one wall to another.

You have to find ingenious ways to solve conventional problems, for compromise is not a word that finds space here. Colour is used dramatically and boldly; textures and surfaces are chosen for maximum impact. Everything exudes precision; every detail is completely perfect and each piece of equipment has its own carefully considered space. Whether it is constructed of natural or synthetic materials, furniture is generally custom-made.

Contemporary style suits those who enjoy clear, clean and open interiors, those for whom comfort means a room that makes them feel soothed and serene. If contemporary style were to have any connection with the past, its minimalism is most likely to have been inspired by Zen philosophy, which aims to create stillness and simplicity.

Employing an architect or designer to help you to create a unique kitchen can be a very successful collaboration; the more you involve yourself in the project the more likely it is to reflect your personality and not just be a showcase for someone else's style.

FORM AND SPACE

Major structural changes can often create a superior kitchen. This basement room (facing page) was made more accessible when an extra flight of steps was added to the original steep and awkward staircase. These new steps were specifically designed to provide most of the storage required in the kitchen. The refrigerator under the original staircase has enough space to allow good air circulation and a slimline extractor hood fitted above the cooking rings is ducted up inside the staircase.

Standard-sized kitchen furniture would have been dwarfed in this high ceilinged room (left). The kitchen design here, therefore, has increased the scale of the furniture but reduced the complexity of each form to a minimum of simple sculptural shapes, carefully proportioned and dramatically lit: a huge slab of steel spreads across a dark blue pedestal and gleams under the row of halogen spotlights recessed into the ceiling; a single block of cupboards follows the contours of the room, each door accented by a thin stainless-steel strip; and a row of stools – bowl-shaped seats perched on sensually curvaceous legs – stand in complete contrast to the restrained geometry of the whole.

You know at a glance that this is the
kitchen of a serious cook: all the plinths
have been adjusted to be at the most
comfortable height for its owner and it
is organized with textbook precision.
Following the classic L-shaped work
sequence, cooking and food preparation
is ergonomically contained along two
walls. The cooking unit, comfortably
ventilated with a large extractor hood,
sits next to a small sink, followed by
work surfaces before turning the corner
to another larger sink with a dishwasher
beneath. Each saucepan has its own
place under the cooktop so that it is
within easy reach when needed, while
wide, shallow drawers safely store and
protect the cook's knives and utensils. A
narrow shelf runs all round the top of
the stainless-steel splashback, a feature
often found in restaurant kitchens where
it would potentially be hazardous –
dangerous even – if doors of upper
cupboards were to be left open. This
shelf houses foods and utensils that are
used regularly, but it also provides visual
relief from the daunting expanse of
stainless steel. The remaining walls are
painted in white waterproof paint, and
the ceiling, with safety sensibly in mind,
has been tiled with fireproof tiles.

PROFESSIONAL

While cooking and preparing food may be low on some people's list of priorities, for others these activities will completely dominate the design of the kitchen: full-time cooks and caterers may only really feel at ease in a room that has been devoted to working with food rather than dining and entertaining. Professional kitchens are planned as workplaces, taking into account the exacting regulations of commercial hygiene standards. And it is worth noting that if you will be producing food for public consumption in your kitchen, the same constraints will apply, even in what you would consider your domestic environment.

This hard-edged, industrial-looking style of kitchen may appear intimidating if you do not cook regularly for vast numbers of people, but a meticulous consideration of efficient ergonomics achieves an unexpected degree of comfort which can be very attractive. An uninterrupted run of work surfaces allows the cook to move around the kitchen at speed; in stainless steel, the preferred surface of professional cooks, it will be extremely hard-wearing and resistant to excessive heat and both acid and alkaline stains. The worktop may also include a large built-in hardwood chopping board, with a pull-out waste-disposal drawer beneath into which to scoop vegetable peelings, and perhaps a slab of cool, smooth marble as well, traditionally the best surface for rolling pastry. Otherwise a freestanding central work station with all-round access may include both cooking rings and a sink for washing fruit and vegetables. The height of all these worktops needs to be carefully calculated because at the wrong height they will make preparing and cooking food unnecessarily tiring.

Most professional cooks prefer to have access to both gas and electricity for cooking. They need bigger ovens to accommodate larger trays and baking sheets and often their stovetops have integrated charcoal barbecues, grills and griddles. Cooking on a large scale generates a huge amount of heat so an extractor hood that more than covers the gas or electric rings reduces heat and steam to maintain a pleasant working atmosphere.

Task-specific lighting is important, so that delicate jobs like filleting and icing can be undertaken without having to fight with your shadow: halogen spots provide glare-free illumination for the front of worktops and some extractor hoods incorporate a good light. Meanwhile rows of spots above the counters offer flexibility and efficiency.

Regularly used pans and utensils are always within reach – either hanging above or immediately beneath the stove. Industrial units, with adjustable shelves and frames, from which utensils may be hung, provide strong, flexible storage; they can either be fitted or freestanding. Open shelves above worktops display more equipment, which may have been chosen for its stackability, while tall, deep shelves at lower levels are used as dry food cupboards for catering-size jars, cans and more weighty items. Many cooks prefer wide drawers so all the contents are visible from above, and can be easily removed and replaced. Razor-sharp knives – a cook's most precious equipment – are carefully protected in a knife rack or felt-lined drawer.

One or even two dishwashers are essential rather than a luxury here, and they need to take a wide range of items: pots and pans as well as the standard dinner service.

UNFITTED

The idea of actually creating an unfitted kitchen is not new; recently, however, and possibly in reaction to the unbroken but rather anonymous lines of units typical of the 1960s and 1970s, the unfitted kitchen has begun to re-establish itself as more than a viable alternative – both with regard to function and aesthetics. By having kitchen furniture as opposed to built-in units you change the whole character of the space, making it more of a room than a work station.

If your aim is to create an entertaining and relaxed living area, rather than keeping cooking and dining areas more formally separated, you will find that unfitted pieces will sit more happily alongside bookcases, desks and sofas than any of their fitted counterparts – of whatever material. But unfitted furniture has other advantages too. You can take it with you should you decide to change home; just as well because a solid wood food cupboard made from quality timber will be expensive, the sort of long-term investment that you would not want to leave behind. You can also vary the height of unfitted furniture so that your work surfaces can vary in height to suit a range of functions: it is, for instance, easy to arrange for a long table with a sink and draining board built into it to be higher than one intended for chopping vegetables; or surfaces at varying levels might be incorporated into a single, movable piece.

Traditional natural materials spring to mind – natural woods with maple, teak, granite or slate work surfaces – in rooms inspired by the simple but exquisite interiors of the American Shaker communities or the vast echoing kitchens of eighteenth-century English country houses. Beautifully made work tables fitted with draining boards and deep butler's sinks, vast larder cupboards with woven vegetable baskets on runners and built-in spice racks, and contemporary interpretations of country dressers all serve to create a traditional farmhouse feel, with all the modern appliances hidden carefully in cupboards to maintain the appropriate atmosphere. You could equally easily, however, use lacquered fibreboard, opaque or clear glass or brushed metal for a more contemporary feel.

ECCENTRIC

An interior perceived by some as eccentric in style might be deemed totally undesirable by others, and greeted with cries of horror. Some brave souls, who have a completely individual style and total confidence in their own taste, do create some stunning interiors. In these kitchens pure whim takes precedence over practicality; visual delight is often wildly self-indulgent; nothing needs to match.

Idiosyncratic kitchens are rarely formally planned; they are more likely to evolve. Furniture and furnishings are accumulated and chosen for their individual merits rather than being selected to fit into a preconceived scheme. Priceless antiques can sit happily alongside chairs retrieved from refuse tips and Japanese simplicity may be juxtaposed with Victorian gothic. The eccentric look is frequently characterized by wit and humour: someone obsessed with photography might create a kitchen resembling a dark room; somebody else might cover every available surface with scraps of broken china and glass for a mosaic effect.

True individualists have a very particular skill; they can improvise in any situation to produce original solutions that challenge accepted conventions and still 'work'. Instead of levelling and covering a scruffy and uneven concrete floor, the eccentric might varnish it – to accentuate the stains rather than concealing them. Similarly, the gleaming white surface of a refrigerator front might be considered vastly improved by several coats of vibrantly coloured spray paint.

It is not possible to copy an eccentric kitchen style because its spirit is the creation of one individual, but you can be inspired by it, admire the confidence of its creator and acknowledge that the style has a real integrity.

PURE STYLE

Very little has actually been changed in the transformation of this sorting office in Paris into a perfectly functional – if rather unconventional – kitchen. But the decision 'not to touch' is just as much a part of creating a sense of style as wiping the slate clean and filling a space with your own new formula. Style has a lot to do with recognizing the character of a place and maximizing its potential alongside, and in conjunction with, your own likes and dislikes.

The immediate attractions of this room (left) are obvious: a massive skylight floods the room with an abundance of natural daylight, and shelves, cupboards and bins that once housed letters and parcels need only the most basic adaptation to accommodate groceries and equipment.

Elaborate cooking does not seem to be a major priority in this kitchen; a real atmosphere and a wonderfully relaxed sense of space are more important. And when you are imagining pale sunny breakfasts in spring, with freshly made coffee, warm croissants and brioches, and simple romantic suppers beneath the stars and the candlelit chandelier, somehow the culinary detail does seem secondary to the atmosphere.

A TOUCH OF THE COUNTRY

In most countries, and particularly those with a temperate climate and definite winter, people naturally congregate in the kitchen, given the opportunity. Traditionally, the range meant that the country kitchen was constantly warm; nowadays its modern descendant, be it an Aga or Rayburn, an American Viking or Westinghouse, a French Bocuse or Ambassade Lacanche, appears as often in the city as in the country – a touch of nostalgia with all the benefits of modern technology ensuring a constant temperature and comfortable atmosphere which encourages relaxed meals with family and friends – a real antidote to a hectic lifestyle.

Understandably, then, country style remains hugely popular today and continues to evolve in a variety of novel contexts. Over-designed and intricately carved furniture has given way over the years to simpler designs, but the kitchen table remains an important focal point, taking centre stage in order to cater for any task, whether that be children's homework, pea-shelling, bean-slicing or bulb-potting. Whether the table is old or new it is likely to be wooden, although highly polished and valuable antiques tend not to be appropriate. Round tables are more sociable but chairs need to be a comfortable height to maximize this advantage. These do not necessarily have to be a matching set, however; a random selection of sympathetic designs can look equally effective. Upholstered cushions will give additional comfort and decorative interest, but removable, washable covers are almost essential as they will inevitably need regular washing with food constantly present. Long refectory tables, on the other hand, almost invite the use of benches – ideal for squeezing in more bodies at a feast.

Although perhaps they lend themselves less to long after-dinner chats, hard benches can hide under the table between meals, making the most of the space available.

Decoration is generally simple with natural materials tending to feature strongly. More expensive initially than other options, these not only last longer, but sustain chips and stains more gracefully, acquiring a desirable patina.

COUNTRY COUSINS

There is something about country living
that appeals to everyone to a degree,
wherever they may live. It may be a basic
existence, particularly if the house is
isolated, or if you are undertaking
extensive refurbishment of a rural ruin,
but the lure of uncomplicated simplicity
is attractive. In this French farmhouse
(facing page) the kitchen table is the
result of some inspired improvisation:
three planks have been glued together
on breeze-block plinths. And the front of
the cupboard is faced with chicken wire.
Both function efficiently, and replacing
the roof beams and windows was more
pressing than fashionable furniture.

   Many city dwellers also emulate the
simple country life in their homes, be it
to add a nostalgic or romantic human
touch to their stressed lives or as a more
self-conscious design style. The focal
point of this vast, low-ceilinged room
(left) is a wooden dining table in the
centre of the room, while the well-tested
stove–work surface–sink–work surface
configuration is confined to one side of
the room. Pans hang close to the cooking
area, and a tiled linoleum floor is easy to
maintain, hygienic, soft and warm under
foot. Devoid of any really rural element,
it is a room with country overtones.

STYLE ■ 35

FITTINGS AND FURNITURE

The best way to start to equip a kitchen from scratch is to examine your cooking preferences and then determine what is important; which pieces of equipment best suit your practical needs rather than your aesthetic aspirations. Once you have the first couple of pieces of the jigsaw fitting together, the myriad decisions involved can often have a direct bearing on each other, and others will fall into place. Start with what is vitally important and always buy the best quality you can afford.

Many serious cooks prefer one single cooking centre that combines the cooking rings and oven. The unit here (right) has four gas rings on a stovetop wide enough to include a central grill plate too – for sizzling steaks or making perfect pancakes. Pots and pans are kept warm and dry on a built-in hanging rail and in the drawers beneath the oven.

The Aga (centre), traditionally synonymous with country kitchens, is now available in a range of attractive colours and feels equally at home in the city. Agas can be electric, solid fuel, oil- or gas-fired; the standard size has two ovens with an additional warming chamber, but there is also a larger model for bigger families or for the professional catering kitchen.

An ingenious solution for making the most of a corner in a small kitchen (far right), this six-ring stove is fitted at right angles to the corner with utensils strung up on butcher's hooks on a fine rail across both walls. A chopping block on the top of a mobile unit can be slid under the worktop when not required. White ceramic tiles provide a tough and heatproof splashback behind the stove while the work surfaces on either side are of hard-wearing stainless steel.

EQUIPPING THE SPACE

Whether, having weighed up the advantages of all your options, you decide to have your kitchen redesigned or merely revamped, and once you have agreed on the layout, you will need to budget carefully for your new furniture and equipment. And while cabinets and work surfaces are obviously important, new appliances must be given priority as they can devour a large part of your available funds.

Appliances

The cooking zone is usually the most important area of the kitchen and your first big decision will be whether to combine cooking rings and oven or to separate the two appliances. Most cooks prefer a gas stove which offers fast and flexible heat; the rings may be combined with wok burners, which is practical if you enjoy cooking Chinese food. Deep-fryers or barbecue grills are other options to consider, but are only worthwhile if you are going to use them regularly. Integrating a stove into a central island unit is becoming increasingly popular as there is space on three sides to prepare food and often seating too, underlining the cooking–eating connection. If gas is not available, opt for halogen, the most responsive of the electric options.

Conversely, it is electricity that offers the best choice in oven-cooking methods. You can buy either single or double built-in ovens and a large household may require the latter, although a single oven and separate microwave might give you greater scope. A microwave is invaluable, both for defrosting, and for providing instant meals for reluctant cooks. When looking at ovens, ensure that the grill is efficient; one with a dual circuit is best so that half the grill area can be used on occasion rather than the entire roof of the oven. An eye-level grill is convenient; so too a self-cleaning facility; and good interior lighting, of course, in order to be able to check on your food's progress at a glance. You can also buy multi-function ovens, which combine a fan-assisted heat function – best for roasting meat – with a radiant heat function, which is better for baking successful pastry and cakes.

You may want to situate all the various cooking functions together and many top-of-the-line stoves today are custom-made, offering you a choice of ovens, a mixture of gas and electric rings, chargrills, griddles and hot plates. Big commercial stoves designed for professional catering kitchens are worth considering too, particularly if you are planning an unfitted kitchen, as they are freestanding. They produce more heat than most domestic stoves so they require good air circulation in the kitchen – and preferably a ducted extractor hood that covers the entire top.

If gleaming industrial steel is not your style, there are colourful enamel stoves on the market, fired by gas, electricity, oil or solid fuel, that may be more appropriate.

Particularly in keeping for a traditional or country look, this type of stove comes into its own where there is no mains gas supply, as it often generates enough heat to warm a kitchen and can usually be adapted to run a water-heating function too. Made in cast iron and designed so that heat comes from all sides of the oven, they have a reputation for turning out good bread and juicy joints of meat.

Before you set your heart on a big brute of a stove make sure that installing it will not present insurmountable problems – either because of its sheer size or its weight. And an industrial stove may not be a wise choice if you have children because the doors can get dangerously hot. Domestic models are often fitted with stay-cool systems to keep doors at a low temperature when the oven is hot.

Even if you have a dishwasher, it is worth having a double or even triple sink as well – to let you wash up, rinse and prepare food all at the same time. Large kitchens with a central island may even have space for an extra small sink specifically for food preparation. A waste-disposal unit will require a second sink, fitted with curved waste pipes to avoid blockages and a reasonable water pressure to flush away rubbish. Good-quality mixer taps will control both the temperature and flow of the water, but it is worth remembering, as you survey what is available, that simple taps of streamlined design are the easiest to keep clean, particularly if the local water produces chalky deposits, and that taps with no washers or ceramic discs will avoid a limescale build-up if the water is hard.

CLEAN AND DRY

A seam-free solid work surface (left) incorporates a small round sink and a draining board that has a slight gradient so that water runs down into the bowl. The chopping board has been tailor-made, chiselled to grip the edge of the sink and the side of the work surface.

Draining boards are not essential, particularly if you have a double sink and if, as here (left), the room has a dishwasher. Only the saucepans are washed by hand and these are left to drip into the sink below. The counter top which surrounds this sink has been treated with several coats of tough waterproof varnish to protect the vulnerable wood beneath.

A modern interpretation of the traditional draining rack (right): water runs off these plates and bowls straight away as they are stacked at a slight angle in the two runs of slotted shelves above the sinks. Fragile, stemmed glasses do not get smashed if they are left to drip-dry after they are washed up, and they are most safely stored hanging upside down from their bases: this arrangement acknowledges both these issues. A monobloc tap swivels over either sink and a crosshead tap provides a separate source of drinking water.

PRACTICAL ADVICE

- Separate oven and rings or combined unit? A freestanding stove can be a major feature, but dividing the cooking areas offers more flexibility.
- Consider the available energy choices – gas, electricity, oil, solid fuel – in relation to your central heating.
- If you cook regularly, a large refrigerator is essential and needs to provide chilled and cold storage.
- Summer gluts of home-grown garden produce will require a large freezer.
- Invest in good work surfaces and get them fitted properly – no dirt traps.
- Every kitchen chore may be made a pleasure if you can access the relevant equipment comfortably.
- Cabinets and work surfaces should be at a comfortable height. Standard units are often adjustable, custom-made furniture is made to measure.
- Doors may be hinged on either side; merely rehanging a door may make more and better use of your space.
- Dimmers give you flexibility, changing lighting levels at the flick of a switch.
- Keep dangerous implements out of reach of young children and put childproof locks on lower cupboards.
- A fire extinguisher, fire blanket and smoke alarm are essentials.

■ 41

ALL PRESENT AND CORRECT

A narrow corridor has been transformed here (right), becoming a wall of well-organized storage. Glasses and tea and coffee pots that are regularly used are displayed on different shelves according to type, style and height, all within easy reach. Maturing preserves which do not need to be accessible fill the highest shelves, while decanters and spirits live lower down. Right at the bottom, in the coolest and darkest place near the floor, is the wine, laid horizontal to keep the corks in contact with their contents.

A washing zone, confined here to a tiny alcove (right below) is lined with panels of stainless-steel mesh. The many shiny pans and lids are hung from their handles on butcher's hooks suspended from a steel bar fixed between the walls. Below them a regiment of utensils hang on a metal rack fixed to the back wall. Table cutlery is kept safe and well organized in two metal baskets above the sink. Part of the charm of this display is the bright lighting above, which emphasizes the gleaming, absolutely grease-spotless metal – grimy varieties need not apply!

Professional cooks definitely favour industrial-quality, stainless-steel sinks while big white Belfast sinks seem to be compulsory in a traditional kitchen – along with a grooved wooden drainer. There are, however, some good-quality acrylic materials available that can be cut and carved, and joined with seams that are hardly visible, in order actually to integrate the sink and drainer into a worktop. Cheaper enamel sinks will probably prove a false economy as they are easily chipped and scratched, and stain readily.

You may be incorporating a dishwasher in your kitchen for the first time – and with a slightly guilty conscience. This time- and labour-saving device is no longer considered a luxury, however, and generally they use less water than washing up in the sink would. If the kitchen is also to be a dining area, it is worthwhile asking to see your preferred model in operation before you buy it: do not dismiss the more expensive dishwashers too quickly for they not only use less water and detergent but tend to be less noisy too.

The cooling zone – and thus your choice of refrigerator and freezer – has recently become more sophisticated, in part because of the development of chilled, ready-made food as well as the frozen alternatives, and in part because of the modern trend for more fresh food, especially fruit and vegetables. Sauces and jams which were previously kept in cupboards once open now have to be kept chilled because they contain fewer preservatives than before. Many refrigerators contain one 0°C (32°F) section for fresh meat, fish and chilled foods, and another at 2°C (36°F) to keep fresh fruit and vegetables in optimum condition.

Big refrigerators do not have to be hidden away behind cabinet doors any more; they are now available in beautiful colours and even, for the organized and tidy-minded, with

SITTING PRETTY

Some storage solutions just cannot be improved upon, so while this well-established kitchen has undergone numerous colour changes over the years, the fundamental design is timeless. White walls and ceramic tiles contrast with the black marble splashback and work surface, creating a background where the shelves and doors may be painted in any colour – an economical alternative to an entire refit of the kitchen when you feel you need a change. The narrow and shallow shelving displays china and glass that has been arranged according to how frequently it is used. Mismatched items and irregular shapes (greedy for shelf space) are hung from hooks on a rail running the length of the wall – even through the bracket supporting the lowest shelf. The old and fragile jelly moulds have been tied up and hung from hoops of string.

Under the shallow sink on two open shelves are a small tin pan and some baskets. This arrangement retains an air of rustic elegance in a space that often houses floorcloths, bleach bottles and untidy collections of brushes. Storage and display have been combined in a simple, straightforward way and yet the overall impression is of sophistication.

■ 43

transparent doors, making all the contents clearly visible. Virtually all refrigerators are now made CFC- and frost-free so that the nightmare of defrosting the fridge is a thing of the past. The refrigerator may be combined with a freezer, and some include an ice-maker which, if it is automatic, will need to be connected to the main water supply.

A tall and capacious fridge-freezer may well reduce your general storage requirements. And it is always better to have extra space in the refrigerator so that its contents do not have to be piled up, but rather are stored in an organized fashion – to be easily accessible. If your old fridge was too small, think in terms of double the capacity this time, and if you have limited space, consider moving your freezer to another room; it may fit neatly under the stairs, in the garage or a utility room.

Storage

A well-ventilated pantry cupboard may well be big enough to store all the food you are not keeping in the refrigerator and you will be able to see all your cooking ingredients at a glance rather than having to forage through lots of different cupboards. Similarly, a tall pull-out pantry unit makes all its contents clearly visible and gives easy, instant access. It is personal preference, however, that will have the greatest influence on whether you decide to keep all the contents of the kitchen behind closed doors or to display pots, pans, china and glass on open shelves or behind wire mesh or glass doors. One large sideboard, whether it is an inherited antique or of a contemporary design, may well provide you with everything you need, not only to display china and glass, and store cutlery and utensils, but with space for dry foods and cans too.

CLOSED DOORS

'A place for everything and everything in its place' seems to have been taken to an extreme in this kitchen (facing page): tiny cube-shaped cupboards arranged in a perfect square appear suspended on a checked pattern of white and cream ceramic tiles. One cupboard holds plates, another stores cutlery, a third is filled with glasses and the fourth is packed with cups and saucers.

In a small kitchen where countertops are limited (right), pull-out units provide extra working surfaces for preparing food. Whereas some such units have only restricted movement – forward and back from their 'built-in' positions – both these trolleys are completely movable; having been positioned where they are required, they are then stabilized by locking brakes on their front wheels. They are topped by thick solid wood chopping boards – ideal as it is easier to chop vegetables on a slightly lower-than-average surface.

White paint and tiles have been used very effectively in this kitchen, with its sloping roof (far right), to raise the height of the ceiling – visually at least. Wall units have been specially made to follow the contours of the room to make the best use of the corner space.

Mixing open shelving with worktops of varying heights – with giant drawers or pull-out wicker vegetable baskets – helps to create an informal atmosphere in keeping with the nature of a friendly kitchen where you would want to spend your time; the regimented uniformity of long runs of anonymous cupboards on the walls and under worktops tends to work in direct opposition to this, and looks a little dated today as well. Unfitted kitchens with freestanding fixtures and furniture have recently become increasingly popular, in part because they allow you gradually to create just such a personal room, adding pieces one by one, from all sorts of different sources – as and when they are needed, rather than to match a design scheme's rules.

When it comes to storing both equipment and food, the golden rule is to keep everything as close as possible to where it is most logically used. And if you don't use it, you don't need it in front of you: the space that the unwanted electric deep-fat fryer occupies might be better given over to a juice extractor, for example. Small electrical appliances should be kept on a worktop next to an electrical outlet, or above or beneath it for easy access and replacement. Mugs and beverages need to be kept wherever the kettle stands; regularly used pots and pans should be stored in wide drawers close to or underneath the stove; spices and herbs, best kept in the dark, should live in cupboards or drawers close to the main food preparation areas.

Central islands may be fitted with a canopy extractor that might itself incorporate shelves for the seasonings you use all the time, and hanging rails perhaps, for utensils and pans. Commercial kitchens tend to have all the pots and other cooking equipment clearly laid out on shelves and dangling from rails to aid the professional chef's furiously fast manufacture of food; but while masses of pans and utensils can make an attractive display, in the kitchen of the infrequent cook they may just become irritating dust traps.

Paying attention to small details can make a huge difference to the smooth running of a kitchen. Having sections in a drawer logically separates different types of cutlery and utensils, for example; choosing pans and china that stack easily will save cupboard space; fitting a wall-mounted magnetic rack or cutting slots into the back of a worktop will keep your knives safely contained whilst maintaining their sharp blades; an open plate drainer over the sink minimizes drying-up time and stores the plates where they are unlikely to get chipped; and a mobile butcher's block can provide extra chopping space where you need it. Be sure that this latter has lockable castors, however, to give your extra work surface some stability.

Furniture

In between all this equipment are all the work surfaces and furniture that coordinate your kitchen's functions. You do not have to spend a fortune at this stage, as it is quite possible to recondition and redecorate units that you might at first feel should be discarded.

Establishing the correct height of a work surface to suit both the cook and the relevant task is a design detail that is often overlooked or ignored. Heavy tasks such as rolling

The lighting system you choose for your kitchen may have to be multi-functional, comprising well-lit work stations and a friendly, atmospheric eating area. You will have to analyse your needs and preferences very carefully before you start, remembering to take into account the variation between daylight and after dark, because you will probably want to conceal wiring where possible.

This charcoal grey kitchen (far left) could have felt cold and unwelcoming were it not for the accents of shiny stainless steel which reflect both the natural light from the south-facing window and the beams of the recessed ceiling downlighters by night. Strip lighting concealed beneath the wall units and extractor hood illuminates the top of the stove and cooking area.

This combination kitchen-cum-dining room has an extraordinarily high ceiling which requires two rows of wall lights at what would be regular ceiling level to illuminate the work areas adequately. Above the dining table tungsten bulbs, shaded by translucent glass shades, direct clear pools of light onto the dining area; they hang as if floating, and, in order to prevent any glare at suppertime, they are crown-silvered.

out pastry or kneading bread are more comfortable and less of a strain on the back if done at a lower level, whereas you need to put less weight behind making a cup of coffee. Some standard kitchen units have adjustable plinths but obviously the ultimate luxury, custom-made furniture, can be designed to 'fit' the individual.

Shelves need to be within easy reach to avoid back strain and rarely used items may be stored even higher up; but do make sure that you have a sturdy pair of steps to hand for when you do need to access them.

Make sure that your choice of seating is appropriate. High stools are fine for quick meals or for a drink while the cook is preparing a meal but they really do need some sort of back support if they are to be your main seating. You must remember to give yourself sufficient leg room too,

Natural sunlight can dramatically affect the atmosphere in any room and kitchens that benefit from masses of warm daylight are a pleasure to work in and joyful places to entertain family and friends. Not only does this kitchen (above) have a south-facing window but a rooflight directly above the island unit as well, flooding the room with sunlight. Reflecting off a natural matting floor, dappled daylight reinforces the bright freshness resulting from the room's green-and-white colour scheme. At night the atmosphere is maintained by a choice of recessed downlighters in the ceiling, wall lights, an electrified chandelier and traditional candlelight.

whether at a bar or at a big table with chairs that would be comfortable for hours. The kitchen table and its chairs are often the most well-used pieces of furniture in the home and they need to be versatile enough to cope with a variety of functions. Dining is just one aspect; the kitchen table is just as likely to become a temporary desk for homework – doing and overseeing – household budgets, or hobbies.

Light and air

A well-designed kitchen is a well-lit kitchen, a sensitive combination of natural and artificial lighting offering the most effective and versatile answer. Food preparation areas need plenty of light – daylight when possible, but artificial at night. A sink near a window, for instance, will probably need an electric light as well to make chores like washing up as painless as possible. And strip lights hidden under wall units illuminate worktops without an eye-tiring glare.

Recessed downlighters provide unobtrusive general lighting and those fitted with eyeball mechanisms may be rotated for more focused lighting – either over a work surface or to display shelves filled with precious china or glass. To create more subdued, atmospheric lighting, you could hang a chandelier of aromatic beeswax candles over the table, or even a light with a rise-and-fall mechanism, especially if you can black out the functional part of the kitchen. As well as being economical, dimmer controls can be very useful too in this respect. Remember that to skimp on lighting is a false economy: lights can always be turned off, but it is more than irritating to work in semi-darkness.

If you are to create a pleasant atmosphere for both working and relaxing in the kitchen, the disposal of both cooking smells and steam, which can cause condensation,

is a very important factor. Fume extractors that fit directly over the stove and which are ducted to the outside provide good ventilation. They are more efficient than those with replaceable filters. These merely re-circulate the air, though they are a perfectly adequate compromise if the stove is so sited as to make access to an outside wall impractical. Many stoves today have integral extractor hoods – with integral steam-proof lighting – which duct the cooking fumes down and away, so you may not be given a choice.

The general ambient temperature of the kitchen is an often-overlooked design detail, particularly if your plans are drawn up in the summer when the weather is warm. The most straightforward option, if space is not an issue, is to incorporate thermostatically controlled radiators at the start, on your plans. Underfloor heating, meanwhile, is as ancient as the Romans and if your new kitchen is to have a hard, cold stone or marble floor it may be worthwhile considering this. Alternatively, perimeter heating pumps out both radiant and convected heat from pipes concealed in trenches around the edge of a room or behind skirting boards, or fitted into furniture plinths. Kickspace convector heaters, which are compact and unobtrusive, fitting neatly into what would often be wasted space in the plinths of kitchen units, are an energy-efficient answer. Switch-operated, they not only provide instant heat, but may also be fitted with a cool-air option for use in hot weather.

Whatever your choice of heating and air conditioning, it is wise to invest in a system that reacts quickly. Intensive cooking generates lots of heat and a flexible and efficient heating and cooling system not only helps to keep cooking pleasurable, but allows you to sit down almost immediately to eat and relax in an appropriately refreshed environment.

LIGHT FROM THE SKY

Painting the walls of a kitchen such a deep blue takes a degree of confidence and a sensitive understanding of light and its effect on colour. These walls (left) remain lively because they are lit by three huge double-glazed rooflights, which provide continuous natural overhead lighting during the day. This illumination is replicated at night by tungsten halogen tubes which, unlike their fluorescent counterparts, give a very flattering light – almost like natural daylight – which is also restful on the eye. The stove and its surrounding work surfaces are illuminated by lights contained in the extractor hood, while the panel of sheet metal that serves to protect the wall from cooking splashes also reflects light back into the room.

If you intend to eat in the kitchen regularly, and particularly if it is also your only dining room, bear in mind that sympathetic lighting can dramatically increase the enjoyment of your meals. Natural light is most flattering for both food and faces, and at night flickering candlelight can make the simplest dish deliciously exciting.

DECORATION

The decoration of your kitchen is the one aspect of its design in which you have almost infinite freedom of choice; it is your choice of colour and texture which puts the individual stamp on a kitchen, making it completely unique. Often the decorative scheme of a kitchen, unlike any other room in a home, seems to evolve, as if naturally, as all the other elements fit together; yet with varying proportions of sensitivity and confidence you will realize your own ideas at the same time – subtle, dramatic or elegant.

COLOUR AND TEXTURE

Many people who feel relatively secure about planning the layout of a kitchen, and who find fitting all the necessary equipment into the available space a satisfying challenge, recoil at the prospect of selecting a colour scheme.

The style and look of your furniture, stove and other major appliances may influence to a large degree your decisions about colours and textures for walls, flooring and work surfaces. Once you have chosen your fixtures and fittings you may find that a colour scheme is developing naturally, or that the amount of wall space remaining is so minimal anyway that it requires no additional colour. Your crockery, glass and other visible accessories may provide sufficient additional spot colour and texture without the need to introduce any more.

WALLS OF COLOUR

A Mediterranean atmosphere has been created (left) with a bold and confident use of deep colours. Midnight blue units and cupboards contrast with a colour-washed wall. This orangey wash was inspired by the range of terracotta tones found in the floor tiles. Painted first with several coats of dark cream emulsion (latex), the wall was then painted with a fine film of thinned-down water-based burnt sienna paint which gives the final colour a luminous effect.

Paint is by far the cheapest decorating medium and, providing it is waterproof, is ideal also for sealing and colouring surfaces of wood in a kitchen. Here (right) complementary tones of soft blue and aqua green cover the panelled walls, ceiling and cupboards, chosen to match exactly the tones of the soft furnishings. The fine red line which occurs in two of the fabrics is repeated as a dado, accenting the transition from dark to light aqua on the walls.

Before committing yourself to a larger expanse of colour, you are well advised to paint a series of small test patches. The shade may look very different from your swatch and really needs to be seen *in situ* in natural light as well as under the artificial lighting of the shop.

COLOUR POINTERS

- Large, sunny kitchens can happily embrace any colour scheme but smaller, darker rooms may need help: light, airy colours will tend to create a feeling of space.

- Kitchens used mainly at night benefit from rich, darker colour schemes which look better artificially lit, and which positively glow by candlelight.

- All surfaces need to be tough and hardwearing; a special paint effect may need the protection of extra coats of varnish to keep it in pristine condition on kitchen walls.

- The wall space between units and wall cupboards needs a tough, durable surface of brightly coloured ceramic tiles, or a solid tone of waterproof paint, or else should be decorated with storage displays, such as gleaming knives and utensils.

- Work surfaces may provide bands of horizontal colour that can contrast or complement kitchen furniture. They may vary in material and texture depending on their use – mix bleached wood with slate or gleaming steel with a matt acrylic composite.

Walls

You may feel that the wall space that remains may be better painted in white or a pale neutral tone to increase the size of the room, at least visually. Today, however, paint can be matched to any colour you choose, which makes it totally versatile: you can either choose to reproduce exactly the shade of another of the decorative elements of your room, or to contrast with it. Alternatively, you might feel that a country-style kitchen would benefit from a range of fresh colours that reflect the natural world – warm cream tones and butter yellow, fresh leaf greens and soft sky blues. Paint is probably the most economical decorative material too, so if you do make a mistake it is relatively cheap to correct it. It is still worth buying test cans of your shortlisted shades and painting patches on several walls – to look at the colours at various times of day and under artificial light too. Washable paint finishes are the sensible choice in the kitchen, particularly near the sink and stove.

PATTERNS & PAPER

Ceramic tiles, and particularly those with a glazed surface, are hardwearing and easy to keep clean on both walls and work surfaces. They need to be laid with meticulous accuracy to avoid leaving gaps that will attract grease and grime like magnets; handmade tiles, which can be slightly irregular in shape, are perhaps better laid by a professional.

A splashback of diagonally patterned ceramic tiles (left) picks up the blue–grey colour of the veins in the marble countertops and dining table. The same tiles are used to line the kick-space between the units and floor. The overall effect is clean and neat.

Many people avoid using wallpaper in the kitchen, but providing it has a waterproof finish, or is treated with a thin layer of clear varnish, it is still a perfectly practical option. The dado rail usefully divides this witty home-made wallpaper from a simple trompe l'oeil paint effect below that resembles a sandstone wall. The combination of the black-and-white wallpaper and the colour of the lower part of the wall is echoed and emphasized by the black wrought-iron storage unit and the naturally mellow wooden tones of the small chopping-block table.

FEET ON THE FLOOR

In any kitchen the part of the floor that needs most protection is the part immediately in front of the working areas: water and food spillages can quickly damage all but the most durable floor surfaces. Here (right) bright yellow and green ceramic floor tiles are used in conjuntion with a wooden floor. This is not only an economical solution, because tiling the entire floor in a large kitchen would be terribly expensive, but also a means of decorating an often-neglected aspect of the room, whilst avoiding an overpoweringly busy effect. The tiles protect the floor below the cabinets, while the main floor area is softer – in simple wood. Linking and dividing the two is a quasi-geometric leaf-design border. The units, meanwhile, have been painted in a paler yellow – to act as a transition between the strong tones of the floor and the harsh white-tiled walls.

You will walk and stand more in the kitchen than in any other room in the home and an old hard floor will be very tiring on the feet and legs. If you like the look of stone or ceramic tiles but not their chilling hardness, why not consider vinyl or linoleum, which have a similar appearance but are much cheaper, as well as being softer underfoot.

You may want to use a more decorative wallpaper if the kitchen is part of a dining or living room but if this is to be hung near work zones it needs to be hardwearing. If you want to use a paper that is not recommended for kitchens you can overcome the wear-and-tear problem by discreetly fitting acrylic panels over the wallpaper in any vulnerable areas – over the worktops, say. Thus, the wallpaper can be continued all around the room to create a unified scheme, whilst being protected with a wipe-clean surface in the kitchen. There are also some wallpapers available which can be painted with a protective covering but this may cause a distortion of the paper's colours.

Floors

Obviously if the rest of the home is carpeted, particularly with coir or sisal matting, it would be highly impractical to continue this surface into the kitchen. However, you can create the illusion of a large, unbroken space if you choose your floor colour carefully. You may want your kitchen floor to be a complete contrast, or you may want to introduce a a chequerboard pattern of several colours, which visually reduces a larger area.

Stone, slate and ceramic tiles will never wear out but are very unforgiving on both your legs and breakable objects. They are also very cold. This is unimportant, of course, in a hot climate and not an insurmountable problem anyway, underfloor heating or washable rugs providing potential solutions.

Solid wood floors need to be laid carefully and sealed with a tough sealant if they are to remain waterproof; chipboard or cork tiles are a cheaper option but these also need to be set on a perfectly flat surface and sealed with

A diagonally-oriented check of blue and white ceramic tiles on the splashback has been repeated on the floor (left above) using blue and white paint. The wooden boards need to be absolutely flat with no gaps, and smoothly sanded, to create the effect of a convincing floor mat. Before you start, each square should be carefully marked and confined with masking tape; then you can paint alternate squares with eggshell or similar oil-based paint. Once you have the right depth of colour, the whole floor (even the unpainted areas) need several coats of waterproof varnish.

Whenever it comes to choosing a decorative scheme for a room it is essential to consider how it relates to any adjoining spaces. The intricate patterns and designs of the traditionally decorated room in the foreground (left below) are not continued in the modern kitchen beyond: the visual link is made by the yellow on the walls and storage units, which picks up exactly the background yellow from outside. This vibrantly cheerful, warm tone contrasts sharply with the cool grey flags of the floor, which will, nevertheless, be more than welcome in a hot Mediterranean kitchen – on both eye and foot.

FLAMBOYANT FINISH

A sweep of matt-lacquered units in deep, relaxing blue (far right) blend beautifully with shiny metal and clear glass, and provide a neutral framework for an incongruous collection of mismatched ceramics and kitchen objects.

High-quality wood has an expressive grain which mellows and improves with age; its warm tone here (right above) contrasts with sharp grey and brushed metal to create a sophisticated and truly contemporary kitchen: edges are sharp, natural and industrial textures combine, and the whole exudes clean design.

Meanwhile a traditonally designed and equipped kitchen (right below) is given a highly contemporary look: the units have simply been given a metallic veneer and finished with wonderfully quirky door handles. It is always worth remembering that it may be possible to recycle second-hand units in reasonable condition – replacing the work surface, repainting the existing doors or fitting new ones. Replacement doors of good-quality cabinets tend to be of standard size and can usually be bought off the shelf. Alternatively, have them custom-made; it will still be sustantially cheaper than a whole new run of units.

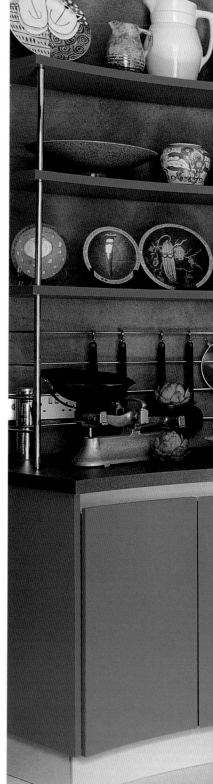

- A solid colour floor may create an illusion of more space, whereas complicated patterns will visually reduce a large expanse.
- Consider how the colour schemes from the adjoining rooms complement or deliberately contrast with the kitchen. Check that the junctions between floor surfaces are safe.
- Refresh colour schemes seasonally by changing a mat or rug on the floor, tablecloths, curtains, cushions – even pictures from summer to winter.
- Natural light is the best form of lighting – if you have it, use it to its maximum potential.
- The darker end of a kitchen may be brightened considerably by hanging a large mirror there to reflect natural light from the window.
- Very bright sunlight can heat as well as illuminate a kitchen: adjustable blinds will give you more control of both temperature and light. Beware of continuous sunshine which fades stained and solid wood furniture.
- If you enjoy constant novelty, use flowers, plants, fruit and vegetables to give splashes of instant, glorious colour that can be changed from one week to the next.

several coats of polyurethane. Working on the existing floorboards is one of the cheapest options. They will need to be sanded and then, to give a soft, muted floor colour, you can paint them with a diluted water-based emulsion paint, before protecting them with a floor sealant. Apply sealant directly onto the sanded boards for a natural look.

Linoleum is a delightfully versatile flooring material: warm and soft underfoot, water-resistant, easy to clean. Better still, it is made from natural materials. Alongside developments in technology, its physical character has been gradually improved; today it is a tough flexible surface available in a wide range of colours, and some textured looks – marble, wood, ceramic tiles – giving it huge design potential. Vinyl flooring is another cheaper option which is available in sheet and tile form. Many of the better quality designs are thicker, making them warmer underfoot and quieter to walk on – important if you have neighbours downstairs. Be sure to look for the best quality you can afford and make sure it is laid well, with invisible seams.

Surfaces that work

Horizontal colour will be provided by the work surface you choose. There is no rule that says that all your worktops need to be of the same material; it is better that they complement the units or cupboard fronts on which they sit. Inevitably, however, worktops need to be durable, and preferably heat-resistant. They also need to fit neatly, avoiding ugly gaps that can be both difficult to keep clean and even unhygienic. Granite and slate are both hard-wearing but they are expensive materials that need expert fitting for perfect joints. Marble is another natural material

PIERCED AND PRETTY

Colourwashing is really only appropriate for large areas and works best on kitchen walls or units. It is particularly effective used on the panels and frames of these cupboards (far left). The mouldings have been defined in a contrasting green dragged finish and this colour is then repeated as a wash on the drawers. And although these cupboards here are new, this finish gives the effect of paint that is slightly distressed and worn with age.

Modern acrylic materials that emulate marble or granite can be cut and carved and joined with invisible seams so that the worktop and walls meet perfectly with no gaps (left). The front of the counter is comfortably rounded; it slightly overhangs and protects the cupboards beneath. The soft muted grey worktop is echoed by the window frame, gently contrasting with the calamine pink of the upper walls and ceiling. The room is subsumed in a peaceful coolness.

A fine mosaic of blue and pink tiles creates a cloudy coloured splashback and countertop (right). To avoid an ungainly joint, the thickness of the counter has been determined by the size of the tiles. Slots cut into the cupboard doors keep the contents well ventilated.

that works well with both painted and plain wood and provides a useful cool surface. Woods such as oak, beech or elm mature and improve with age, but require sealing at regular intervals with oil or polyurethane. On the other hand, teak – used extensively in boat-building – naturally repels water, although even teak does appreciate regular oiling if it is near the sink or if you chop directly on it. There are also many acrylic surfaces available nowadays in a rainbow of colours and effects; these may be custom-made to fit the space exactly and can be shaped to form sinks, avoiding any jointing.

Ceramic tiles may be laid as work surfaces: matched to vertical splashbacks, or arranged in a decorative design between the countertop and cupboards above, or even co-ordinated with a tiled floor. Be sure that the tiles you select are recommended for work surfaces and ensure that they are laid completely flat on hardwood or a particle board surface with waterproof grouting. Even with this proviso tiles may not provide an even surface for food preparation – unlike stainless steel, which features in most professional kitchens. It is durable and easy to clean, but you will need to build in separate wooden or marble areas – or blocks – for chopping vegetables.

By far your cheapest option would be to choose from the vast range of laminates on the market, but it is certainly a false economy to buy the very cheapest; it may not be heat-resistant and if it stains and scratches easily, it will become a constant irritation. Better quality laminates, on the contrary, offer all the advantages of natural materials as well as offering you the opportunity to combine a coloured work surface – be it sober or bright, plain or patterned – with an integrated wooden chopping area.

COUNTERS OF CONVENIENCE

Accommodating both a double sink and drainer and a stovetop, fitted with a glass lid, this island unit (far left above) still maintains a feeling of space; nothing seems crowded in this compact working area. The glass lid not only helps to keep the stovetop clean; it also acts as a protective screen between the steam or spitting fat of cooking and the food being prepared on the other side of the island. Cupboards above the sink offer convenient access to essentials.

The muted tones of this blue-, green- and stone-coloured splashback and the matt green, painted cupboards (far left below) sit well with the display of opaque glass jugs and bottles above it. A solid wood worktop reinforces the natural feel that pervades the kitchen, generated by the colours of the tiles.

A narrow galley kitchen (left) has been built in the corridor that links one end of the house with the other. Natural wood, white paint and brushed steel have been juxtaposed to provide a highly sophisticated and stylish interior with overtones of café chic, but one which will also prove an efficient functional environment: easy to maintain, with everything within reach and well lit.

Picking up on details

The most cautious colour scheme can be made flamboyant if you put colourful accessories, crockery and utensils on display. If you have a kitchen table, a bright vinyl tablecloth will provide colour and protect the top. The chairs give you lots of scope too: paintwork or upholstery can be movable highlights or spots of contrast in the overall scheme.

Vases of fresh flowers or a huge jug filled with buds or branches refresh any room and temporarily alter the colour scheme. Similarly, bowls of bright red peppers or seasonal fruits can treat a monochromatic room to a burst of colour. House plants last longer and can also soften the hard edges of an interior's design. You do need to select them to suit the micro-climate available, however. And do not place plants high up on wall cupboards; they rarely receive sufficient light unless there are skylights, and are too easily forgotten. Aromatic herbs, citrus trees or fragrant jasmine all appreciate a kitchen's warmth and relative humidity: a row of herbs along the window gives you fresh natural colour and a constant source of culinary flavourings. A windowbox outside could be planted up with bulbs for a change of scenery in spring, or filled with evergreens or perennial plants to create a natural screen.

Window dressing

Maximizing the amount of sunlight in a kitchen is a vital design consideration, but you may find striking a balance between light and privacy a problem if you live very close to your neighbour. Ventilation is crucial too, so access to the window needs to be simple and safe, and you should select styles that are easy to open but which provide adequate security. You could actually increase the number of

DESIGN ACCESSORIES

A collection of antique colanders, pans and moulds (left) can make an attractive and sometimes colourful collage on a plain white wall. It is vital,however, if this idea is to be successfully replicated, that all the individual elements be kept clean and shiny. Saucepans hanging from rails must gleam too (right below) if they are to be decorative as well as merely being to hand. Here the horizontal axis of these rails is further echoed by the recipe-book holder's runner; all the little details build towards a bigger effect.

If you have a warm sunny windowsill, meanwhile, it will be ideal for growing herbs (right), such as parsley and basil, chives or chervil. Both the plants and bunches of freshly picked herbs will be a decorative bonus in any room, providing greenery, a pleasant aroma and fresher-than-fresh flavourings for your cooking.

It is not uncommon for a fashion designer to choose a different motif for each button on a jacket. Less expected here, the concept is extended with ease and style as a variety of leaf designs become handles for a flight of drawers (far right above). The darker, painted beading on each drawer not only creates a more interesting profile for the whole but consciously frames each handle too.

windows – not forgetting the massive potential of skylights – and this might prove the best investment you could make in terms of renovation. And then your window dressing must be flexible enough to address all these requirements.

Blinds are the obvious choice. Roller blinds may be fitted at the base of the window and drawn upwards to allow light from above whilst concealing the interior of the kitchen below. Café-style curtains create the same effect while Venetian blinds control the amount of light entering the room as well. And wooden shutters are a neat, clean-cut option which can add a degree of warmth.

If the kitchen is not well ventilated and the window is close to the cooking source, it is wise to choose an easy-to-clean window dressing because it will quickly be covered with a layer of grease which attracts dust and grime.

LIGHT AND SHADE

Wooden shutters may be adjusted to maximize the light in this kitchen (facing page); they can be made in sections so that the upper doors may be left open during the day while the lower ones ensure complete privacy from the street outside. At night they are completely closed and then they merge with the walls and retain the warmth in the room. While here they are painted white, they can just as easily be left as natural wood or painted a tone to contrast with the wall colour. These shutters are louvred like Venetian blinds and the fact that the sunlight can thus be filtered makes this a very attractive form of window dressing: wooden furniture, which can be quickly faded by really bright sunlight, is here given a degree of cooling shade.

A beautiful view from the sink (left above) is enhanced by four slender windows that help to provide sufficient daylight in the room; keep the kitchen cool; and, by virtue of their narrow shape, act as an important security feature in this isolated country house.

Roman blinds do not restrict the delightful view from this kitchen window (left below) but neatly fold into a wide pelmet by day and are released to just above the level of the plants at night.

SMALL
KITCHENS

Preparing and cooking food in a space where everything is within easy reach and logically located is a real pleasure, and much less tiring than it would be if you had to keep walking the length of a huge room. Designing a kitchen to fit into a small space in a large room can often be a deliberate decision; perhaps the only way to stay sane as a cook in a room where entertaining and people are priorities is to contain the work area. Careful planning, however, will fit a fully functional kitchen into the tiniest room.

MACHINES FOR LIVING

The famous French architect Le Corbusier once described a house as 'a machine for living'; the definition seems just as appropriate for a well-designed kitchen, particularly a small kitchen, where all the living functions seem concentrated in a limited space – from cooking, eating and even entertaining, to dish- and clothes-washing, and drying – all cogs in a well-oiled machine. This exaggeratedly high-ceilinged room has been converted into a fully-equipped kitchen without compromising any feeling of relaxed space. A floor-to-ceiling unit tucked into what would otherwise be dead space beside the window contains and conceals all the intestines of the central heating system, simultaneously creating a small but effective drying cupboard – located in an ideal spot conveniently close to the washing machine.

An extra-wide windowsill serves as a breakfast bar, which makes the most of the panoramic view from the window, while the stool that tucks neatly underneath can also be opened out into a set of sturdy steps, tall enough to provide access to the higher shelves.

INSPIRATIONS

When you are planning a small kitchen you should follow all the basic principles but you will probably end up doing more research, and having to employ more ingenuity. All this will pay massive dividends, however. Whereas in the past one-room living was usually forced upon people when their financial situation allowed nothing else, nowadays all the social stigma has gone and it is not only popular but chic, particularly in cities where space is at a premium and property expensive: from concept to execution, designs ooze practicality and efficiency.

It may be worth visiting some show flats in buildings where architects have been employed to divide up huge spaces into apartments of varying sizes; sometimes they have managed to fit the kitchens into really tiny spaces. Alternatively, you could go to a boat show and take a peek at the galleys of ocean-going cruise yachts where marine designers have designed kitchens that can cater for the appetites of a hungry crew in a situation where space is at a real premium, and where there are other considerations, such as safety, that have had to be taken into account as well. Not only may many of the general concepts be worth a second thought as the plans for your kitchen evolve, you might also come across some compact and streamlined appliances that are just what you need.

Designing for small spaces is all too often seen as problematic rather than as an exciting challenge. Yet many people deliberately choose to have a small kitchen. Those who generally eat out may decide to limit themselves to a mini-fridge and microwave, a designer toaster and the finest espresso machine, but even these few choice items

need to be accommodated with care in any design scheme if they are not to look uncomfortable. And keen cooks should take comfort from the knowledge that many of the best cooks actually prefer working in a small kitchen designed specifically for their own style of preparing and cooking food, with everything within easy reach.

For those people who enjoy entertaining but for whom the luxury of a big, social kitchen is out of the question, the idea of a self-contained working area along one side of a longer room may appeal. The first kitchen I designed for myself measured approximately 2.1 x 1.8m (7 x 6ft); a breakfast bar separated my 'kitchen' from the room proper but friends could still sit or stand and talk to me while I was cooking, and I could easily converse with people at the dining table on the other side of the room. It worked

TALL IS BEAUTIFUL

An entire wall here (left) comprises cupboards and drawers to provide ample storage capacity in this very narrow, irregularly shaped kitchen. Even access to the lockers right at the top does not pose a problem, because a metal bar has been fixed to run along the length of the wall for a simple ladder to be clipped over. For the faint-hearted, perhaps, this may look a little precarious, but, on a more practical note, it does mean that every inch of space is working hard – essential in any small room, but crucial in a work station like a kitchen.

The D-shaped handles are, in fact, more interesting than they at first appear. And it is worth noting that, ergonomically speaking, this design works better – is easier to use – if it is fixed vertically for opening doors and horizontally for pulling out drawers.

One of the drawers has been adapted to contain a small pull-out table; when not being used, it slides back and sits flush with the rest of the units.

One alternative to the small kitchen is to combine cooking, eating and living in one open-plan space. In the 1960s, in cities like New York, former industrial buildings were transformed into single-floor apartments where all the separate elements bar the bathroom – and even that, sometimes – were designed to fall into one space. The attraction of this style of living is the luxurious feeling of open, clear and light space. Areas like the kitchen still need careful planning, and good ventilation is essential if you intend to sleep only a few feet away from where you cook. Unless you are a coffee-and-toast cook, an extractor fan or a window that can be adequately opened is advisable. In fact, even the smell of burnt toast can linger without help from a fast-acting extractor fan. This kitchen (left), positioned under one of the room's windows, is arranged in an L shape and equipped with a powerful extractor above the stove. In order to maintain an atmosphere of spaciousness, there are no wall-mounted units; the storage space has been confined to the floor, while three transparent shelves are used to display a small collection of glass and chrome.

perfectly except that there was not enough space for two people to wash up! It proved invaluable having a recycling hood, as well as an extractor fan and a window that was easily opened, as the amount of heat generated by four rings and an oven would have become unbearable in a tiny space, particularly on top of the pressure of cooking.

Sometimes drastic and bolder measures are necessary. If your kitchen space is too claustrophobic then you may want to consider taking down a wall and combining two rooms. If you do this it is worth consulting an architect to ensure that all the proposed structural changes conform with building regulations as most countries now have strict fire-and-safety regulations as regards kitchens. If open planning does appeal, you will have to think through the ramifications of combining the functions of the kitchen and another room. Easy maintenance is crucial, for example, so that you can switch off from work mode and relax in the other half of the room without being reminded constantly about clearing up – a dishwasher may be deemed essential, so that dirty plates can disappear from sight immediately. Alternatively, the whole kitchen can be hidden behind screens or folding doors, or well-directed spotlights and low-level lamps can put the work area into virtual darkness whilst the rest of the room is illuminated.

To compromise ...

For those with a conventional lifestyle but only a small kitchen, compromises may have to be made on equipment: you may have to content yourself with two cooking rings; a single sink instead of a double; and a refrigerator with a freezing compartment rather than a freezer. There may be other multi-functional space-saving solutions that are suitable too: a double sink with a fitted chopping board as an optional extra provides a vital work surface, and similarly, some cookers (stoves) have covers or hinged lids that are flat and strong enough on which to prepare food.

Machines for both washing up and laundry are very greedy as regards space. The dishwasher must still be the greater luxury of the two and thus should go top of the hit list. And if your bathroom is small too, and cannot double up as a laundry, you will need to look for a combination washer–drier instead of two separate units.

Or not to compromise ...

Fashion consultants advise their clients to get rid of anything they have not worn for a year, and you might do well to apply the same advice in your kitchen – think of that dinner service you bought in a sale but which has not emerged from its box yet. If you cannot part with it, store it under your bed and use the space it vacates for things you do use. Similarly, the set of fish knives you are keeping for sentimental reasons, but which you always forget to use have no place in a small kitchen. Rarely used gadgets and appliances need to be given away, or swapped for others that you might use more. If you only use an electric juicer in the summer, for instance, store it somewhere else for the rest of the year, rather than wasting space.

A way of life

You may need to adapt how you shop to suit your kitchen. Nowadays shops have much longer opening hours – ideal for the small kitchen owner who can then shop daily on the way home from work. If you have been used to shopping once a fortnight, you will probably find it difficult limiting the amount of perishables you buy to the capacity of a

UNDER THE COUNTER

Conventional store-bought units may not be appropriate for odd-shaped kitchens and particularly where the available space is very restricted. You may also inherit appliances that might not appear to fit, but with some initiative you can create great things. In this kitchen a dishwasher and a place to eat have been combined in one space, a pull-out counter on a wheel being stowed away above the appliance and below the countertop proper, sliding back neatly to give access to the dishwasher beneath. The little 'breakfast table' is also useful as an additional work surface.

Historically, in a great house, the kitchen would be located 'below stairs' as a service area; in more modest houses it would probably be hidden at the back of the house on the ground floor – closer to wood or coal supplies and water. As dwelling units decrease in size, and bigger houses are converted into flats, many kitchens today are situated under the eaves. A sloping roof is unsuitable for wall units or shelving, but a series of rails can provide hanging storage for – and instant access to – mugs, cups and jugs, at the same time liberating the base units for stacking items, such as plates and bowls, or even food products.

CULINARY CORRIDOR

Even in the smallest kitchen there is usually some means of squeezing in somewhere to eat. The previous layout of this kitchen included only a rather narrow shelf beneath the window to serve as a breakfast bar. Recognizing that this was a perfect place to dine, given the view and the abundance of natural light, the new owners decided to build a platform just big enough for a table for two. Now they can sit and enjoy the garden rather than having to stand up to appreciate it. And by containing the kitchen area within four narrow partition walls, they have managed to hide the working area from sight when they are dining. These partitions also provide support for two shelves on either side of the kitchen so there is space under the worktop – even in a small kitchen – for an oven, dishwasher, and a washing machine, as well as a cupboard and drawer units. Low-voltage halogen spotlights light the shelves; much smaller than standard bulbs, these give a very concentrated beam of bright white light. And there is strip lighting concealed beneath the lower level to illuminate the work surfaces.

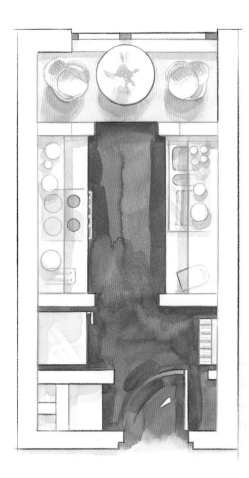

Furniture

There is always space for a pull-out counter or fold-down table and many stools and chairs fold flat to hang up when not in use. A sturdy stool with folding steps is useful too – for getting things down from high cupboards or shelves.

Custom-made furniture may be more feasible in small kitchens than in larger rooms where the cost might be prohibitive. The interiors of drawers and cupboards can be carefully designed to accommodate your crockery and gadgets. The narrow shelves that maximize space in a well-designed refrigerator can be reproduced on the inside of a cupboard door to house all your herbs and spices quite visibly in single rows. And if you have no draining board, you could install a bottomless wall cupboard fitted with a draining rack above a single sink, and store your plates wet. Large serving platters may even be better stored vertically.

A long, narrow pull-out drawer unit which starts close to the floor and runs right up as far as you can safely reach is the ideal answer for a small – often disproportionately tall – kitchen. With access on both sides, shelves at varying levels and all the contents visible, this may provide all the dry-food storage you need. And delving in the back of an untidy cupboard, where everything always gets piled on top of each other, will become a habit of the past.

Stemmed glasses are more efficiently stored hanging upside down between two pieces of dowelling than in a cupboard. And stackable china and glass, saucepans and storage containers will use less room than a mish-mash of ill-matching equipment. What is most obvious in a well-designed small kitchen is the way each item's needs have been analysed and answered, with every available inch used in the most logical way possible.

reduced-sized refrigerator, even if you are aware that you will probably be eating more healthily under this system. More economical bulk-buying of cans and dry goods may still be possible although you may only be able to store enough to hand for your immediate use; the rest will have to be consigned to somewhere less accessible. The lockers under the berths in boats are often filled not with clothes but with long-lasting food for unexpected weeks at sea.

LITTLE REMINDERS

- Conventionally sized units may be inappropriate in a very small space, whereas custom-made furniture can be designed to make the best use of every fraction of the room.
- Do not clutter precious space by keeping equipment you never use. And stacking crockery is probably better for everyday use.
- Do not scrimp on lighting. A small space may become claustrophobic if it is not well and imaginatively lit.
- Every space behind closed doors needs easy and safe access. Consider using the back of doors for narrow shelves or fixing wire racks.
- Good ventilation and an efficient heating system are vital to maintain a pleasant atmosphere all year round.
- Simple, bold decorative schemes are best; avoid over-complicated patterns or too many colours and textures.
- Small-scale equipment can often be found at specialist kitchen shops and catering suppliers. Alternatively, you might find that nautical fittings from a chandler are suitable.
- If space is tight, can you move the washing machine into the bathroom, or into a built-in cupboard in the hall, or is there room under the stairs?

Containing your kitchen in a space the
size of a wardrobe is not uncommon –
variations on the theme are found in
countless pieds-à-terre all over Paris.
Choosing to live in the centre of a major
city anywhere in the world means
compromising on space, unless you are
very wealthy. But because cafés and
restaurants are generally located close
by, it is possible to confine the kitchen
of such establishments in a tiny space;
the inhabitants can eat out whenever
they like, and so have no real need for
elaborate cooking facilities; any cooking
can be kept simple and minimal. If the
owner happens to love cooking, another
room will have to forfeit a few metres.

ALL LOCKERED UP

In this tiny apartment in the centre of
Sydney one wall has been transformed
into a kitchen and all but the sink and
fridge–freezer have been concealed
behind a series of custom-made doors
and drawers. The overall impression is
of a Constructivist relief sculpture, a
series of white geometric shapes and
shallow layers of white.

   Each section has been tailor-made for
the appliance or untensils that it stores.
The cooking rings are contained in a
drawer, the flip-down door of a cupboard
storing breakfast-making equipment
doubles as a work surface, with a section
at exactly the right height and width for
an electric blender. The same style of
cupboard in reverse, with a flip-up door,
held open on a locking metal arm,
contains a microwave oven which can
also be used to cook conventionally.

   When the cook has served dinner for
his/her guests, or is simply relaxing in
front of the television for the evening,
the kitchen can disappear discreetly
behind its flush white doors.

■ 77

INDEX

PUBLISHER'S ACKNOWLEDGMENTS

Conran Octopus would very much like to thank the following photographers and organizations for their permission to reproduce the photographs in this book:

1 Eric Morin; 2-3 James Mortimer/World of Interiors; 4-5 Albert Roosenburg; 6 -7 Schöner Wohnen/Camera Press; 7 Joshua Greene; 8 Alexander van Berge; 9 Richard Felber; 10 Arc Linea; 11 Pascal Chevalier/World of Interiors; 12 Mark Darley/Esto; 13 left Verne Fotografie (architect: Sluymer/Van Leeuwen); 13 right Hotze Eisma; 14 Arc Linea; 14-15 Andy Whale/Homes & Gardens/Robert Harding Picture Library; 16-21 James Mortimer(architect: Anthony Hudson); 22-3 Tim Beddow (architect: Dennis Mires)/The Interior Archive; 23 Simon Upton/Homes & Gardens/Robert Harding Picture Library; 24-25 Simon Kenny/Belle/Arcaid; 25 C. Simon Sykes (architect: Nicholas Haslam)/The Interior Archive; 26 Trevor Mein (architect: Colin Rofe)/Belle; 27 Ray Main; 29 Alexander van Berge; 30 Smallbone of Devizes; 31 Headley James; 32-3 Antoine Rozes; 34 Gilles de Chabaneix (Marie Kalt)/Marie Claire Maison; 34 -5 Nicolas Tosi (Catherine Ardouin) Marie Claire Maison; 36-7 Fritz von der Schulenberg (architect: Nico Rensch)/The Interior Archive; 37 Ray Main; 38 left Mark Darley/Esto; 38 right Henry Wilson/The Interior Archive; 39 Mark Burgin (architect: Elizabeth Watson-Brown) Belle Magazine ; 40 Trevor Richards/Country Homes & Interiors/Robert Harding Picture Library; 41 left Richard Felber; 41 right Alexander van Berge; 42 above Rodney Hyett/Elizabeth Whiting & Associates; 42 below Simon Kenny/ Belle/Arcaid; 43 Hotze Eisma; 44 Hotze Eisma/V.T. Wonen; 45 left Hotze Eisma/V.T. Wonen; 45 right Tim Beddow/The Interior Archive; 46-7 Ian Parry/Abode; 47 Dominique Vorillon(architect: T. Bosworth)/SIP; 48 left Richard Felber; 48-9 Verne Fotografie (architect: Domus); 50-1 Alexandre Bailhache (stylist: Julie Borgeaud) Marie Claire Maison; 51 Paul Ryan/International Interiors; 52 Paul Ryan/International Interiors; 53 James Merrell/Woman's Journal/Robert Harding Picture Library; 54 left Alexander van Berge; 54 right Simon McBride; 55 Mike Parsons; 56 Alexander van Berge; 57 above Otto Polman/Ariadne; 57 below Henry Wilson/The Interior Archive; 58 above Verne Fotografie (architect: Jo Crepain); 58 below Simon Brown (architect: Justin Meath-Baker)/The Interior Archive; 58-9 Tim Beddow (architect: Colin Childerley)/The Interior Archive; 60 left SpikePowell/ Elizabeth Whiting & Associates; 60 right Christian Sarramon; 61 Marie-Pierre Morel (stylist: Daniel Rozensztroch)/ Marie Claire Maison; 62 above Albert Roosenburg; 62 below Deidi von Schaewen; 62-3 Alexander van Berge; 64 Hugh Webb/Belle; 65 above left Hotze Eisma/V.T. Wonen; 65 above right Witney Cox (Designer: Charlotte Milholland); 66 Simon Kenny/Australian House & Garden; 67 above Simon McBride; 67 below Alexander van Berge; 68-9 Paul Ryan/International Interiors; 69 Otto Polman/Ariadne; 70 Nick Carter/Elizabeth Whiting & Associates; 71 Verne Fotografie (architect: Jean de Meulder); 72 Hotze Eisma/ V.T. Wonen; 74 Ralf Stradtmann/Schöner Wohnen; 75 Ophüls/ Schöner Wohnen; 67-7 left Geoff Lung/Vogue Apartments.

AUTHOR'S ACKNOWLEDGMENTS

I would like to thank everyone who has let me into their kitchens over the years – whether it be to explore or to be entertained – and Terence Conran, Malcolm Riddell, Virginia Pepper and Audrey Slaughter, who have encouraged me to write.

I would also like to thank the editorial team at Conran Octopus, who made this project possible, and in particular Sarah Sears, whose sense of humour and determined calmness has made this book a joy to write.

On a more personal note, I would also like properly to thank my parents, who have supported me, whatever I have chosen to do and whatever the consequences!

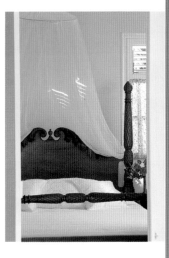

MAKING
THE MOST OF
BEDROOMS

MAKING
THE MOST OF
BEDROOMS

KAREN HOWES

CONRAN OCTOPUS

For Pooks

Commissioning Editor	Denny Hemming
Project Editor	Sarah Sears
Art Editor	Ruth Prentice
Picture Research	Clare Limpus
Production	Jill Beed
Illustrator	Sarah John
Editorial Assistant	Paula Hardy

First published in 1997 by
Conran Octopus Limited
37 Shelton Street
London WC2H 9HN

CONTENTS

BASIC PRINCIPLES

The four walls of your bedroom surround a very private world; its style, colour and contents will be stamped with your personal touch. The role played by a bedroom will vary, however, and to define the requirements of these different roles should be your first consideration when you are planning from scratch. Nevertheless, if you carefully assess the available space and follow some basic rules, it should be both easy and enjoyable to create the perfect bedroom sanctuary.

PLANNING

The flexibility of today's lifestyle and the wide variety of environments which we choose to call 'home' ensure that more than a degree of thought has to go into deciding on the location of the bedroom.

Traditionally, in a house, bedrooms are located upstairs and near a bathroom, separated at a discreet distance from those rooms – living room, dining room or kitchen – in which you entertain. So for those with the means to have a whole house at their disposal, there is generally less scope for originality because the bedrooms will have been planned as part of the fabric of the building. For the majority of city dwellers, living in apartments, basements, houseboats, converted lofts, schools and even converted warehouses, choosing the location of the bedroom can be a more personal and original decision.

Most people have already decided which room will be where before they purchase or move into a new property, their decisions governed – or at least influenced – by the dimensions of the available rooms. The living room nearly always acquires the only available fireplace and the largest floor area. But it does not have to be like this.

Take the time to sit down right at the beginning, over a large mug of tea, and analyse your lifestyle and your requirements. Do you entertain a lot? How much time are you likely to spend in your bedroom? Will you use it for anything other than sleeping? How much time do you actually spend awake at home? The list can be endless!

Depending on how honest you are, your bedroom could easily, and should perhaps, occupy the largest room you have available; leave your friends to sit on top of one another in a kitchen-cum-living room instead. If you live in a *pied-à-terre* or studio you will inevitably entertain in your bedroom, as it will be the only room. You could easily apply the same principle in a loft conversion or a barn, however. In all these cases, one large room can prove to be remarkably adaptable. You can designate one end as 'the bedroom', and hide the bed behind a screen, raise it on a gallery, or disguise it during the daytime as a large cupboard (closet), whether it be upturned and stored inside or perched like an eyrie on the top.

On the other hand, why not make a focal point of the bed? Why disguise it? Do this deliberately, however, rather than by mistake, for it can be very expensive to buy a bed that becomes a white elephant. And it is all too easy to make mistakes amidst the excitement and enthusiasm that always surrounds a new home. Buy the bed to fit the room, or you may suffer the consequences: one of my friends fell in love with a substantial four-poster, which became the talking point of the village because it had to reside in all its glory in the centre of his living room. No other room in the cottage was able to accommodate its girth and weight.

A bedroom that has a permanent status as a bedroom gives you great scope. First of all, bearing in mind reference points such as windows and doors, built-in cupboards (closets) and existing lighting sockets, as well as specific items of furniture that you cannot live without, decide on the best location for the bed. What sort of bed do you see yourself in? Are you intending to fill up your room with lots of furniture? If you have the space, what about a separate dressing room, or storage room, for shelves and additional

A PLATFORM PERFORMANCE

Platforms are an increasingly fashionable solution to the dilemma of finding a suitable bed. In this Japanese-style studio, architect Nico Rensch has successfully incorporated a central clothes storage unit into the platform, which acts as a headboard and as a base for flexible lighting, as well as providing hanging space. Built-in drawers make an architectural feature of the back wall and flank a minimalist blue glass washbasin. The shower is a glassed-in cubicle in the far corner of the room.

An emphasis on light wood in this airy, clapboard bedroom (previous page, left) unites walls, ceiling and floor with an interesting, if mannered, use of horizontal and vertical planking. A simple, painted, wooden bed, its crisp blue and white cushions and bed cover echoed by other cushions on the window seat, completes the fresh look, while rush matting adds to the overall natural feel.

Orderliness does not have to be crisp and empty. This storage unit for the clothes-conscious male (previous page, right) illustrates that it can be idiosyncratic too.

PLANNING

■ Decide on a style for your bedroom
and stick to it. Don't compromise.

■ If your bedroom is 'on show', drape an
interesting cover over the bed and
scatter it with cushions to transform it
into a day bed. Store your bedclothes
in an old-fashioned blanket box or
wicker basket at the end of the bed, in
specially designed drawers under the
bed, or in a cupboard (closet) –
wherever space permits.

■ Establish what furniture has to be
accommodated in addition to the bed
before you choose potentially too
small a room. Then choose a bed that
suits the shape of bedroom.

■ Do not allow the guest bedroom to
degenerate into a junk room. Have
ample drawer and cupboard (closet)
space or store junk in such a way that
becomes a decorative feature.

■ Allow the limitations of the space to
dictate the terms in awkwardly
shaped rooms. If an attic, design a few
shelves or cupboards to fit the
irregular wall pattern if traditional
furniture is inappropriate.

■ Do not economize on lighting. Explore
the various systems available until
you find an effect that is right for you.

■ 9

hanging space, leaving the bedroom free for the more unusual paraphernalia of your life? If you are sharing a house with friends, incorporating some sort of sitting room into the bedroom might be useful, in order to give you a little additional privacy and to avoid having to watch television endlessly from the bed.

Guest bedrooms tend to be the smallest rooms in the house. The size of bed is therefore very important. If this room does not have to perform a dual role, functioning as part-time study, work room or dumping ground when not inhabited by guests, you should give as much thought to its layout as a bedroom as you would to your own. Guests like

to feel that you have taken some trouble. A pretty chair beside a small table that can double as dressing table and desk, some interesting pictures, a few strategically chosen books by the bed, ambient light and flowers for a personal touch go a long way to making guests feel welcome.

En-suite bathing

Incorporating a bath into your bedroom will require considerable thought. Although the romantic appeal of being able to roll out of bed straight into a hot bath, or vice versa, carries great sway, the practical problems created by lack of privacy, general plumbing installation, and the

OPEN SPACES

A master bedroom should know the luxury of space. The location of the bed is important if the room is not as large as this one (far left) and built-in cupboards (closets) can contribute. If two rooms are opened up into one, the resulting skeleton support can become a feature of the much-enlarged new look, and you can incorporate a cosy sitting area, too. If the bedroom is at the top of the house, why not enlarge your space still further by building upwards: you could have an eyrie up in the roof space, only accessible via a ladder.

Guest bedrooms (left) tend to occupy smaller rooms, often devoid of interesting features. Just because these rooms are only used irregularly, however, it does not mean that you cannot liberate your imagination in them. Some tend to double up as a dumping room, so make sure your junk is constantly hidden from the surprise guest – here concealed under a table draped in fabric which serves as a headboard. While wardrobes (closets) are really unnecessary for the temporary visitor and take up valuable space, ensure that there is a chair for their suitcase and a couple of hooks with coat hangers on the back of the door.

■ 11

effects of steam and condensation must be considered, especially in cold climates. Where space is at a premium – in guest rooms, for instance – you might be able to plumb in a small handbasin or modern shower unit in one corner to give you a little additional privacy. Those of you with a romantic inclination, but without the means, could always introduce an antique water pitcher and basin, either for purely decorative purposes or, as it was originally intended, as a functioning, portable washbasin.

BATHROOMS LAID BARE

Accommodating bathrooms in small living spaces – especially for guests – can prove expensive on space as well as posing nightmarish plumbing problems. One alternative is to place the bathtub in the bedroom itself. To have your bath as close to the bed as it is in this converted and modernized attic room (left) can be very convenient for the indolent, but the tiled floor and general austerity of the room are especially suited to a warm climate. Practical problems such as steam and condensation perhaps account for the absence of curtains, carpets and bed hangings.

An alternative scheme might be to conceal a handbasin and storage shelves behind the headboard of the bed (far left). The bath, located against the far wall, is open along the side but screened at either end for a little privacy, creating an environment that is conducive to long, luxurious soaks. This layout will also go some way in reducing the problems of condensation in the bedroom, especially if an extractor fan is also installed. As a means of saving space, this arrangement provides a very workable solution while the design clearly defines the room into two areas.

■ 13

SPACE EXPLOITATION

Guest bed, your own bed or comfortable den – in any case, this half landing under the eaves displays not only an aesthetic but an ingenious use of space. Again, the platform bed has been employed, though here it is a little impractical as far as making the bed is concerned – and access might be rather inelegant, too. But it does leave the bed at the right level for the clever cupboard (closet) units, and the proportions of the room, governed by the low ceiling height, work well in relation to it. As an alternative to the oil painting which is used here as a headboard, you could paint an imaginative bedhead on the wall or hang up an interesting and colourful piece of fabric. As a multi-purpose area, this bedroom combines as study and library. To create a really cosy and inviting lounger for reading, the bed could be loaded with comfortable cushions in muted, but co-ordinated colourways. The choice of pale wood for the shelving and cupboard doors, the uncluttered surfaces and the white-painted floorboards all combine to enhance the light atmosphere in this roof conversion.

Dual-purpose space

Multi-purpose rooms require discipline, particularly at the planning stage. If your bedroom is to double as another room on a permanent basis, it is important to establish a balance between the two intended functions at the very beginning. If you envisage sleeping in your library/study, your wall space will probably be taken up in housing your collection of books. Where will you put your clothes, shoes, hats, handbags and the clutter that tends to accumulate in the bedroom? Free-standing storage units may prove useful in this context. Choose bedside tables with drawers, boxes and plastic storage containers which can slip under the bed; perhaps you can leave one wall free for a wardrobe (closet). If you need a writing surface in the room, take over some of the drawers of a desk for clothes storage. An additional wall could be saved if you designed one of the bookshelves to fit around the bedhead, and building lights into the shelving saves space, too. If you have a television, position it at a good height in one of the bookshelves opposite the bed, and then find a similar home for your stereo, remembering that you will want frequent access – stylish and practical space-saving.

BARE ESSENTIALS

Modern can often mean minimal and this bedroom is no exception, located on a landing of a very slender house and benefiting from the light from numerous narrow windows. Minimal also means 'no clutter' and even in a room designed to serve several purposes, there is a distinctly economic use of furniture. The table or working surface collapses neatly against the central partition of the room, leaving a single chair and side table. Discreetly concealed behind this partition and accessible by the short set of stairs, is a bathroom, luxuriating in the sunlight. There are no paintings to break up the architect's clean lines. Instead, texture provides the decoration by way of rattan, metal and polished wood. It is a clever manipulation of a small and awkward space.

One-room living

One room or studio living – the way many of us live in large cities – is generally a euphemism for personal chaos! An environment in which you combine living, working, playing and sleeping is often achieved with minimal expense but with maximum stress levels. There is no greater challenge than condensing your belongings to fit your current living space. What to take and what to leave behind – and where? Attics and storage rooms of long-suffering friends and relations suddenly mushroom with dustbin bags containing valuable chunks of your life, yet the conundrum of how to accommodate the items you insist on keeping with you can produce ingenious storage ideas.

The motto for living in one room has to be 'Keep it simple'. It must be applied to the style of furniture, the decoration of the room, the objects and personal clutter. It is important to maintain a sense of space, particularly if the room is a modern unit and has a clean and streamlined look. Remember that the way you light the space is equally important and can make a boring room much more atmospheric – you can use low pools of light rather than overhead blanket lighting, candles for softness, or even small uplighters in the corners of the room.

If you are to live in a room that does not belong to you, studio rooms in old Victorian terraces, with their high ceilings and bow-fronted windows, accommodate more readily the personal touches you bring with you; living in a modern space requires a knack. Swathes of fabric can transform the grimmest room, helping to disguise ghastly wallpaper and less-than-perfect furnishings and cocooning you in a cosy refuge from the outside world, without causing undue damage to walls or ceiling.

Awkward and unorthodox spaces

Imagination and patience are required in equally large quantities when you are planning a bedroom in an awkward space – and any room that is not square is awkward. Variable wall and ceiling heights can pose problems too, when the eaves of a roof come right down to floor level; effectively where there is no 'room' at all but where an area has to be created. Following the one-room-living principle, the simple approach is normally the most successful. Adventurous ideas can lead, if you decide to cope by yourself, to disastrous consequences. It is essential to seek professional advice if you are thinking about an attic conversion and any other building work that requires a knowledge of structural engineering.

It is fun to sleep in unorthodox areas, however, so creating a platform for a mattress where before there was no space for a bed at all, can be extremely satisfying. If you hoard clothes and possessions to the point where nothing else will fit into your designated bedroom, build a strong platform above your wardrobe (closet) and sleep up there! If the room is tiny, create a platform under the window. Be adaptable and you cannot fail.

As everyone is obsessed with utilizing space, rooms take shape in the most unlikely locations (below left). Place a mattress on an extended window seat, use the deep cupboards beneath to store the duvet and any additional pillows, and you have created a bedroom out of nothing, lit by natural light and one small reading lamp. And although it has essentially evolved out of practical constraints, this bedroom is characterized by compactness and originality, making it nestlike and cosy.

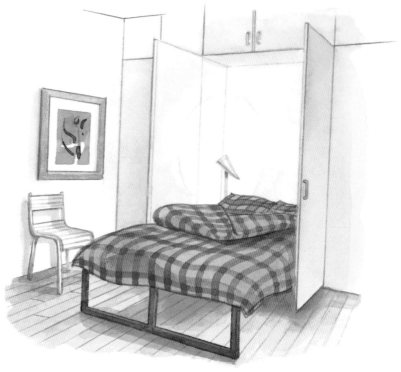

UP AND AWAY

Dealing with awkward spaces is always a challenge and trying to accommodate beds will magnify the difficulty as their length and weight create obvious problems. One way of sidestepping this problem (opposite, right) is to put the bed in a cupboard (closet). Built of light aluminium, with neat folding legs, these beds can be literally folded into a specially designed cupboard (closet) and shut away, together with slim duvet and pillows – a great way to avoid that daily chore of making the bed. The space they vacate can then be occupied by a table and chairs, and the room given a totally different function.

Lofts provide additional space but often in a very restricted form. The angle of the roof can be so acute that the only place a bed will fit is right in the middle of the room, where there is barely sufficient space for any other furniture. In this example (left) dormer windows not only shed more light, but also mean two single beds can be situated neatly side by side under the eaves.

■ 19

Storage

Few of us are naturally tidy-minded and a tidy bedroom seems to be one of life's more unattainable aspirations, but do try not to design a bedroom environment that is completely inappropriate to your lifestyle. If your clothes tend to lie around in heaps for days, the minimalist bedroom is not for you. You need rows of cupboards (closets) and bottomless drawers. Invest in a few high-sided storage boxes to contain the debris that normally ends up under the bed, or buy a bed with built-in drawers – ideal for packing away the duvet. If short of space, be economical with non-functional furniture. It is very easy to transform an old school trunk, by covering it with a kelim or old rug, to provide additional storage space at the foot of the bed and a surface for books and magazines – and it is far more space-effective than a mere bench.

Storage can be decorative as well as functional. Doors can be imaginatively painted or stencilled, or clad in fabric to match the bed linen or bed hangings. Cheaper alternatives include using coloured paper, or creating collages of postcards and memorabilia. You could remove the doors completely and replace them with rattan blinds. There are lots of ways to bring a cupboard (closet) to life.

Storage units can also become a structural feature of the bedroom. If space is short, you could place your mattress on top of free-standing storage units and make a

Storage at its most basic, yet most effective, is illustrated in this small understated bedroom (left) in which industrial metal shelving units have been erected along one wall, the only concession to decoration being the extravagant wrought-iron bedstead and the lengths of bright red fabric used as rudimentary blinds. Hat stand, basket-weave tray and a universal drawer unit provide a plethora of storage possibilities (above), while a more organized and stylized approach to storage has been taken in the bedroom (right). The basic divisions have been achieved using single rows of bricks, painted white, while the various compartments have been alternately curtained-off or fitted with simple plank doors.

BEDROOM STORAGE

- Try and combine more than one function in any one storage element. Wall-to-wall fitted cupboards (closets) could include mirror doors or incorporate a washbasin and, in addition to hanging space, provide storage for all those cumbersome bags and suitcases which always end up under the bed.

- If averse to mirrors, use glass-fronted cupboards (closets) and display your clothes. As a focus of the bedroom, the cupboards (closets) will provide additional depth to the room and can be discreetly lit. Serried ranks of underwear, shirts, etc., interspersed with books and objects and even the occasional picture, will turn your storage into a conversation piece.

- Open shelving can take care of those problem areas under the stairs and eaves but can gather dust and leave clothes less than pristine. Simple curtains or individual storage boxes can be used to protect delicate items.

- Storage units can also be used as room dividers; clothing rails in bedroom corners can be hidden behind screens covered in either fabric or paper.

self-styled sleeping platform. If aerial suspension does not appeal to you, use the units as room dividers – either as a series of screens or around the bed to create some privacy.

Lighting

The importance of lighting in a room cannot be over-emphasized. Strategically placed lamps can transform the most unimaginative room. Retailers have finally recognized the need for sophisticated and appropriate lighting, and there is something to suit everyone's requirements. You can choose from a great variety of standard bases, high-tech flexible stems, spots, uplighters and downlighters. Experimenting with lighting is not cheap, however, so it is probably better to start by looking at some basic principles alongside what you already have.

Forget overhead light: it will kill any atmosphere – particularly important in the bedroom. If you have always used standard bedside lamps but find that they are too harshly bright in their new environment, use bulbs of a lower wattage. Experiment with different shades; drape dark-coloured fabric over the existing shade to test a tone; have your lights on a dimmer switch so that you can adjust them to suit your immediate requirements; *in extremis*, place the lamp base on the floor to act as an uplighter.

Candles are cheap and will guarantee atmosphere. Metal-backed wall sconces reflect the candle light and so increase illumination in the room generally, but silver foil will achieve the same effect. You must remember to consider all aspects of bedroom life in your lighting plan: vanity units and dressing tables will need brighter, more directional lighting, and equally vital is the positioning and efficiency of reading lights.

SWITCHED ON

Lighting can make or mar the overall effect of a bedroom. Your first consideration should be practical for there is nothing more irritating than trying to read in bed with inadequate light, or having the shadow of your head thrown onto the page because of a badly placed lamp. However, the exciting variety of lighting available in the shops means that boring old bedside lamps on tables can be a thing of the past.

This light, white bedroom (far left) admits natural light through internal glass bricks. The choice of artificial light creates an interesting architectural focus. The lamps, on flexible arms, can be turned down for reading or turned away to reflect against the wall for a more muted, atmospheric effect.

Similarly, this plain white room (left) with decorative headboard and matching bed cover, has been transformed by the sculptural style of the lighting scheme. Positioned at each corner of the bed, the standard lamps are sufficiently tall to throw light on the bed as well as around the room, with two shelves positioned within the metal structure for necessities – an alarm clock, for example, and even a book or two.

STYLE

Style is a personal attribute which
requires neither extraordinary wealth
nor valuable possessions; if you have
style, you will be able to create
an environment in which you can live in
harmony with your surroundings. For you
will understand, and be able to
interpret, what works for you and your
day-to-day existence. The elusiveness of
style creates gurus out of interior
designers, and yet style is really only a
subjective synonym for good taste –
'You've either got it, or you haven't.'

COUNTRY

It is all too easy to be patronizing in interpreting what is meant by 'country style'; the concept as it is defined by magazines and marketing today is romanticized and often insulting to the rural world. Just as country themes tend not to work in the city, big city ideas for a humble country cottage can prove equally out of context.

Every property must be allowed to retain its individual atmosphere, even in the search for that elusive country idyll. After all, what undoubtedly attracted you to living in the country in the first place was the house or cottage and its location; its isolation, perhaps; the scope it has for a wonderful garden; the sense of getting back to nature. We all tend to over-romanticize our need for fresh air and wide open spaces, yet within that heightened sensitivity lies the true interpretation of our innate sense of country style.

The bedroom is naturally the most susceptible to the country influence, since here you can create an atmosphere of rustic tranquillity to suit your own interpretation. Often cosy in proportion and with small, low windows, cottage bedrooms tend to be dominated by the bed, leaving little room for other furniture. If this is a weekend retreat, then seasonal influences must play their part in the style of the bedroom. Muslin curtains, or no curtains at all over small windows, would allow summer's early light to filter gently into the bedroom. Heavier duty curtains could be substituted for those cold winter nights and sluggish, wet country mornings, when your inclination is to snuggle deeper under the colourful quilts and layers of thick blankets that transform country beds into nests for hibernating humans.

The city bedroom's country cousin can happily adopt an eclectic look: odd pieces of furniture from local antique shops, with no obvious function but fantastic form. Objects and well-worn textiles can also contribute to the rustic charm of a country bedroom. Rooms are usually smaller, so less furniture is required, with less emphasis on the finish of uneven walls and scrubbed floorboards. Armchairs should embrace you like old friends, tables and cupboards (closets) should be softened and rounded with age, beds should creak at your approach, linen sheets and quaint quilts redolent with the scent of freshly picked lavender should flow over the bed, with a pitcher of clover and meadow flowers on a neighbouring table. Each detail is important in setting the scene, creating a very special atmosphere that you can metaphorically bottle and carry with you.

RURAL RETREATS

These two images typify country style. Both rooms are small and have low ceilings, the bed in each case occupying most of the available space. Simple beds can be made cosy and inviting by combining colourful cotton quilts with a variety of pillows in similar tones, or by hanging a simple calico curtain around the bedhead to soften the austere effect of a wrought-iron bed.

Style in the bedroom can be as simple as an imaginative detail of a headboard (previous page, left). Located in a room with walls painted a glowing colour, the room needs no other visual adornments. Old printing-block storage units have been positioned on the wall between two barley twist posts, topped with a golden setting sun. The arrangement of pillows in a variety of stripes is a cheap and jolly way to liven up the bed, creating an eye-catching effect.

Counterbalancing this image is a detail of crisp lace on the turndown of a sheet and a lovely, dainty bolster cover, tied with pale blue ribbon (previous page, right). Antique sheets and lace pillowcases make a romantic addition to any bed.

HELPFUL HINTS

- Have the courage of your convictions. If you lack confidence in your own sense of style, you can glean a lot from the myriad books and magazines available on the subject. Remember, though, that every style has its place.
- Be daring in your use of colour and fabric. Combine different elements to create a new and exciting effect. If something does go wrong, you can always rectify it.
- Be inventive with your furniture. Practically no item has to be used solely for the purpose for which it was originally intended.
- Never turn up your nose if friends or relatives offer you a chance to hunt for treasure when they are cleaning out their attics. Amazing results can be achieved from unlikely beginnings: priceless antiques have been found at rummage sales, after all!
- Experiment with different looks until you find the one that feels right for you. This can often take several attempts, so do not get depressed.
- If in doubt, choose one strong element – a piece of furniture, a rug or a length of fabric – and let your design develop around it.

SHABBY CHIC

You do not necessarily have to have lots of money to create a shabby chic bedroom. However, you do need plenty of self assurance if you are going to combine successfully a selection of apparently incongruous elements in the same room. While magazines might suggest that anything goes in shabby chic, what separates the sheep from the wolves is one person's ability to see which faded fabric will work with which piece of distressed furniture, and which ancient mirror would add the appropriate sense of faded grandeur without looking self-conscious. Do not try too hard or you may find that you have created a disastrously unkempt effect instead. To produce the look that makes old and worn look rich and welcoming, you need a good eye for design – and enough historical knowledge to ensure that you use styles that are sympathetic to each other.

It may be the acquisition of an antique mirror, or a vast wardrobe (closet), or even some chintz curtains originally designed for windows much larger than yours that tempts you to consider opting for a shabby chic bedroom. What do you do with this kind of legacy? You must experiment. Now is your chance to luxuriate in quantities of antique fabric that would otherwise be totally out of your financial reach. Indeed, if you have none, you should search for antique curtains that you can use for bed hangings as well as for your windows; alternatively you could unstitch them and transform your bed by making a new bed cover with a half tester, or adapt them to drape in great swathes over a simple four-poster frame. If there is still fabric over at the end, you could cover a cushion or re-upholster that little chair: well-worn fabric will never look brash or out of place.

Employing strong and impressive pieces of furniture in a bedroom can be more difficult because they can take over a room. Any reservations you might have about mixing antique with modern furniture should be dispelled if you choose pieces of similar line and proportion. You can emphasize this visual link by employing a distressed paint finish or an appropriate fabric to unify the various items. A linen press or *armoire* is ideal for clothes storage, and just right for a shabby chic look, but if bedroom space is at a premium, perhaps it will have to stand on a landing – an item of furniture to be admired.

Shabby chic is ideal for wandering travellers who arrive home from exotic lands laden with ethnic acquisitions; these textiles and objects tend to combine much more happily with faded and worn furniture and textiles than with brand-new upholstery and a selfconsciously designed scheme. For the budget-conscious decorator, for whom buying a property stretches resources to the limit, shabby chic can conserve funds. You can still put together a wonderfully theatrical effect. You can make a considered decision not to invest in 'bright and shiny new' but to celebrate 'well-built and old' instead. What does it matter that an arm of a chair is worn or that your sagging shelves are propped up on piles of books? The chair must be comfortable, and a straight line is less important than surrounding yourself with books.

The overall look of shabby chic, from subtly coloured distempered, peeling walls to big, cosy furniture that seems to have been there for ever, even the mellow lighting, is inviting; the room feels well lived-in.

FANTASTIC BEGINNINGS

Creating your own particular style depends to a certain degree on the furniture and accessories you have available. Few people are likely to inherit a wonderful four-poster bed, and yet they can be constructed in varying shapes and sizes from all sorts of odds and ends. Remember that in a poorly proportioned room a four-poster can appear dumpy, stealing what little height a room may have. Assuming that you do have the space, however, four-poster beds can be constructed from wood or metal, from DIY kits – even scaffolding poles. Once the frame is *in situ*, you can experiment with curtain permutations: formal and fixed, tied with ribbons, or unfinished lengths of fabric just thrown or draped – a constantly moving feast of ideas and whims. In this French château, the relative simplicity of the bed frame is disguised by the prodigious lengths of rough linen draped loosely over the poles, while an ancient narrow serving table at the foot of the bed bears candle and leather-bound volumes to further the fantasy. Why not try to create your own fairytale world!

MEDITERRANEAN

In a hot climate, interior decoration in the bedroom tends towards the minimal. The use of fabrics is negligible and more practical than decorative, with mosquito netting as bed hangings and cotton voile or calico curtains or blinds at the windows. Painted shutters will protect from sun and rain alike, the slats casting long and interesting shadows on bare walls and floors during the heat of the day. Furniture tends to be of bleached or pale wood, floors either scrubbed or tiled, and beds of a simple local construction, whether of wood, rattan or wrought iron.

Whitewash abounds, but dramatically juxtaposed with bright blue, yellow and pink highlights that bleach in the sun's heat to produce softer, quieter, faded shades which are more suitable for bedrooms than the bolder, brighter versions that preceded them.

Natural reds and oranges are popular too – terracotta colours that characterize those refreshing, tiled floors you find all over the Mediterranean. Marble, stone and wood are equally typical and easy to build into your design.

In a Mediterranean-inspired bedroom, arrestingly shaped bits of driftwood might gather as trophies on mantelpieces and window sills, along with fragile shells and seaside pebbles polished in rough waves – muted echoes of the bright outside world in a simple and uncluttered interior, essential for keeping cool.

This tranquil, underfurnished style of bedroom is ideal in the heat of the summer, but might lack in cosiness in winter, despite central heating. Plan for this in advance and incorporate a degree of flexibility: seasonal bed covers, for example, and curtains you can remove for the summer.

Warm climates encourage simplicity of style. In this refreshing, pared-down bedroom, the bed itself is uncomplicated by a frame. The fine mosquito net above it serves both a decorative and a functional purpose and the blind against the window has a similar translucency. The walls, ceiling and floor have been limewashed, together with the small chest and even the frame of the picture beside the bed. The model boat, the painting and the portholed shutters laid against the far wall combine to strike a cool, nautical note.

COOL BLUE

Everything about this bedroom is cool, from the cool blue of its thick, ancient walls, the metallic silver of the bed and the fan in the rafters to the natural terracotta tiles underfoot. The sheer uncluttered emptiness of the room is set off by the simple cement staircase running up the far wall, lending a sculptural quality to an otherwise featureless expanse of blue. There is no attempt to overstate this bedroom; its minimal decoration and furnishings – a blend of traditional and modern – reinterpreting its Mediterranean origins. Its style is functional, the wide metal shades on the lamps attached to the back of the headboard designed to give as much reading light as possible, the stubby bolster providing good back support. The adjoining room, small and light, is a bathroom, where clothes' racks, piles of shoes and faded T-shirts which cannot be accommodated in the bedroom are stored out of sight.

MODERN

A bedroom with a modern theme means there can be no half measures in its application. A style which relies heavily on structure and form and a significant use of space needs only one or two strong elements to enforce it. Stylish storage systems will help to emphasize the theme by preventing inappropriate belongings from upsetting the balance, while flooring can make a positive contribution to the design: use sympathetic colours, textures and finishes, or combine materials, such as wooden boards or even cement, polished to a marble finish, with rugs to soften the effect.

In a room where little is left on view, texture can play an important visual role. Fabrics for bed covers and even the bed linen can be made to toe the modern line.

While paintings may be out of financial range in the early years of property ownership, prints and black and white photographs are becoming increasingly popular. Alternatively, an interesting empty frame can give a wall a three-dimensional quality, while the strategic use of mirrors or even a strong architectural shape – a piece of furniture or free-standing sculpture, be it a 'find' or intended for display – can add interest in a dead corner.

Modern can be romantic as well as minimal. Here a small, low chair upholstered in fresh white linen with a silvery metallic appliqué, and a day bed, simply draped in a lace sheet and scattered with a few white-clad cushions, combine to sharpen up a fairly empty room. The pale blue tone of this corner, the transparency of the long, blue curtain, the drunken chandelier and the empty, ornate frame perched on the mantelpiece lend the room an air of mystery. The fireplace surround has been clad in reflective beaten metal, which gives the room another dimension. The overall effect is stylish, the minimum of possessions creating the maximum effect.

DRAUGHTSMAN'S DISCIPLINE

It takes great discipline to live in a modern interior. The architect John Pawson has designed this bedroom (far left) with the bed on a simple raised wooden platform, the warmth of the wood contrasting with the stark whiteness of the rest of the room. A row of recessed cupboards (closets) along one wall hints at orderly ranks of sharply pressed shirts and disciplined suits, racks of colour-coordinated shoes and pigeon holes for socks and knitwear. There are no bedside tables, no chairs, no mirrors or paintings to distract you from the minimalist look, the only concession to comfort being the soft duvet over the bed. The lighting has also been used to enhance the strictly architectural emphasis of this bedroom: strip lights run the length of the cupboards (closets) with additional wall strips behind the bed recess. The introduction of an Anglepoise lamp for reading is a surprisingly classic touch.

OUTDOORS

Sleeping out-of-doors requires few props, irrespective of how grand and memorable an occasion you wish it to be. A sleeping bag beside the dying embers of a picnic camp fire under the stars at the end of a mellow evening; a simple cotton hammock strung up between two trees, their spreading branches sheltering the incumbent from the afternoon sun; a tent in the back garden – all spontaneous suggestions that are instantly achievable.

Themed tents and special beds can be hired for one-time occasions. There is also a whole range of campaign furniture available – beds, tables, even wardrobes (closets) that derive from Napoleon's original designs. He wanted to be surrounded on the battlefield by familiar and, above all, comfortable furniture, designed to be collapsible and to fit into special trunks for ease of transportation. Authentic campaign furniture is rare, but it is quite possible to find inexpensive alternatives that will create the right feeling in your tented summer holiday quarters.

In an attempt to recapture something of the spirit and adventure encapsulated in Karen Blixen's novel *Out of Africa*, recreated so memorably by Sydney Pollack for the big screen, it is increasingly fashionable to take to canvas on exclusive wildlife safaris. The *frisson* of excitement or terror which results from being separated from a prowling night predator by only a thin expanse of canvas, coupled with the pure romance of eating outdoors by the light of a flickering storm lantern, listening to the noises of the bush, has to be the experience of a lifetime.

TOUCHING THE HEAVENS

The romanticism of sleeping in the open air surrounded by diaphanous clouds of mosquito netting, structured in the shape of a tent, surely cannot be bettered. Low camp beds on a floor of rush matting share a bedside table in the form of a campaign folding stool, with a paraffin lamp and a cup of sweet-smelling jacaranda standing on it. This outdoor bedroom in Kenya is enclosed only by the roof of the world, a multitude of tiny stars penetrating the netting of its transparent shelter in the dark. It is certainly an exotic, glamorous setting, but there is no reason why the same effect cannot be reproduced anywhere on a steamy summer's night. Sleeping under the stars is an experience not to be missed and generally it is not difficult in practical terms to set up. So exchange the security of your bed for a night in the back garden – you will be amazed by the plethora of stars.

DECORATION

The bedroom can occupy more or less any room in the house, from the tiniest shoe box to the airiest attic. Whether its look is spartan or luxurious, the bed will naturally play the starring role, its style and shape dictating the whole tone of the room. It is the happy combination, however, of paint and wallpaper, fabrics old and new, rugs or simple floorboards, wicker baskets or built-in cupboards – even Granny's chest of drawers given a new lease on life – that gives a room its intensely personal nature.

DECORATIVE PLANNING

That feeling of wanting to stamp your own personality upon your surroundings in exactly the way you would like, whether you are renting a room or have bought your own house, can often be frustrated by a shortfall in means. However, with very little expense and practically no expertise, a room can be transformed by a single pot of paint or a length of fabric.

Decorating never fails to take longer than you think, especially if you have little or no experience, so allow enough time to complete the job and reinstall the furniture before inviting your friends around for dinner

and an inspection of your work. Try to finish the project in daylight; you will be surprised what a difference it makes if you work in good light.

You are probably more likely to encounter problems if you take on a more unusual site. You may be restrained by planning permission or the need for appropriate interior colour schemes in a period property, or the size or proportions of your rooms in a cottage in the country. Or you may be working on a space with quirky

architecture, a former warehouse perhaps, or a self-consciously modern and minimalist apartment. With so many constraints, it would be best to consult a professional with specialist knowledge, in the early stages in particular, because 'going it alone' is likely to become a minefield.

Every time you move, your bedroom is almost bound to change in character. In fact, as different architectural styles will reinterpret the same style in very different ways, it is unlikely that you will want to retain the same scheme when you move. Your sense of colour, style and coordination will develop and improve each time you decorate a room, however, just as your knowledge and experience grows, giving you more and more confidence to experiment with original and imaginative themes.

Colour and texture

Although paint is probably the first option, you can use paper or fabric to cover walls and ceiling, and you can cover your chairs and the bed – anything you choose, in

SIMPLE COUNTRY EFFECTS

Simplicity in decoration is always effective. In this rustic bedroom, with its low ceiling and thick, uneven walls, decoration has been kept to the bare minimum. The bulk of a somewhat solid, unforgiving carved wooden bed is relieved only by an upright painted chair beside it and a narrow cotton runner on the scrubbed, wooden floor. However, the walls have been washed in a pretty yellow, instead of being left whitewashed, which offsets the austerity that characterizes the furnishings, The bold use of a contrasting darker colour below an imaginary dado level emphasizes the warmth of the yellow above and improves the proportions of this little room.

fact – with checks or stripes, with traditional floral chintz or with just plain colours. Texture plays a very important role, coordinating not only colours but also combinations of patterns and fabrics: flat cottons with slub silks, appliqué and lace – even a soft, old, worn paisley shawl.

Choosing the dominant colour for your bedroom is a matter of courage. If you have inherited a tired set of walls, or a room papered in some ghastly pattern, you will be obliged either to strip everything down and paper it, or to conceal such horrors by covering them up with a dark colour. Choose a colour that complements or echoes a favourite painting or bedspread, or a piece of painted furniture that will be housed in the room.

It is worth poring over a practical decorating book before you decide anything, in order to look at examples of all the different effects you might want to achieve, be it with paint, wallpaper or fabric; to learn how easy or hard they will be to effect; and to understand fully the problems and advantages of each. It is very easy to choose the wrong paint, or to paint where wallpaper would have been better.

WARM WOOD

Pine panelling is typical of Alpine chalet architecture. Its warm yellow tones can be rather overwhelming, precluding the use of many bright, primary colours for bed linen and furnishing fabrics. Carved features, columns or detailing define the panels on the wooden walls. Enhance the natural beauty of the grain of the wood, its whorls and idiosyncracies, by varnishing, staining or even colour-washing walls and floors. You can incorporate more wood in the furnishing of the room with turned wooden lamp stands with pale shades, for instance, or hang simply framed paintings on the panelling – perhaps contrasting woodgrain and patina for additional texture. A glorious antique painted wardrobe (closet) would add the final touch, or you may want to paint your own modern equivalent.

With a low ceiling, the size of the bed is important. The brass finials of the four-poster touch the ceiling, but the frame has been left bare in order not to exaggerate the lack of space. Instead, the eye moves instantly away from the ceiling to the pretty white lace bed cover and crisp duvets.

Wallpaper is a traditional wall treatment; if the previous occupant of your bedroom left walls full of cracks and holes, wallpaper is an easy and effective cover-up.

Stripes provide a solid base for the decoration of any room (opposite), but ensure that the room is square, or your lines will not end up straight. If you are papering a small room, striped wallpaper will help to disguise its size.

A plain paper is useful if you are dealing with uneven or lumpy walls. Paint applied over the paper will reveal fewer of the damaged patches. When you have finished, any spare paper left over could be used to re-cover old hat boxes to make decorative storage units.

Look at the age of your room first; it may have a bearing on how you proceed. For example, although you will have to kerb your rasher impulses, and decorating a period property authentically can be an exacting exercise, it can also be quite stimulating, and there are now a vast number of heritage paints – period colours and paint recipes – on the market to make a successful job easier. If you do wish to pursue this option in your bedroom, there are umpteen books on the subject to offer advice on all the relevant areas: architectural detailing, wall colours, curtain and furnishing styles – appropriate patterns and fabrics too.

Modern rooms tend to be less demanding. It is not unusual to encounter unfinished walls in a warehouse context and you can exploit the textures of raw breeze blocks, bricks, rough metal supports and cement walls to advantage if you incorporate them into a simple bedroom design. Tall ceilings and large rooms provide ample area for trial and error and, with an emphasis on space, your possessions can happily take on gigantic proportions.

Big needs to be bold, so you cannot be tentative. Dramatic colours, bold designs on bare walls, or a commitment to a smart, monochrome theme: without historical constraints, this is perhaps the closest you will come to being given true freedom to express yourself. If you do choose pale, less overwhelming colour schemes, they are likely to benefit from accents of colour: decorative

FLEXIBLE FABRIC

Fabric is an adaptable wall covering that can be used very successfully in a wide variety of rooms. More formally, the fabric would be battened: narrow strips of wood would be tacked onto the wall as a base onto which the lengths of material would be attached. This produces an effect similar to wallpaper, although the texture and colour combinations of fabrics create a softer and often warmer atmosphere.

Hanging fabric loosely around the four walls like curtains creates an interesting textural effect; here (left) the lengths of crisp, white cotton hang in unregulated folds, from a narrow bamboo pole which runs around the room, tied by short lengths of matching fabric. Its effect is immediately to soften the harsh austerity of the box structure of the room and to avoid the need for any additional accessories in the shape of mirrors, pictures, etc., as these would be difficult to hang successfully on folds of material.

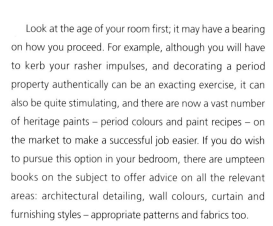

details, such as wall hangings, paintings or mirrors, a bright bed cover or an interesting bedhead will fulfil this brief.

If you are working in a rustic environment, steer clear of those dark, vibrant colours that work well in the city: with low ceilings and small windows, rooms will begin to resemble dungeons. Keep colours light and bright and keep the whole scheme simple. Either paint beams, picking up a tone used for window frames to tie the whole scheme together, or to lend emphasis to the ceiling, or stain them to bring out the wood's grain and natural colour.

If you are decorating or restoring a panelled room, it may be difficult to replicate the original wood – almost impossible if it is antique. A *trompe l'oeil* paint effect executed by an expert will probably come closest; or you might like to brighten up the panelling by painting it. You could even create simple mock-panelling on a blank wall.

Above all, experiment, for bravery brings rewards: using bright, clashing colours might create a surprisingly exciting bedroom environment. If it proved disastrous, you would only have to repaint the walls or buy a new set of less outrageous sheets.

Flooring

Spend time and money on flooring; it is an important and often neglected aspect of a decorative scheme. A uniform floor covering can offer a continuity of flow between a series of rooms or, if you choose wildly differing styles and colours on the walls of different rooms, can pull the overall design scheme together. If expense is a factor, you can leave plain wooden floors, or put down coir or seagrass matting throughout to provide a natural background for individual rugs and kelims, chosen for each room.

COSY CARPETS

Carpets tend to be one of the first things you replace when you move. In many cases they are laid wall to wall to disguise the indifferent surface of the floor underneath, but it is a good idea to check on the condition of the floorboards, as many are in surprisingly good shape and an industrial sander would soon have the surface smooth and splinter-free. If you are lucky enough to discover a proper parquet floor (left), a good polish is all that is required to bring it up to scratch. Other wooden floors may not be quite so easily salvaged, in which case you might consider painting the floor – either in a deep gloss or with a pale Scandinavian-style wash. Then you need only throw a few loose rugs on top – kelims or Indian dhurries, for example.

Otherwise you could choose a carpet that will provide the main decorative theme of the bedroom. A carpet resembling jaguar fur brightens up the quiet modernity of this room (right) and has been used to cover the platform base of the bed as well. The strength of its statement means that other elements pale into insignificance: bold white for the duvet cover is safe.

Visually, a wooden floor can provide pattern and texture, depending on how it is laid. Tiles, marble slabs and even bricks can add interest in a less traditional style of bedroom but, as all these materials are cold to the touch, it is probably worth scattering them with carpets, runners, rugs, and innovative floorcoverings for comfort's sake. Bedroom floors need to be cosy; that first toe needs to be tempted out of bed in the morning.

There are paint varieties on the market that are actually recommended for floors – hard-wearing enough to sustain scuffing and scratches. So you could design your own kelim and paint it on the floor of your bedroom, and then the colour scheme of the floor could reflect the tones of other objects and textiles in the room, without the need for a long-winded and expensive search for a proper rug. More simply, you could paint the floor a dark, high gloss – you will be amazed how it changes the atmosphere.

Do not forget more traditional forms of floor covering. You can use strong colours or patterns in a carpet as the leading element in a decorative scheme, choosing fabrics and wall finishes to coordinate with it, rather than the other way round. If you only own moth-eaten rugs, you can still create an opulent effect by overlapping them on your floor Middle-Eastern fashion, ensuring that the good part of one covers the holes in another. You should be able to cover most of the floor with minimal cost and effort.

Window dressing

Practically speaking, when money is any sort of consideration, there is little that you can do with the structure of the windows you inherit with your property, but there is no shortage of exciting and imaginative ways –

both simple and elaborate – in which you can disguise, dress, or emphasize their form from the inside. Consider all the alternatives rather than limiting yourself to traditional treatments straight away.

The function of window dressing is primarily protective – insulating you from the prying eyes of the outside world – and many people do indeed resort to pinning an old sheet or blanket up against their bedroom window when they first move into a room. It may stay a while because finding more permanent protection is a crucial step that should not be hurried; your choice will play an important part in the overall decorative scheme of the room, so be sure rather than investing in fabric and fittings that do not look right.

Different window treatments can change the atmosphere of a room dramatically. In this distinctly summer bedroom (above) a single voile curtain hangs from an unobtrusive wrought-iron pole over each French window. It billows in the gentle breeze but does not change the quality of sunlight entering the room.

The tiny window above this neat bed under the eaves (right) would be dwarfed by the addition of curtains. Arched shutters shaped to fit the rounded window take up little space and could reveal a painted mural – a moon and stars perhaps, or a pastoral scene – when closed.

BEAUTIFUL BLINDS

For many people living in large cities, being visible to neighbours is a constant problem. New and exciting decorative ideas have now been explored, however, that can replace the twitching net curtains so often turned to as a last resort in the past.

You can hang translucent blinds, made of cotton voile, or sheeting, or anything pale that lets in the light, from the top of the window frame in your bedroom to cover the window permanently. When you have two or three old sash windows in the room hang a blind at each, so that you can raise and lower them independently as you wish, according to the amount of light required.

The decorative theme of the windows can be extended by hanging a similar length of fabric as a wall hanging behind the bed. Oriental-style stencils in gold on each blind (right) can also create a striking window covering, reinforced by the central motif on the white cotton bedspread; the lamp base and wide shade pursue the theme. The overall decorative effect is that of soft, filtered light, cocooning the bedroom and successfully shutting out the world beyond.

Many period properties retain their traditional internal shutters which, on top of their decorative potential, provide additional security. However, when closed at night the bare wood may be look dull. Lliven up the shutters by tacking bright tin or even copper to them, or paint a pastoral or moonlit scene on them to gaze at from the bed.

If you live in a basement and your bedroom gets little or no light, you could exaggerate this to dramatic effect. Instead of putting up expensive curtains, intersperse the standard, clear glass panes with coloured glass or, even simpler, stick a coloured gel across the window pane. The glass can be decorated in other ways too: frosted, engraved with an interesting motif, or covered in an opaque rice paper that has been cut ornamentally. Daylight would be filtered and soft, casting gentle shadows over the interior of the room – ideal for a room with no view.

Blinds are very useful for awkward windows but are sometimes considered rather a poor solution in a bedroom, compared with warm, voluptuous curtains. Given an original and individual treatment, however, painted with

scenes, or cut with a pattern of holes so that sunshine or
street light will illuminate the motif, making it glow with
life, a parchment blind can be a very decorative feature.

With blinds of natural materials such as rattan, bamboo
and cane, which allow the sunlight to filter through the
loose weave, you could add an edging in a fabric that
matches the bed cover, or the upholstery of the bedroom
chair, for a more coordinated decorative effect. Instead of
adjusting the blinds traditionally with a simple cord, you
could fix them permanently in one position with ties in the
same edging material or in a coordinating colour.

More austere Venetian blinds suit modern spaces; they
can be wooden and kept natural, or painted, or even more
sophisticated. You can then control the amount of light
allowed into the room and adjust it according to the
prevailing weather conditions.

Ultimately, fabric will always be by far the most
flexible raw material for dressing windows. Choose the
design and the material at the same time as you
are planning the colour of your bed linen and walls.
Curtains can sweep dramatically and fall luxuriously,
and do not have to be complicated to make.

Furnishing fabrics are surprisingly cheap and come in
widths appropriate for large-scale ideas. It is important to
remember, when measuring, that to match stripes and
patterns will require considerably more fabric than your
initial measurements might suggest; you must also allow
for a certain amount of shrinkage. Either take into account
a possible 10 per cent shrinkage and cut accordingly, or
wash the material before you start to cut it into lengths.
This first wash should also dispose of any stiffening in the
fabric and make it easier to work with.

WINDOW DRESSING

If your bedroom is not architecturally
interesting, make a special feature of
the window: a little can go a long way.

Not all translucent curtains have to be
white or ivory. Indeed, this fabric (left,
above) comprising pale blue-and-white
checks, allows quite a lot of light to
filter through. It has been gathered into
curtains and fixed permanently in place
across the bay window, tied with
matching fabric to create a fuller shape.
The table in front of the centre window
is draped in a coordinating blue-and-
white striped cotton, and stacked with
tiers of fabric-covered boxes, flanked by
tall lamps that pick up the blue theme.

Curtains and window treatments for
skylights and awkwardly placed windows
in lofts or under the eaves, where
window shapes tend not to be standard,
can pose problems. Roller blinds can
satisfy this requirement but tend to be
pretty basic. Alternatively, you could
introduce some sturdy plants (left,
below) to act as a screen, or use them in
conjunction with a blind. Your decorative
theme would influence the style and
colour of the pots and the plants would
provide additional pleasure and colour if
they produced flowers or fruit.

CLEVER DISGUISE

Accessorizing the bedroom is probably more fun than anywhere else in the house. The variety of bed linen, pillows and cushions, blankets, duvets, throws and rugs on the market today means that you can basically change the look of your bedroom every time you change the sheets. You can have plain, striped, checked or patterned sheets or duvet cover in all the colourways imaginable, with coordinated blankets and even lamp bases and lampshades to match. If you are more ambitious, you might dress up that anonymous side table in a check or stripe to complement the week's bed linen. In fact, who is to know that there is a table under there at all? Many a serviceable table has been revealed as an upturned cardboard box cleverly draped in fabric!

A successful scheme does not always have to be an immaculate mix and match combination, however. You can play around with your existing bed linen, rejuvenate ancient blankets by sewing a colourful cotton border around the fraying edges and go through Granny's trunk searching for old patchwork quilts and pretty embroidered bedspreads that would add the finishing touch.

Few bedrooms have the space to house a dressing table as a specific piece of furniture, and in essence it is an old-fashioned notion; but the necessity of a set of drawers for those small, personal items and a flat surface for a good mirror is still high on the agenda.

Unusually shaped bedrooms sometimes incorporate strange niches, often either side of a chimney breast or in a former fireplace, which can be exploited to advantage. Position a stray table, preferably with a couple of drawers in it, to fit into the alcove, and add a lace tablecloth. Delicate reading lamps and a pretty, decorative mirror will complete the picture, while all those bowls of rings and bracelets, keys, pens, hairbands and bows that invariably go missing for want of a more permanent home will add that final, personal, finishing touch.

If you do not find formal curtain-making an appealing prospect, there are plenty of other ways to hang fabric. The haberdashery department of any big store is like an Aladdin's cave of loops, curtain rings and eyelets of every conceivable metal and material; colourful arrays of braid of all descriptions with matching tassels; ribbons of widely differing textures and shades. All you need is a little imagination and the courage of your convictions.

Equally, if making curtains is beyond you, the old blanket tacked to the window frame can be replaced by a more dramatic alternative until you have discovered a seamstress. Last summer's faded sarongs will liven up your windows with their unusual colours and designs. Or a tea towel might fit a narrower window. Instead of tacking it to the wall, you could add a degree of permanence by punching brass eyelets into the two top corners, to hang the tea towel from hooks screwed into the window frame.

If you want to be more unorthodox, experiment with a simple curtain pole: try draping your fabric over the curtain pole and playing around with the general fullness of the swags – curtain fabric can be quite stiff but cotton voile or lengths of mosquito netting will hang beautifully. Finials can be added afterwards to complete the look.

Street lights are often a problem, if you are an urban dweller: even lined curtains do a poor job of keeping out the glare in the small hours of the morning. Hotels use blackout blinds which are concealed by day behind smart dress curtains; a double set of curtains might also solve the problem, and would prove less austere in your own bedroom. Alternatively, you could cover a screen and put that in the window to block out the light or simply move a cheval glass or similarly tall piece of furniture into position.

Furniture and fittings

When you come to furnishing your bedroom, you will be using your imagination and creative assets at maximum capacity. With your basic colour scheme now firmly in place, and the proposed treatment of walls, windows and floors agreed, the selection and arrangement of your furniture and the fine-tuning of your own accessories will require thought and discipline.

SCREENED OFF

The soft furnishings in a bedroom
contribute in large part to the personal
atmosphere that is ultimately created.
Although nothing is standard and beds
can come in a wide range of styles and
sizes, it is the way the pieces of furniture
are pulled together; the use of fabrics
and colours to soften their edges; and
the introduction of new ideas that
ensures the final look's overall success.

Here, in what might be considered by
some a slightly gloomy bedroom, there is
an all-embracing tranquillity, making it
the perfect resting place at the end of
a stress-filled day. The narrow metal
twin beds are painted an interesting
pale blue-grey, their striped covers
echoing the blue of the bed frames.
There are no cushions, however, to
break the line at the head of the bed,
no light touch on the side table, no
flowers, no sense of levity.

The folding screens on one side of
each bed, their wrought-iron frames
threaded with lengths of white broderie
anglaise with a pretty scalloped edge,
are both decorative and functional,
shielding the occupant against draughts
and providing an essential sense of
enclosure and privacy.

You may have decided on a new bed. As the one essential item in any bedroom, spare no expense. There are many aspects to consider when you buy a bed (see page 60), not merely its style and size.

Apart from the bed, there is no absolute need for any other furniture in the bedroom, although if you have space available, a bedside table, a comfortable reading chair and stylish, effective storage for all your clothes and personal belongings are all luxuries that could be incorporated into a decorative scheme to advantage.

If your bedroom is very small or a difficult shape for some of your furniture, then you will have to adapt. A chest of drawers with a small mirror perched on it can replace a dressing table. Tables, whether round or square, are good corner fillers: the flat surface can be used for books, a vase of flowers, ornaments, photographs or other personal items and, if you drape it in a coordinated fabric or an antique oddment, it can liven up a dead corner and can conceal boxes of junk beneath the folds.

Beautiful old wardrobes (closets) are can be expensive; they can be cumbersome; very few fit easily into a bedroom and many appear even heavier than they are because of the rich colour of the polished wood. You could, however, look for a smaller, cheaper cupboard (closet), which you could paint as an integral part of your decorative scheme. You could add a chair in the same tone, too. A fabric tent, constructed around a simple frame across the corner of a room, could also provide space to conceal clothes and overnight bags without dominating the room visually. Just like a Victorian changing tent on a beach, this self-styled wardrobe (closet) can blend into its surroundings or take centre stage, depending on how elaborately you dress it.

Storage and display

Try not to over-clutter your space because the fewer pieces of furniture you put in a room, the larger it will appear, and the bed will already take up a substantial proportion of the available room. If you have a low ceiling, leave the walls free of large paintings and mirrors as these will draw attention to it. Accessories should be kept small and simple, too: a few pictures or photographs by the bed, a sampler, or even a few pretty plates on the wall.

How you choose to display your favourite things can play as large a part in the overall decoration of your bedroom as the paint and fabric. Ultimately, however, if you intend to drill the wall full of holes to display a vast array of pictures and photographs, you will not have to worry so much about the finish you achieve with your paintbrush. As the months go by, the pristine

LOVE OF LINEN

Collecting linen can become as obsessive as any other fad and those of you prepared to do battle in street markets, antique fairs and rummage sales will find a vast array of antique and monogrammed linen sheets and pillow shams, Victorian lace nightdresses and comforters, laundry bags, shoe bags and antique cushions to take your fancy.

From a storage point of view, the most satisfactory aspect of such a passion is that piles of neatly ironed sheets and pillowcases occupy so little space! Imagine tying up each pile with silk ribbon and keeping them on show – in a special glass-fronted cupboard (closet) in your bedroom.

There is no need to be elitist here, though: the pleasures of crisp linen are only marginally superior to those of Egyptian cotton sheets or any other cotton for that matter, and you do not have to collect antique linen. If you like to alternate your bedroom image on a regular basis, you will undoubtedly have several different sets from which to choose: whether it is the turn of the embroidered cotton or the well co-ordinated colours of designer linen, the pleasure is the same.

exhibition of frames will inevitably become augmented by flotsam picked up along the way: souvenirs of a recent trip will find a vantage point on the edge of a heavy mirror frame, together with postcards from friends; while hats, scarves, ties and handbags will nearly always end up perched on the knob of the bedstead or hooked on the edge of a picture.

Making collections of personal souvenirs can sometimes take an obsessional turn but some of the more interesting trophies can be put to a practical purpose. Collections of colourful empty tins could be used for storage, for anything from coins to safety pins, while antique luggage, which has become highly collectable, especially grand leather suitcases embossed with some stranger's initials and lined in green silk, can be piled up in a prominent position to act not only as a decorative focus, but also as containers for your spare bed linen and blankets. A leather trunk at the foot of the bed could be filled with all those difficult things that you can never store tidily, like maps, unruly electrical cable, and maddeningly shaped baskets, while magazines and books – even last night's discarded clothes – could rest on the top.

Decorating ideas are constantly changing, although at a different rate to the volatile fashion world, and there will always be a new look to try. Decorating trends move backwards and forwards from exotic to minimalist, from dark, vibrant colours to pastel and natural tones, from opulent to austere. As in the fashion world, however, an over-enthusiastic adherence to a new trend can sometimes prove an expensive mistake. Be careful.

The bed in this spacious attic (right) has been positioned at an angle, taking up more room than it would otherwise. The sloping walls and jutting roof beams restrict the possibility of other furniture and the only item on display is the oval mirror on its wrought-iron stand, which occupies a prominent position in the middle of the floor.

The layout of your bedroom depends entirely on the number of possessions you like, and need, to have around you. And a lack of storage space may mean that some of your belongings have to be on display so you must be extremely orderly.

DRAMATIC DISPLAY

In contrast to the more self-conscious attic space, this bedroom of normal proportions loudly proclaims the personality of its owner (right), even to providing clues to his initials emblazoned in red above the bed. Although average in size, this room has been given over to a conscious display of eclectic bits and pieces: a curious collection of framed chequer boards and coats of arms, a snooker score board and a shelf of childhood toys. At the foot of the bed, valuable space is occupied by a low wooden stool bearing four large cylindrical tins, which could house socks, underwear, or any other useful things.

As purposeful as this room is in its display, the storage elements of those more private possessions must be equally so. At the opposite end of the room to the bed is a built-in cupboard (closet), glimpsed briefly in one of the horizontal mirrors that hang above the bed.

DECORATING TIPS

- Have the courage of your own convictions. Don't be inclined to ask too many friends' advice. A bedroom designed by committee will not be a success.
- Start with one strong element of colour, whether floor-covering, textile or item of furniture, and let that influence your overall design.
- Register any problem areas before you get too involved. An expert's opinion and help at the beginning will save time and tears later.
- Don't despair of your furniture – an indifferent wardrobe (closet) or worn blanket box can be scrubbed, painted, stencilled or just disguised to give a new and more appropriate look.
- Take time over the details of your decorative theme. Specific ideas often take longer to come together and it is worth waiting for the right fabric or other element, rather than cutting corners, to achieve the best effect.
- Never throw anything away until after your bedroom has come together. You may find that the very item you so eagerly disposed of during the initial turn out is the very thing needed to finish off your new image.

FURNISHING THE BED

In any bedroom, the bed takes centre stage. And whether formal and tailored or soft and casual, the bedroom is the place where fabric can be used to convey a sense of sophistication and elegance, or warmth and comfort; the secret lies in the blend of colours and textures of bed linen and fabrics.

Bed curtains or drapery, country quilts, pillowcases and duvet covers, fine linen or pure cotton sheets – all have a decorative potential when you come to furnish the bed.

MAKING CHOICES

The universally accepted fact that the majority of us spend one third of our lives in bed underlines the importance of finding the right mattress. Hand-made mattresses can be ordered to fit any shape and configuration of bed, new or antique, while a range of mass-produced styles can be tried and tested for size and comfort in showrooms everywhere. It is essential – in the interests of a good night's sleep – to have a good bounce on a mattress before you buy it.

It is equally important to search out the right pillows and in today's allergy-conscious society, feathers may be a problem. It is wise to check what the pillows are filled with and to test the relative comfort/support of the different types available. Pillows of different shapes in various colourways and combinations can create interest on a simple bed with a plain headboard, or one that has to be jammed against the wall. There are square versions called Oxford pillows as well as the standard oblong variety. And then there is a huge range of smaller cushions, be they tapestry or lace, circular, square or heart-shaped, ornamental or just comforting, possibly filled with fragrant lavender or sleep-inducing remedies – personal touches with a decorative edge.

Finding the correct duvet and trying to understand variable tog (density) values and the different merits of different filling products is just one more challenge. Moreover, you may still prefer to be tucked into sheets and blankets, for there is just nothing quite like slipping into wonderful starched, crisp linen sheets. Freshly laundered linen, and traditional wool blankets edged with satin, must still be the ultimate in luxury. Although the ubiquitous duvet seems to have relegated blankets to second place, they still make a cosy bed. If you prefer neatness, a duvet has a habit of looking perpetually untidy, whereas blankets tuck firmly under the mattress with sharp, mitred corners.

FRESH TO FORMAL

Beds come in all shapes and sizes. Wicker beds are an unusual feature (previous page, left), the warmth of their natural colour accentuated by a predominant use of red in this otherwise simple Balearic bedroom. A four-poster bed, by contrast, in a small room, makes an imposing and altogether less flexible impression. Simple beds, like this pretty wrought-iron framed example (far left), can be made to appear softer with a squashy duvet and an abundance of pillows.

Bed linen nearly always comes in a variety of colourways: a large blue-and-white check alternated with striped blue-and-white and plain white pillowcases, with a variety of blue edgings, gives the bed a freshness you can almost smell. You might create a more exciting effect by mixing the colours – perhaps red-and-white with yellow-and-white pillowcases instead of more traditional blue combinations.

A traditional four-poster bed with festooned bedhangings creates a more formal decorative style (left), here tempered by the lightness of the bamboo-style posts, complemented by the bamboo bench at its foot, and the simple white cotton bed cover.

Whatever the bed and wherever it is situated, you can disguise a tired look if you use fabric cleverly. You can transform an occasional guest bed in the study into a day bed if it is covered with a smart tartan rug with a few cushions scattered on it. Colourful cotton dhurries or light kelims introduce a novel texture; they can be used to great effect as bed covers, while patterned paisley, silk saris and other ethnic fabrics give any bed an exotic feel.

The bedstead

If you are buying a bed for the first time, you may be uncertain as to what to look for. Divan-style beds are the most readily available; they come with or without a headboard. The advantage of this type of bed is its accessibility, for although it may be unimaginative to walk into a showroom and buy your bed 'off the peg', as it were, you do, at least, have a chance to try out the different styles, testing the length and width of each bed, the degree of support, and looking carefully at any other factors which will affect your final decision.

Antique beds tend to be small when compared to the vast 6ft (183cm) king-size beds available today in the shops. If you are tall or share your bed with a large person, think twice before opting for a 4ft 6in (137cm) variety. If discussing this style it would be wise at the planning stage to include in your costings the price of a mattress, too.

Similarly, an authentic French *bateau lit* is almost bound to require a base and a mattress. This style of bed may prove well worth a big financial outlay, however, as it seems to suit masculine bed linen and romantic and whimsical drapery equally well, making it truly versatile – a lasting investment. The style is gaining widespread

popularity and modern reproduction versions are now being manufactured in standard sizes to meet this demand. If you decide on this Continental type, a duvet is essential, or making the bed will be a nightmare.

If you want to find a more interesting and more unusual option, it will take time. Everyone seems short of time today, but it may seem shorter still if you are spending sleepless nights on an old mattress on the floor while you search for the ultimate bed. If you are looking in an antique shop or at an auction, you will need a little imagination: brass and wrought-iron bedsteads are often hard to envisage as beds when seen out of context, stacked as

Another way to maintain the decorative drama of your bedroom if you are short of paintings and accessories is to emphasize the sense of colour coordination and focus attention on the bed itself, rather than on the room in general. Blue and white are two colours eternally linked and always popular. The interesting use of varying shades of blue on this bed – the two-tone headboard and contrasting blankets, dark blue pillowcases edged in white and even a blue trimming on the sheet – all compensate for a rather ordinary room.

DIAPHANOUS DREAMS

Fabrics can change the atmosphere of any room, softening a spartan interior, disguising its shortcomings and harmonizing any rough edges. An eclectic mix of materials and textiles will bring out the best in any bedroom.

There is no feature in this room (left) to distract your eye from a large expanse of bed. The walls are without pictures, there is no furniture, not even a lamp. However, because of an appropriate choice of wall colour and the gentle combinations of the right fabric and textures, the overall effect is one of tranquillity, conducive to sleep. The pale *eau de nil* of the walls sets a calm and peaceful mood; the dreamy transparency of the mosquito netting hanging from a frame in the ceiling reinforces the effect.

The intricate patchwork quilt is draped casually over the wide bed disguising the disarray of unmade blankets, and ticking pillowcases are just visible. The bright Persian rug provides a glowing block of colour on the floor, yet its faded red tones are not remotely intrusive.

HEADBOARD HEAVEN

Styles of bed differ so much that the term headboard may seem somehow inaccurate. Many brass and iron beds come with a top and a tail of differing heights, four-posters are often without either, and a vast number of beds simply improvize.

If you possess a mattress and a base but no specific frame as such, you can invent or design your own bedhead (right). A set of disused shutters, a wall hanging or an interesting rug would provide a focus for the eye in the same way, and would supply a new texture at the same time. A large, unwieldy picture in need of a home might be happy standing against the wall behind the mattress or hanging heavily above it.

Why not try using a screen, whether clad in fabric, covered in postcards, or just painted? Remember those Victorian screens covered in a collage of images and then varnished? It would also add a very feminine touch as the surround for a pretty guest bed, and you could expand the idea by using chintz for the curtains and bed cover, even a floral wallpaper.

heads and tails against the back wall of a shop. Remember to make sure that all the pieces are present and intact; that the iron runners which attach head to tail fit comfortably into the retaining section at each end, so that you do not find yourself on the floor again, with only ironwork for blankets and pillows.

If your bed-hunting proves fruitless, you can combine the possibility of tried and tested comfort with an imaginative setting, by buying the divan of your choice from a standard outlet, together with its mattress, and designing your own bed around it.

You need not limit yourself to personalizing the headboard; you could construct an entire frame. If you are not entirely happy about entrusting the safety of your prone body to your creation, ensure that the store-supplied base carries all the weight and that your homemade frame is free-standing around it.

Once again, junk shops and auctions will reveal a host of potential components: extraordinary bits of architectural salvage, furniture, columns, ironwork, paintings and posts. Fabric, ribbon, pieces of carpet, tassels and braid can be used to disguise any unattractive seams or areas which do not fit as neatly as they might. Odd lengths of silk and ethnic embroidery can be incorporated into the drapery of a four-poster bed. Things do not have to match; it is the overall effect that is important.

The headboard

If you lack the time or confidence to launch into a full-scale project, keep your ideas simple. You can still give your bed a personal touch if you choose to concentrate purely on the headboard and its surroundings. Design a mural, and

A blank wall, even if laden with an interesting selection of pictures, can look rather conservative and unexciting. However, a strong image has been created in this case (left) by using a series of pen and ink drawings, all identically framed, above a wooden headboard which has been softened with a long flat cushion, upholstered in white cotton. As the piles of books either side of the bed would suggest, this headboard has been designed with an avid reader in mind.

Test your artistic talent and paint your own style of headboard onto the wall, as here (left). In this particular case, the design is little more than an outline, painted in a colour to match that of the blanket cover, its shape reflecting the design of the two lights on either side of the bed. What gives this bed an additional perspective is the stone wall above and behind the bed, which reinforces the colour scheme and provides a shelf at the same time. In cases like this, when the bed has been squeezed into a small space with no room either side for tables or even a chair, any thought of a bed frame has also had to be abandoned.

BRILLIANT BED HANGINGS

Bed hangings can be an imaginative and creative way of changing the whole look of your bedroom. You do not necessarily need to invest in a four-poster bed, but if you are lucky enough to have ceilings sufficiently high, improvizing with this style of bed can be fun.

Whether the frame is wood or metal, covered with a canopy or left open to the ceiling, you can attach your chosen lengths of fabric in a variety of ways – threaded over a pole, attached by ribbon or fabric ties, hooked onto curtain track or simply draped. Wooden posts can be carved or painted, iron or metal frames treated with different paint effects or wrapped in fabric.

The curtains around the bed can be of diaphanous light cotton or heavier, warmer material. Four-poster beds conjure up images of vast, draughty bedrooms in cavernous houses or castles, so curtains to keep you warm and cosy and protect you from draughts are traditional. However, lighter curtains can seem just as appropriate when you draw them around the bed as protection from the bright afternoon sun during a siesta in a warmer Mediterranean bedroom, and they lift in the breeze.

EASTERN AND EXOTIC

An ornate brass and iron single-bed frame has been draped very simply using a continuous length of striped fabric to produce a looser, more informal style here (right). Two rod supports are fixed securely to the wall along which the bed stands. The fabric is allowed to hang loosely down to the ground at either end, to enclose the bed like a canopy, rendering any further decoration of the clapboard wall behind unnecessary.

Instead of scented candles in the bedroom, their gentle perfume permeating the folds of material long after the candles have finished burning, a coil of incense swings at each end of the bed. A heady mixture is slowly released, lending an exotic and smoky atmosphere to the room. Incense creates little heat after it is first lit, but be wary of the proximity of burners to fabric.

The colour of the bed linen is picked up by that of the overhead drape, and a couple of additional colourful cushions on the bolster are linked visually with the red and purple stripes of the woven rug to form an exotic corner in an otherwise unremarkable room.

sketch the outline on the wall behind the head of the bed; or hang a gilt-framed mirror or a large painting horizontally above it; or cover the wall with an array of small, framed pictures – formally disposed or randomly scattered – or even a wall hanging.

If you are more fabric-minded, and your ancient, much under-used sewing machine is still at the bottom of your wardrobe (closet), why not see whether you can make bed hangings? The traditional four-poster bed is obviously made to be decorated like this, which means that curtains or swathes of fabric can be hung about it with relative ease, tempting even the beginner to try to produce some fantastically dramatic effect. Remember that the fabric can always be draped into position instead of sewn into a more formal hanging, if the hardware around your bed is appropriate. And there are, of course, other ways of experimenting with drapes.

For instance, if your bed is situated along a wall, you can fix a metal or wooden rod to the wall above the centre of the bed and drape your fabric, tidily seamed or left fraying, across the support, allowing the ends to hang loosely over the head and foot of the bed. The impact of the sweep and drop of falling fabric can be increased dramatically if you move the support higher up the wall.

Alternatively, hang your fabric from a coil of wire attached to the ceiling, like the frame of a mosquito net. Buy a corona or some such similar device and drape the fabric around it above the head of the bed. If your bed is situated under a sloping roof, attach a length of fabric to a suitable rafter with a staple gun. You will curtain it off, effectively transforming it into a four-poster.

Bed linen

You should never be in a hurry to buy new bed linen; as long as you are sleeping in comfort, you can always put up with sheets that are too small for the bed, or the sorry sight of faded, washed-out pillowcases and the occasional patched blanket; even the wrong-coloured sheets can be hidden, if necessary, under a decorative cover. Remember that by far the most economic time to acquire luxurious new bed linen is at the end of the season, and discontinued combinations are worth a look, too.

UNDER THE EAVES

Creating a very bold scheme is often the answer if you are dealing with restricted spaces or where the architecture dictates the limits of your design. In this masculine attic (left) a single four-poster has been constructed to fit in under the eaves. Although there is little space to be too elaborate, using contrasting checks here has proved very successful. Matching checked silk throws have been used as a bed cover and hanging while a larger check in different colours is used for the carpet. Using strong textiles has avoided the need to add very much decoration on the little wall space available.

This airy summer bedroom (right) by contrast, although also an attic space, has a high ceiling; architectural interest surrounds you, from the exposed rafters and old-fashioned ceiling fan, to the high window. Storage space above and within the curtained cupboards (closets) enclose a comfortable window seat. Seen through the filter of a mosquito net, the clapboard interior of the room is painted white throughout. White muslin curtains cover the cupboards (closets); the sheets, pillowcases and quilt are all white and blue.

If you are in the happy position of being able to rummage in the family blanket box to see what you can plunder, now is the time, for although there is always an abundance of new designs to suit any decorative scheme, the quality of some old linen and blankets is unbeatable, and deserves a little loyalty. Moreover, although the more practically minded of you will shudder at the idea of ironing – and starching – so many yards of sheeting, perhaps if you have resisted buying new linen, you should on this occasion take advantage of a local laundry service.

If you are short of a suitable cover for the top blanket, a lace tablecloth would make a pretty cover during the summer and can be replaced by a tartan travel blanket when the nights start to get cooler. If you are more concerned with a coordinated end result, why not design an interesting original bed cover – perhaps a patchwork using up scraps of curtain material, or a more sophisticated American-style quilt with a personal motif. You can pick up on colours or motifs from the linen when you come to cover your reading chair, perhaps, or if you have cushions on a window seat.

Some ideas for bed linen may be entirely original, while others may be inspired by a set from a period drama on the big screen or on television. Your own choice may be influenced by a display in a shop window, an imaginative photograph in a colour magazine or even by the acquisition of a particularly beautiful fabric. It is your interpretation of each of these trends that makes your bedroom personal, intuitive and fun. Whatever direction you choose to take, analyse the colour and pattern in schemes that you like, the contrasts of scale and proportion, and use this as your guide.

CHILDREN'S BEDROOMS

A very particular set of criteria come into play when you design a child's bedroom. You must place the emphasis on bright, bold fun, but be aware of the constant need for space and sufficient storage. An older child's bedroom should incorporate areas for more serious occupations and many children's beds nowadays build work and storage units into their general design, providing a vast array of adjustable shelving, drawer and table space – ideal when there is homework to do, or a computer to house.

STARTING OUT

Children are likely to spend a lot of time in their bedrooms. For those not fortunate enough to have a separate nursery or playroom, the room will have to assume a number of important roles. Primarily it is where the child sleeps, and there are beds to suit every child's fantasy. Some are disguised as buses and trams; modular beds incorporate writing areas, television and computer stations and sleeping platforms. Bunk beds will enable you to accommodate easily any unexpected guests, but truckle beds, inflatable mattresses or even camp beds can lend an impromptu stay a certain *frisson* of excitement.

Sleeping should be fun and planning the whole room around a favourite cartoon or television character is one way to create a sympathetic environment. Decorate the walls with cut-outs, posters and friezes, and retain the theme in your soft furnishings: bed linen today is developed to follow every new trend, so characters from literary classics and stars of the big screen appear on duvet covers, pillowcases and matching pyjamas to boot.

Children are acquisitive by nature and notoriously untidy, so storage must be near the top of any agenda in a child's room. They like to be able to see their toys, which means that increasingly, nowadays, the traditional toy box is being replaced by transparent plastic bins. If you make tidying up fun, you will encourage your child to help, so plan your storage carefully. Use bright and colourful units; keep shelving, boxes and drawers within easy reach. A bed with built-in drawers underneath is a popular solution to housing everything from clothes to toys; or big wicker baskets which are light enough for a child to move around.

TOY TOWN

A bright colourful room is always popular with a younger child, with an abundance of storage space to accommodate the ever-increasing number of toys. Remember to position shelves with the height of the child in mind, so that the games, puzzles and books that are used on a daily basis are always easily accessible. The bed should be big enough to accommodate both the child and a huge family of teddy bears, the overflow perhaps living in a painted trunk. The floor is another important feature of a child's room because many games happen at this level. It should be smooth and practical, avoiding the possibility of splinters in knees and hands, and for reasons of hygiene, but at the same time it should provide the optimum surface for car chases, battles and general high jinks.

It is unusual today to meet a child who is not fascinated by either the small screen or the cinema. If you intend to let your child have a television, insist that it is situated sufficiently high up to be out of harm's way; perhaps you could use the same shelf to store videos. Remember, too, that electricity can be lethal so wires should be inaccessible.

■ 71

Nursery

One of the joys of expecting a baby is building a cosy nest for it. Although initially it will be unappreciative of your efforts, a baby's smile as it grows gradually more familiar with the colours and shapes in its bedroom will bring pleasure to everyone.

Plan the room to incorporate the essentials: cot (crib), grown-up's chair, changing mat and storage for clothes and nappies (diapers). Try not to take up valuable space with bulky chests of drawers. Instead, you could simply screw a hanging rail to the wall and suspend colourful plastic buckets from it, to keep everything in one area.

You might find the number of coordinated ranges of nursery wallpapers and fabrics overwhelming. They can be brightly primary-coloured or quietly pastel (less interesting for the baby but more peaceful for you), purely decorative or educational, featuring animals, clowns, flowers, or nursery rhymes. Or you can invent your own design.

The nursery of your first-born will be the object of infinite thought: not only the colour of the room but the position of the cot (crib), changing table, wardrobe (closet) and clothes rail will have been the focus of much agonizing. You may decide to employ an old-fashioned iron cot (crib) in a corner of the room (left) next to your own bedroom, and paint animals of all shapes and sizes around the top half of the walls (right).

Practical considerations at this stage revolve around safety: for your own sake, check the height of the changing table, and ensure that you have easy access to nappies (diapers) and clean clothing as you cannot leave a baby at a height to go off in search of either.

Junior bedrooms

The transition from nursery to first real bedroom and from cot (crib) to proper bed is an important step for both child and parent. Until the young child becomes accustomed to sleeping in a bed, it is wise to restrict its height off the ground to the minimum, in case the child should fall out.

If your child is hugely excited by the change of sleeping arrangements, harness that energy and try to ascertain what they want in their first bedroom. The demands may be extraordinary, prompted by peer pressure at school in the main, but listen and adapt to make it a happy room.

Young children tend to be very sociable. Nowadays, as more mothers return to work, more children than ever before will be obliged to socialize with school friends on a regular and frequent basis. If the child-minding parents are without a garden, a decent-sized child's bedroom seems the only escape from chaos. Although children take up less space than adults, if the bedroom is to become meeting-place as well as playroom and bedroom, it will either need to be bigger than you planned, or you will have to employ space-saving devices to exploit the space available.

To this end, manufacturers are designing more and more themed and modular beds. Simple bunk beds are no longer enough. Today they have to be incorporated into complicated units of shelves, drawers, tables or drawing surfaces, with special slots for computer screens and television sets. The bed units themselves tend to have built-in drawers constructed with the child's strength and size in mind, for not only are they within easy reach for someone of restricted height, but access to the drawers is simple. These will provide ample storage for anything from train sets and tin soldiers to furry animals.

Super-trendy is usually super-expensive, however, and a child's desire to keep up with his or her peers can be very oppressive and disheartening for the average parent. If your child is to have a more traditional style of bedroom, you can take infinite care over its decoration instead which will go some way to mending the situation. And involving your child as much as possible in any of the decisions that have to be made, whether concerning the size, shape and colour of the bed, or deferring to them when it comes to choosing the bed linen, will produce a rewardingly positive response. You will be well advised to avoid sheets and blankets because making beds properly is relatively difficult and time-consuming, while persuading a child to tidy a duvet each morning should be comparatively easy.

Keep an inflatable mattress on hand for unexpected overnighters; it can be stored with a duvet and pillow in a wicker basket or blanket box in a corner of the bedroom, or at the foot of the bed. If you have enough space, you might consider having a second bed in the room. It could stand against a wall as more of a day bed, used predominantly to house the overflow of soft toys from the main bed.

You can magnify the sense of excitement and adventure that a child will feel when a friend stays the night by adding some apparently spontaneous decorating touches. When the extra bed materializes, you could make up both beds to match: both with tartan blankets, or with duvets featuring opposing cartoon characters like Tom and Jerry. You could even drape sheets around the room to resemble tents or teepees, replacing the sheets on the beds with sleeping bags. You could stick silver glitter or tiny stars onto a dark ceiling to further the camping image, even hang up a mobile of a large yellow moon.

A CHILD'S CHOICE

The modular style of bedroom (opposite page) can combine every little girl's fantasy of living in her own doll's house with a clever storage idea. Each unit here is designed to resemble a house – complete with pitched roof. Easily accessible drawers with large finger holes can be approached from either side of the unit and the three units together create an effective screen for the bunk beds. The house at the head of the beds contains a bedside lamp, while the unit furthest away is equipped with a black-board and drawers for chalk and dusters.

The decoration and furnishings in both the bedrooms (left) appear simple and traditional, but both contain clever, more contemporary features. A simple, low, pine bed in a sparsely furnished room (above) has a system of wicker baskets underneath as inventive storage, making the most of the little space there is. The sponged red-and-white check paint effect (below) is ideal in a room dominated by iron-framed beds; busy, bright and cheerful, it lifts any austerity in the atmosphere. At the same time, the friendly sponged finish helps to ease the child's tastes towards the more formal designs of adult fabrics and papers.

KING OF THE CASTLE

Teenagers are always demanding so there is no reason to suppose that decorating a teenager's bedroom will be easy. The room must take on its more serious role as a study at this stage so you will also need to establish what that will require in terms of space and storage. Tidiness will be increasingly important as the child continues to grow in a finite space. If you are lucky enough to have high ceilings, you can save floor space by employing a scaffolding structure (right) with a bed platform on top. Bolted to the wall for safety, this is an imaginative, hard-working piece of furniture with a bookshelf as one end of the bed support and the access ladder as the other. The desk is positioned directly below the sleeping platform, resting on wooden trestles and supported by the central filing cabinet. An extra shelf at the side of the bed stores books and an alarm clock, as well as preventing the occupant from rolling out of bed.

As they require minimal care, duvets are perfect for a teenage bedroom, and particularly here, where bed-making is difficult and untucked sheets and blankets would spoil the structure's line.

Life in a teenage bedroom

Most teenagers will have very strong ideas of what they want and how it should be arranged, so it may be difficult to have things exactly as you want them. Remember how important that private space will be for a developing adolescent; how vital it feels to have some freedom to create your own environment; how stamping your own personality on your room is crucial to your general self-confidence and to the development of your self-image during those confusing years. It is at this age when the bedroom doubles as a study, but also where those intimate conversations with best friends over the first adolescent agonies take place.

Requirements can far exceed the size and suitability of the bedroom, with every conceivable inch of wall space taken up with magazine cuttings, postcards and pin-ups of

favourite idols. Overladen shelves will inevitably stagger under the weight of the latest in hi-fi equipment and pounding speakers. Compact discs will vie for space with cassettes and paperbacks, and the floor is bound to be piled high with magazines and heaps of discarded clothing and shoes, and probably dirty coffee mugs. As every available cupboard (closet) and drawer disgorges its contents to add to the chaos, you will doubtless be told that everything has a place in this disorderly scheme of things. Manufacturers continue to market new ranges of sophisticated bedroom units, meanwhile, in an attempt to help parents and children alike bring order to this mayhem.

Some children, of course, will be keen to be involved in creating a special style for their bedrooms. The mysterious disappearance of an old rug from the corridor, or some cushions from the sofa, may be the first indications that your teenage child is developing decorating fever. Traces of lurid paint in the bathroom basin and protracted periods of time behind closed doors should probably be encouraged, at whatever cost, as signs of a developing personality.

BLACK AND WHITE

Decorating monochromatically can lend an air of style and sophistication to a teenager's bedroom (centre) – just as effective and a refreshing change from bright colours. Black-and-white mattress ticking – chic and affordable – has been used for the bed cover and festoon blind to set the scene, with black-painted floorboards and wicker chair to match. The narrow strip of coordinated braid running around the top of the otherwise plain walls is a subtle touch. Marilyn Monroe could have been joined by several other black-and-white photographs to liven up the wall.

Too often a teenager's bedroom is not large enough to accommodate a spare bed for occasional overnight guests. Bunk beds may be the easy answer but they will probably be deemed juvenile; there are modular beds on the market, however, which have adapted the idea of storing a small trestle bed under a standard one, and these will solve your problem. The version illustrated here (left) comprises a base and simple mattress, forming a more than serviceable bed; it can be pulled out into the centre of the room on demand – probably by the children themselves.

INDEX

PUBLISHER'S ACKNOWLEDGMENTS

Conran Octopus would like to thank the following photographers and organizations for their permission to reproduce the photographs in this book:
1 Jean-Francois Jaussaud; 2 Paul Ryan (designer: Myra Frost)/International Interiors; 3 David Parmiter; 4-5 Deidi von Schaewen (interior designer: Françoise Dorget); 6-7 John Hall; 7 Heiner Orten/Jalag/Sabine Oppenlander Associates; 9 Fritz von der Schulenburg (Architect:Nico Rensch)/The Interior Archive; 10 Ingalill Snitt; 11 Pascal Chevallier/Agence Top; 12-13 Jerome Darblay; 14 Nicolas Tosi (stylists:Julie Borgeaud & Anne-Marie Comte)/Marie Claire Maison; 15 Tim Street-Porter (architect: Jeffrey Tohl); 16 Peter Cook (architect: Sergison Bates)/Archipress; 17 Peter Cook (architect: Sergison Bates); 18 left Henry Bourne/Elle Decoration; 19 William Waldron; 20 left Stephane Couturier (architect: Nouvel)/Archipress; 20 right Hotze Eisma; 21 Christophe Dugied (stylist: Catherine Ardouin)/Marie Claire Maison; 22 Stephane Couturier (architect: Colomb)/Archipress; 23 Pascal Chevallier/Agence Top; 24-5 Ingalill Snitt; 25 Jean-Pierre Godeaut; 26 David Parmiter/Homes and Gardens/Robert Harding Picture Library; 27 Ianthe Ruthven; 28-9 René Stoltie/The World of Interiors; 30 Jerome Darblay; 31 Eric Morin; 32 Tim Beddow (Architect: John Pawson)/The Interior Archive; 33 Richard Waite; 34-5 Tim Beddow (designer: Ricciardi)/The Interior Archive ; 36-7 Fritz von der Schulenberg (designer: Mimmi O'Connell)/The Interior Archive; 37 Simon McBride; 38 Hotze Eisma/V.T. Wonen; 39 Guy Bouchet/Stock Image Production; 40 Ingalill Snitt (Stylist: Daniel Rozensztroch)/Marie Claire Maison; 41 Christian Sarramon; 42 Paul Ryan (designer:Marla Weinhoff)/International Interiors; 43 James Mortimer/The World of Interiors; 44 Hotze Eisma; 45 Mark Luscombe-Whyte/Elizabeth Whiting & Associates; 46 Jerome Darblay; 47 Henry Wilson/The Interior Archive; 48 Hotze Eisma; 49 above James Mortimer (designer: Wendy Harrop)/The Interior Archive ; 49 below Marie Pierre Morel (stylist: M. Kalt)/Marie Claire Maison; 50 Polly Wreford/Woman & Home/Robert Harding Picture Library; 51 left Chris Drake/Homes & Gardens/Robert Harding Picture Library; 52 Christian Sarramon; 53 James Merrell/Homes and Garden/Robert Harding Picture Library; 54 Tim Beddow/The Interior Archive; 55 Trevor Richards/Abode; 56-7 Fritz von der Schulenberg (Mimmi O'Connell)The Interior Archive; 57 Christian Sarramon; 58 Gilles de Chabeneix/Designers Guild bed and bedlinen, Kings Road, London; 58-9 Fritz von der Schulenberg (Adelheid von der Schulenburg)/The Interior Archive; 60 Hotze Eisma/V.T. Wonen; 61 Thomas Piek; 62 Marie Pierre Morel (le Signe & Puech)/Marie Claire Maison; Top; 63 above Pascal Chevallier/Agence Top; 63 below Nicolas Millet/Agence; 64 Simon McBride; 65 Marie-Pierre Morel (stylist:Marion Bayle)/Marie Claire Maison; 66 Nadia Mackenzie; 67 John Hall; 68-9 Wayne Vincent (designer: Lesley Saddington)/The Interior Archive; 69 Schöner Wohnen/Camera Press; 70-1 Jean-Francois Jaussaud; 72 left Scott Frances/Esto; 72 right Hotze Eisma/V.T. Wonen; 73 Jan Baldwin/Domain; 74 Schöner Wohnen /Camera Press; 75 above John Hay/Voque Living; 75 below David Brittain/Domain; 76 left Jean-Paul Bonhommet/ Elizabeth Whiting & Associates 76-77 Tom Leighton/ Elizabeth Whiting & Associates.

AUTHOR'S ACKNOWLEDGMENTS

I would like to thank the professional team at Conran Octopus for their help and moral support in putting this book together. To Clare Limpus and Ruth Prentice, to Sarah Sears for showing me a glimpse of the diplomacy of editing, and to Denny Hemming for keeping me on the straight and narrow.

A final thank you to my team of stickers in the office, to Pooks, Zoe, Nancy, Sophie and Fred, for their laid back attitude in moments of crisis.

MAKING
THE MOST OF
BATHROOMS

MAKING
THE MOST OF
BATHROOMS

C A T H E R I N E   H A I G

conran
OCTOPUS

Commissioning Editor	Denny Hemming
Project Editor	Helen Ridge
Copy Editor	Tessa Clayton
Designer	Liz Hallam
Design Assistant	Amanda Lerwill
Picture Research	Claire Taylor, Clare Limpus
Production	Mano Mylvaganam
Illustrator	Sarah John

First published in 1996 by

Conran Octopus Limited

37 Shelton Street

London WC2H 9HN

a part of Octopus Publishing Group

Reprinted 1998

British Library Cataloguing-in-Publication Data
A catalogue record for this book is available from the British Library
ISBN 1 85029 827 0

Printed in China

CONTENTS

This stylish bathroom has two clearly defined roles – bathing, at left, and storage, at right – visually separated by the design of the floor tiles. The wavy black-and-white dividing line is echoed by the serpentine-fronted cupboards. These create a much greater feeling of space than a straight wall-to-wall arrangement and help to soften the rectilinear, galley-like shape of the room.

The circular basin, encased in the same wood as the cupboards, and the cast-iron bath with its ball-shaped feet continue the curvy theme. As the taps and mixer spout are wall-mounted centrally above the bath the bather can lie facing either end of the room and there are, accordingly, two niches in the tiled wall for soaps and shampoo.

INTRODUCTION

The past one hundred years have seen a remarkable revolution in bathing and bathrooms. A century ago, the once-weekly familial bath, taken in a tub laboriously filled by hand in front of the living-room fire, was gradually being superseded for the lucky few by the first Victorian and Edwardian bathrooms, complete with vast baths and substantial plumbing. As technology improved and demand increased, so bathroom fittings began to be mass-produced on a scale more suitable to the average-sized home. Today, thanks to sophisticated modern plumbing and design, most of us can enjoy a piping-hot bath simply at the turn of the tap, at any time of day or night.

These advances in design and technology mean that the modern bathroom is a much more flexible and personal room than ever before. At its most minimal, it can occupy remarkably little space, carved, for example, out of an existing bedroom or a redundant attic. At the opposite extreme, it can be one of the most luxurious rooms in the house, wholly dedicated to the comfort and wellbeing of the user. While single-room apartments require ingenuity to incorporate even the basic minimum of fittings, most houses today offer the option of one bathroom and an extra toilet and many have the extra space for an en suite bathroom, a separate shower room or a downstairs cloakroom.

Whether installing a brand-new bathroom or revamping an old one, initial planning is of vital importance. There has been a huge expansion in the range and variety of bathroom fittings available, all designed with maximum hygiene, comfort, practicality and convenience in mind. No longer is the bathroom seen as the poor relation in terms of design, and manufacturers are vying with one another to produce the most elegant, as well as the most comfortable and economical, bathroom suites on the market. For the purchaser, this excess of choice can be more than a little confusing and it is essential to know exactly what sort of fittings you require and whether they will be suitable for the intended location. Taking time to plan ahead, armed with tape measure and graph paper, can help to translate ideas into reality and to ensure that you really do end up with your perfect bathroom.

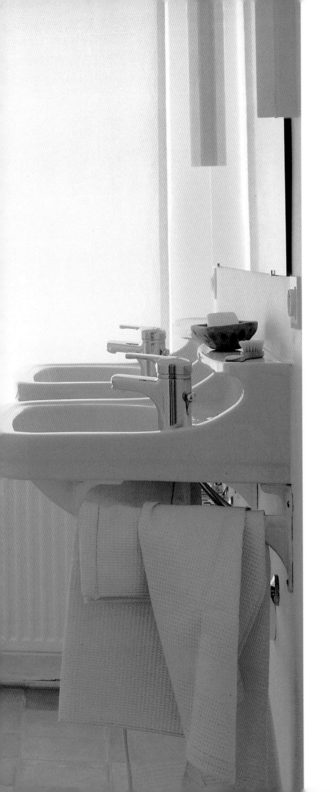

PLANNING

Planning a new bathroom can be a daunting prospect. Not only does it involve choosing the right fittings but it may also mean extending and, in some cases, completely reorganizing the existing plumbing in order to accommodate them. Whether you want to install a completely new bathroom or make improvements to an old one, there are still the same decisions to make and problems to overcome. The first step is to define the role and requirements of the new room; the rest will follow.

TAILOR-MADE

A bathroom must be tailored to personal
requirements and every plan will vary
according to the likes and dislikes of the
planner(s). This spacious bathroom
(previous page, left) is shared by a
couple. They opted for double basins,
centred against the wall at right, with
storage units, bath and toilet set against
the opposite wall. A low tiled wall
projects between the bath and toilet,
providing privacy for the latter as well
as completing the splashproof surround
for the bath. Storage takes the form of
simple, open shelves with plenty of
space for piles of towels and linen.

Others may prefer closed or concealed
storage space such as this built-in
ottoman with a hinged lid (previous
page, right). The space inside is ideal for
use as a laundry basket or for storing
towels, cleaning supplies and toilet
paper, and the ottoman doubles as a
seating area when closed.

Planning a bathroom involves more
than the positioning of the basic fixtures
such as the bath, basin, shower unit and
toilet; make sure your plan allows plenty
of floor and wall space for 'extras' such
as a towel rail, mirror and laundry
basket (right).

ASSESSING THE SPACE

Whether you are planning a brand-new bathroom or making improvements to an old one, taking a moment to think about the exact role of the room may save expensive mistakes later on. Ask yourself the following questions: Is the bathroom to be used by the whole family, just the children, a couple or a single person? Should it be en suite with the main bedroom? Is it for guest use only or will it serve the whole house? Will it require any special adaptations to suit the elderly or young children? Will it need to double up as a dressing room, exercise area or a laundry with facilities for washing and drying clothes?

The answers to these questions will determine almost every decision you make concerning the bathroom, from the choice of fittings to the choice of decoration. You may have always dreamed of having a super-powerful shower but if the other potential users of the bathroom are all under five years old, you may wish to think again. Similarly, a luxuriously carpeted room may be unbeatable in terms of comfort but it will certainly not give much pleasure or last very long if it is permanently soggy thanks to careless teenage bathers. The bathroom is a much-used room and both its design and decoration must be strictly tailored to suit its occupants and their requirements.

The next step is to establish whether the intended space can be plumbed. Take advice about local water and plumbing regulations; they vary from area to area and it is vital to understand their implications before you start. Secondly, unless your house is very new, the existing plumbing has probably 'evolved' over the years and it may be necessary to make changes so that the system can accommodate the new bathroom. It may be that your hot water tank is not large enough to cope with the extra demand. Existing pipework and plumbing may influence the siting of the bathroom itself and the positioning of the fittings within it: for example, it is much easier to connect a new toilet if it can be linked into an existing waste pipe.

Once the space has been allocated and the plumbing considered, begin to plan the layout of the bathroom. Use graph paper to map out the position of the fittings. Most bathroom catalogues include a sheet of graph paper for this purpose and some even provide line drawings to scale of toilets, basins, bidets, baths and so on. Cut them out and juggle them around to see how best to incorporate each piece. Don't forget to allow for access as well: you need enough space to get from one fitting to another and to use them in comfort; this is especially important if more than one person will be using the bathroom at any given time. Keep plumbing guidelines in mind: a toilet may be easiest to connect when sited against an outside wall; toilet and bidet should ideally be placed side by side; basin and bath water need to be channelled away in the same direction.

When choosing the fittings, keep your earlier definition of the bathroom in mind. If the room is to be used by the whole family, a separate shower unit might be preferable to a shower over the bath, as it would allow more than one person to wash at any time. Double basins are also worth considering. If space permits, install the toilet in a separate room to avoid delays at peak hours. Choose serviceable, splashproof materials for floors and walls and invest in a large mirror, a laundry basket and plenty of shelving.

PLANNING AHEAD

- Take professional advice before planning a bathroom. Take into account local water regulations, existing plumbing facilities and the construction of your house.
- Draw out the area on graph paper and study how best to divide up the bathroom for different tasks. Look at the options of various 'dividers' such as double or sliding doors, archways, curtains and changes in floor level.
- Ensure that space is available not only to accommodate your chosen fittings but also to move them into position. For example, a heavy cast-iron bath is awkward to manoeuvre. If the staircase is too narrow, could the bath be winched up and brought in through a window? Will the floor take the strain once the bath is full of water?
- Be realistic about the possibility of future plumbing problems and allow for access to potential trouble spots such as the shower pump and boxed-in toilet cisterns. Fit removable panels instead of sealing these utilities in behind fixed walls.
- Build in utilities such as good heating, ventilation and lighting. They are vital to ensure that the bathroom both looks good and works efficiently.

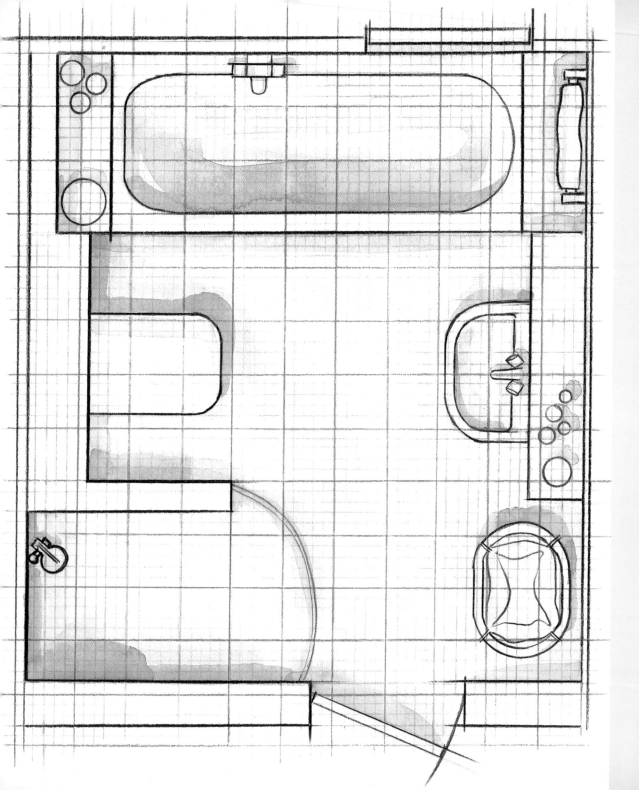

DRAWN TO SCALE

When planning a bathroom it can help
to map out the fittings to scale on graph
paper first. This floor plan (left) relates
to the bathroom shown at right and on
the previous page. Note the division of
space: the bath runs almost the whole
length of one wall, with tiled 'extensions'
at each end filling in the gaps. The toilet
and basin face each other while the
shower is partially separated from the
rest of the room by a full-height
projecting wall. Basin and toilet are
wall-hung and, in each case, a false wall
has been built out from the original
bathroom wall to accommodate the
necessary pipework and plumbing. Tiled
and painted to match the rest of the
room, these projections are hardly
noticeable but give the room a much
neater, more streamlined finish. The
basin wall has also created a handy
alcove for the laundry basket.

Shelf space around the bath, basin
and shower was planned before work
began. The false wall behind the basin
created an instant shelf (see previous
page) and the recessed wall above was
lined with mirror. The areas at both ends
of the bath were tiled to match the walls
and a niche was carved out of the shower
wall for soap and shampoo bottles (right).

If young children are going to be the main users of the bathroom, choose fittings that will accommodate short legs: a wall-hung basin, for instance, that can be set at an appropriate height; a toilet with a low-level cistern and a lever that is easy to reach; a bath with a relatively low side and a flat, non-slip base; a shower with a sliding shower head rather than a fixed one and, if possible, a thermostatic safety control to prevent small hands suddenly causing a surge of scalding water. Many an accidental bang on the head can be avoided if you wall-mount the bath taps and mixer spout; this will also keep the controls out of reach.

Make sure that at least one cupboard is fitted with a secure lock to keep medicines and cleaning agents out of harm's way. Buy a rubber suction mat for the bottom of the bath and a large, absorbent bath mat for the floor outside. Flooring generally should be non-slip even when wet and this applies especially to the areas by the bath, the shower, the basin and the toilet. If you fit a lock on the inside of the bathroom door, position it well out of your children's reach.

Some of these guidelines apply for the elderly as well, such as a shower with a thermostatic safety control and non-slip flooring. A shower door that opens inwards or slides will reduce the likelihood of water dripping on to the floor, making it slippery. The bath should similarly have a flat, non-slip base but in this case a high side is a help rather than a hindrance, allowing access to the bath without too much bending or straining. Some sort of bath chair on a swing arm may be required for the very infirm; position the bath to accommodate the fixings. Choose taps or levers that are easy to turn and add helpful 'extras' such as grip rails in the bath and shower and judiciously placed seats.

A bathroom plan should also incorporate changes of floor level, if appropriate. Here, the shower area is defined by a lowered floor (above) which, together with the partition wall, retains most of the fall of water, allowing the shower to be used at the same time as the rest of the bathroom. The flooring throughout the room runs to skirting-board height and the join with the tiles is well sealed to prevent any water seeping through. The wall-hung toilet and basin (above and above left) stand clear of the floor, making it an easy-to-clean surface. Both bath and basin are fitted with streamlined modern taps, and a white ladder-rack towel rail (seen on page 10) makes good use of the otherwise redundant space at one end of the bath.

UTILITIES

A well-designed bathroom does not just function well, it is also warm, cosy and inviting to use. Make sure you take time at the planning stage to think beyond the basic necessities, such as fittings and fixtures, to elements such as lighting, heating and ventilation. These are easy to install at the time of building, but expensive and disruptive to alter or add to later on.

Water and electricity are a lethal combination and it is vital that the accommodation of these utilities is carefully and safely planned. Some of the bathrooms shown in the pages of this book do feature electric sockets, but in many countries safety rules and regulations do not allow them, or specify their location. In the United Kingdom, for instance, there must be no socket outlet within the bathroom at all, unless it is a special low-voltage shaver unit, and any light fitting or other electrical supply must be worked by means of a pull-cord if it is within reach of the shower or the bath. If in any doubt at all, seek expert advice.

The bathroom tends to be used most in the early morning and late at night and good lighting is of paramount importance. Normal ceiling lights and wall lights are permitted in bathrooms, provided they are correctly wired in and safety guidelines are adhered to. A permitted alternative to pull-cords is a switch on the wall outside the bathroom door. If the ceiling is very low or the light is to be positioned over the bath or shower, pendent lights and ordinary inset spotlights are not recommended. Instead, choose from a wide range of specially designed bathroom lights, including sealed bathroom spotlights which are designed to function in a wet, steamy atmosphere.

SAFETY FIRST

When space is restricted, it may be necessary to extend the bathroom's role to include washing – and sometimes drying – clothes and bed linen. Appliances can be installed within bathrooms but they should be positioned well out of reach of the bath and shower and must be safely wired. In this bathroom (left and right), for reasons of safety and aesthetics, the machines have been concealed behind sliding mirrored doors. When the doors are closed, the mirror serves to increase the feeling of space within the bathroom, creating no break in the all-white scheme; when open, they offer easy access to the appliances and, with the doors sliding back one behind the other, take up minimal space.

Washing machines and tumble dryers tend to generate a lot of condensation, and if you plan to install such appliances you should make sure the bathroom is well ventilated. As this room has no windows, the owners have installed ventilation ducts, which also provide a casing for the inset spotlighting.

It can be hard to decide where to position the lights until you have actually started to use the room but, as a general rule, over-light rather than under-light. Taking a light source out later on is far less expensive and disruptive than adding one after all the decoration has been completed. Place a light near the bath to allow for reading or shaving; light the mirror over the basin, positioning the fittings to throw light on to you rather than the mirror in order to reduce glare, and ensuring that the light or lights are sufficiently wide to illuminate the sides as well as the front of your face. Pay particular attention to dark corners or recesses; a judiciously placed light focused on an object or picture can transform a dreary corner into a feature of the room. If the room contains cupboards, fit lights inside that come on automatically when the doors are opened; this is one example of a highly practical and effective 'extra' that is easy to install while the bathroom is undergoing construction, but awkward later on.

Heating and ventilation are also of prime importance. A heated towel rail will provide a modicum of warmth but most of this will be absorbed by the towels. A bathroom radiator or a radiator and towel rail combined can help to increase the heat, as can underfloor heating if installed during construction. Don't forget that towel rails warmed by the heating system will not function in the summer when the heating is turned off. Even in hot weather, it is still much nicer to have warm, dry towels so either choose a rail that can be connected to the hot-water system or substitute an electric one.

It is not essential to have a window in a bathroom but, given the hot, steamy atmosphere and the inevitable condensation, it is vital to have adequate ventilation. Building regulations require that an extractor fan be fitted in the absence of an openable window and it is most usual for the fan to work in conjunction with the light. Fans can be programmed to stay on for some twenty minutes or so after the light has been switched off.

Hair dryers, fan heaters and similar electrical equipment are not permitted in bathrooms but larger appliances such as washing machines or wall heaters can be installed, provided that they are permanently wired into sealed sockets. They must not be positioned within reach of anyone using water, so should be well out of the way of the bath or shower.

Telephones are permitted in bathrooms but again, for reasons of safety, it is not advisable to have an ordinary telephone socket in the room. The effects of steam and condensation on the telephone itself must also be taken into account. One solution is to have a telephone on an extra-long lead in the next-door room or to install a portable, cordless model which can be carried in and out of the bathroom.

ON SCREENS

As well as the siting of fixtures and
fittings, planning a bathroom also
involves making sure that there is
adequate space for washing and bathing,
for storage, and for any additional
activities such as dressing or exercising.
In a small room there is less room for
manoeuvring, but in a larger room, the
different areas need to be carefully
planned and defined.

Screens are useful tools for creating
both a decorative and a practical
division of space. In this spacious, high-
ceilinged bathroom (right), a triple-
panelled screen serves to create a cosy
area around the bath and acts as a visual
divide between the two ends of the
room. Made of wood, it has been
painted to tone in with the decoration of
the room. In addition, at the far end of
the room long curtains suspended from a
wooden pole hide the contents of the
shelving system from view.

DIVIDING SPACE

Maximizing the potential use of any bathroom depends on an appropriate division of space within the room itself as well as the way in which it is connected to the rest of the house. Again, this involves considering the list of questions at the beginning of this chapter: you can only decide how best to allocate space once you are sure of who and what the bathroom will be for.

Division of space involves defining the boundaries of the bathroom. You may wish to carve up an existing bedroom, or create an extra room in the attic. You might choose to extend a room by taking in all or part of an adjoining room or passage. Or you might find extra space under the stairs or in a hallway, for example, for a toilet or shower room. Within the bathroom, it involves allocating space for the different items that may be required: for example, a shower fitted over a bath, or a bath and separate, self-contained shower unit; double or single basins; storage; a dressing-room area; or utilities such as washing machines and tumble dryers.

The dividing lines may be either decorative or structural. Breaking up the space may simply be a case of installing a screen or different flooring or tiling to indicate a change of use within the bathroom, or it may involve physically separating a bathroom from its en suite bedroom. Whatever the situation – and it will be different in every case – the division of space must be decided at the planning stage. Walls, doorways, floor levels, positioning of fittings and fixtures are all still fluid at this point and with the help of a tape measure, a pencil and a sheet of graph paper, it is possible to experiment before making any unalterable decisions.

Within the bathroom itself, divisions of space can be decorative and/or practical. A raised floor around the bath might separate that area from the rest of the room and, if tiled to match the surrounding walls, might also create a waterproof 'platform' within an otherwise non-waterproof floor. Screens are economical options; they can be fixed, as in sliding doors or panels, or freestanding, either painted or decorated, or fabric-covered for a softer effect. In its freestanding form, a panelled screen can be placed around the toilet, for example, to increase privacy, or near the entrance to the room to cut down on draughts, as well as providing a useful place to hang towels or robes.

Separating the toilet from the rest of the room or, if space permits, installing one toilet within the bathroom and another elsewhere in the house, can greatly increase

MAXIMIZING
POTENTIAL

Partitioning space is an easy way to increase the potential use of a bathroom without having to divide it into separate rooms. In this room (above and right), the bathroom area is divided from the dressing area beyond by partition walls which visually separate the two, though access remains open. In addition, the toilet, bath and shower, ranged along one wall, are separated by a trio of tiled projecting walls. These serve to give privacy to the toilet area and to create a splashproof cubicle for the shower. They also enclose the bath and provide enough space to hang a towel rail.

Note how changes in flooring can be used further to define different areas: here, the toilet area is tiled throughout in the same black border tiles used to edge the main floor-covering.

the potential of a bathroom used by more than one person. A standard toilet and a wall-mounted basin can be fitted into a surprisingly small space, requiring only about 140cm x 90cm (55in x 36in) in total. Alternatively, a toilet can be screened or partially screened from the main area of the bathroom by a partition wall – with or without a door. Even a low-level partition wall, rising to about 90cm (36in) in height, would serve to increase privacy, as well as doubling up as a useful shelf to house toilet paper and accessories.

If your shower is to be open-plan with the rest of the room, some sort of screen or partition may be appropriate to keep the basin and toilet area dry. Even if the whole room is tiled and therefore entirely splashproof, it may still serve to increase the potential use of the bathroom if both shower and basin can be used at any one time without both users getting soaked.

Dual-purpose bathrooms

Dual-purpose bathrooms may work better if the two areas are divided or semi-divided. In a bathroom-cum-dressing-room, for example, the storage area for clothes would benefit from being separated in some way from the moisture and condensation of the main bathing area. This might involve fitting a standard cupboard with hinged or sliding doors or creating a large, walk-in closet. It might simply be a case of hanging a curtain which would cut down on dust and add a decorative touch.

In certain countries, such as the United Kingdom, regulations dictate that appliances such as washing machines have to be positioned out of reach of both bath and shower, and the installation of some sort of screen or divider would enhance the safety factor as well as conceal

these less-than-decorative items from the rest of the bathroom. Sliding doors are a space-saving option, while double doors look attractive and can be designed to fold back flat for ease of access. A word of caution about boxing-in any appliances, especially washing machines or tumble dryers: take care to ensure that there is sufficient ventilation and that installation instructions are correctly followed. A tumble dryer, in particular, generates a great deal of condensation and most models require a vent leading to an outside wall.

One possible drawback of dividing space within the bathroom is that each individual area may have to be independently lit, but powerful angled spotlights and clever use of mirrors can help overcome the problem.

OPEN OR CLOSED?

The division of space between a bedroom and its en suite bathroom can be as formal or informal as you like. These two rooms (right) are virtually one, separated only by a wide curtain-lined arch. The striped ticking fabric is tied back to reveal the cast-iron bath on its elegant grey slate plinth. The shape of the splashback echoes the archway, and brass swan-neck taps complement the brass bedstead. Wide oak boards run, almost uninterrupted, throughout the two areas.

By contrast, the illustration (far right) shows how a bathroom can be carved out of a bedroom, the two separated for reasons of logistics by conventional walls and a sliding door. Every inch of wall space within the bathroom is needed to accommodate just the basic fittings and there is no room for decorative manoeuvre. As the entrance to the bedroom has virtually been reduced to a passage, cupboards occupy the remaining space, freeing up the rest of the room for bed, armchair, table or bookcase as required.

EN SUITE

Once experienced, an en suite bathroom is a luxury that it is hard to give up. Even if you think you have no spare room in the house, it may still be a possibility, given careful planning and clever division of space. If your children have

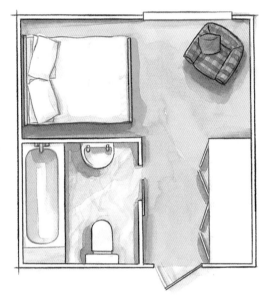

grown up and left home, then a bathroom adjacent to the main bedroom, supplemented by a smaller shower and toilet elsewhere, would be a practical arrangement. If your house has sufficient bedrooms, then it may pay dividends to convert one into a bathroom and knock through the adjoining wall. If an existing bedroom is large enough, there may be space to fit a bathroom within it, either screening or semi-screening off the two areas or simply leaving them open-plan.

However the two are arranged, an en suite bathroom is designed first and foremost to be used in conjunction with an adjoining bedroom and the division of space should reflect this. A conventional doorway is the most usual 'divider' but if space is at a premium and a door takes up too much room – particularly if you feel that it will always be left open anyway – then there are alternatives.

Depending on the positioning of the two rooms, an archway between the two can create a decorative visual divide. An arch is always a graceful architectural feature in a room and, large or small, it allows easy access while keeping the bathroom at a discreet distance. It can be hung with a curtain for a decorative effect or for extra privacy, or left elegantly open.

A difference in floor levels can also create a visual divide between a bedroom and bathroom. Perhaps combined with a doorway or archway, steps either down or up help to define the separate areas.

ONE ROOM OR TWO?

An en suite bedroom and bathroom should ideally be planned as one unit, taking into account access between the two, the view from one to the other and a sense of continuity in terms of decoration.

Given the size and proportions of this room (left), it seemed unnecessary to divide the space at all and the bathroom has been largely incorporated into the bedroom scheme. Toilet and bidet are housed in another room but the decorative period-style bath and basin blend easily with the white Lloyd Loom chair and lace-covered bed. French windows ensure ample ventilation and the polished wooden floor is suitable for both bedroom and bathroom use.

An archway and a change of floor level serve to separate this bedroom and bathroom (right) while matching paintwork and floor-covering unify the two spaces. The classic black-and-white theme of the bedroom is carried through to the bathroom, echoed in the smart black bath and the thick, white towels.

Double doors can provide a flexible alternative. They allow the two rooms to be closed off from each other completely when shut, and yet virtually made one when open. They would be particularly appropriate in cases where an en suite bathroom has another access and might, on occasions, be used by people other than the occupants of the adjoining bedroom.

An en suite bedroom and bathroom should be planned in conjunction. Not only should they look good together, complementing each other in decorative terms, but they should work well together. Depending on the positioning of the two rooms, the less-than-decorative items such as the toilet and bidet should be discreetly placed out of sight from the bedroom. If they cannot be hidden, then folding wooden screens, either painted or decorated with decoupage or fabric, a curtained canopy, an opaque glass screen or a simple semi-partition wall can all be brought into play. Another ploy is to focus attention elsewhere, making a decorative feature of the bath or basin.

Continue the style of decoration through from one room to the other. The bathroom need not be a replica of the bedroom but should echo the same themes. Use matching fabric at the windows or complement the wallpaper in one room with a fabric in the same design in the other, and run the same floor-covering throughout both rooms, if possible, for an added sense of continuity.

One final consideration: particular attention should be given to heating en suite bathrooms, especially if the bathing area is not sectioned off from the bedroom. Large rooms are difficult to heat evenly, and you might want to consider additional heating near the bath to ward off post-bathing chills.

HIDE AND SEEK

Conventional storage units can be adapted to contain fixtures and fittings in bathrooms where, for reasons of privacy or aesthetics, it is necessary to screen off certain elements. The key element of this peaceful, contemplative retreat (below right) is the large marble soaking tub which stands squarely in the middle of the room. Plain white panels line the walls, cocooning the bather and screening off the other areas of the bathroom. Hidden behind this all-white wall are the toilet and bidet, storage space and the V-shaped marble basin with its simple spout and chrome extending mirror just visible here. All clutter and activity is contained within and nothing intrudes upon the soothing atmosphere of the bathing area.

MADE TO MEASURE

Once all the bathroom fittings and fixtures are in place you may find there is little room left for free-standing cupboards and shelving, so it is vital that storage is considered at the planning stage. Returning to the graph-paper floor plan of your bathroom, assess the available space. Remember that no elements, except perhaps the windows, need be constant. Building a false wall a few feet out from a real one might create an ample walk-in closet. Alternatively, build out to either side of the basin or the bath, creating a decorative alcove (which could be mirror-lined) and providing twin storage units. Use the space above and below the fittings: set the basins into cupboards and utilize the otherwise wasted area above the bath with a row of shelves or a towel rail. Modular shelving units need not necessarily stand against a wall; projecting at right angles, they can also serve as decorative room dividers.

Built-in storage units are a good way to make use of every available inch of space. Made to measure, they can be fitted into awkward alcoves or under sloping attic ceilings. A row of floor-to-ceiling cupboards will give a room a streamlined finish, as well as disguising less decorative elements such as the hot water tank or cluttered shelves.

BEHIND CLOSED DOORS

Twin storage units have been built out from the wall to either side of the basin in this sunny, well-lit bathroom (right). The 'cupboard' on the right houses a toilet; the other provides ample space for a shower. The shower's interior is fully tiled and the unit has a conventional shower door, which provides a better seal than the exterior door. Linked by the pedimented mirror above the basin, the two units add an architectural note to the room, creating a decorative feature out of necessity. For good measure, the design of the doors neatly echoes the shutters at the window and the panels on the bath.

STYLE

With the practicalities of planning under way, it is time to turn to the more creative side of bathroom design. The style of your bathroom requires careful consideration as it will dictate your choice of fittings and decoration. To help you build up a picture of the effect you want to create, keep a file of ideas: jot down points of interest from other people's bathrooms, and tear out magazine articles for inspiration. But most important of all, allow yourself to dream a little.

Creating the style and atmosphere of a bathroom need not necessarily be complicated or expensive. Tiled in a bold chequerboard design, this cream-and-turquoise bathroom (previous page, left) combines great style with simplicity and practicality. Bright Mediterranean colours lift the tiling out of the ordinary and, together with the hand-finished effect of the tiles themselves, create the feeling of being inside an Italian *palazzo* or an ancient Roman bathhouse. The broken run of cornice above one end of the bath enhances the atmosphere. All that needs to be added are soft white towels and plenty of hot, scented water.

Sometimes the fittings themselves can dictate the style of a bathroom. A feature as striking as this beautiful antique blue-and-cream basin with its original brass taps (previous page, right) would lend instant charm and character and establish the look of the rest of the room: plain cream walls and the simplest of curtain treatments would be all that would be required to show it off to its best advantage.

COUNTRY

Whether it is designed to complement a rose-covered cottage or as an escapist retreat from urban reality, the country look always works well in a bathroom setting. Easily created, involving inexpensive materials and simple techniques, the effect is pretty, fresh and appealing.

The classic country look is perhaps best associated with sprigged floral wallpapers and flowery fabrics, which, together with accessories such as bunches of dried flowers, are readily available and have a timeless appeal. The country-style bathroom, ceiling included, is often entirely decorated with floral wallpaper, complemented by wall-hung flower-patterned plates or prints. A window curtain decorated with spring blooms might be matched with a basin frill in the same material or, for an original touch, a curtained canopy around the bath. The scheme can also be extended to fixtures and fittings: Victorian basins and toilets were often decorated with fresh blue floral designs and though the originals are much sought after and difficult to obtain, reproduction models are easily available.

Variations on the gingham theme, with one-colour or multi-colour checks, work just as well in a country-style bathroom as in a classic country kitchen. Try simple and uncomplicated curtain treatments with gingham fabric hung from a painted wooden pole or tied with bows on to a wrought-iron one.

The country style implies a certain nostalgia and fittings usually follow a traditional theme: large, old-fashioned washstands with brass legs; cast-iron baths with ball-and-claw feet; high-level toilet cisterns worked by pull-chains; wooden toilet seats and towel rails.

Walls and floors should have a rustic feel. Plain white paint, evoking traditional whitewash, creates a crisp, fresh background while natural matting, painted or stained floorboards or terracotta tiles might cover the floor. Stencilling allows a decorative motif, perhaps taken from the curtain fabric, to be repeated on walls, cupboard doors, floors and the sides of the bath. Cupboards and shelves are in rustic pine – sanded and sealed rather than painted – with doors and windows to match, evoking the wooden beams of old country cottages. Wicker baskets, filled with soaps and potpourri, add an inviting touch.

RURAL RETREATS

Rustic wooden beams and whitewashed walls evoke the spirit of the country in the two bathrooms shown here. The brickwork above this basin (left) has been left unplastered and the white-painted shutters provide a little privacy during the daytime when the checked curtains are open. White walls in this spacious, airy bathroom (right) provide a fresh, light foil to the row of maplewood cupboards. These, in turn, complement the beamed ceiling, with the natural grain, texture and colour variation of the wood playing their own part in the decoration.

In the larger room, the bath takes centre stage. Unusually, it stands on a pair of wooden brackets, rather than cast-iron legs, and still has its original lever-operated brass plug.

BACK IN TIME

Pictures and accessories play almost as great a role as fittings and decoration in creating a traditional-style bathroom. An old document, mounted and framed, hangs above the bath (left), while prints, photographs and memorabilia cover almost every remaining inch of wall space. A portrait (right) is flanked by two framed panels of antique blue-and-white tiles. Collections of silhouettes are grouped to either side and a large gilt-framed mirror hung over the basin makes a striking statement.

TRADITIONAL

Recent years have seen a great revival in 'traditional' bathrooms that evoke the stately, rather masculine style of the Edwardian era, when bathrooms were sumptuously – if rather cumbersomely – decorated. Original fittings have come back into vogue and architectural salvage firms are flourishing as home decorators scour the country for old brass taps, basins, roll-top baths and commodes; these are invariably beautiful to look at but they need careful restoration to function properly and a lot of time and effort is required to keep them looking good. Luckily for all those who have little time to seek out the genuine article, manufacturers have been quick to respond to demand and

most bathroom showrooms and catalogues now offer well-designed and authentic-looking traditional ranges.

The centrepiece of most traditional-style bathrooms is a large, cast-iron roll-top tub with decorative ball-and-claw feet and polished brass taps. Alternatively, a standard bath can be set into a marble surround with side panels of glossy, dark-stained wood, evoking the mahogany fixtures of times gone by. Whatever its size and shape, however, the bath is always a cast-iron one; these rooms look back to the days well before the invention of acrylic.

Basins are usually capacious affairs, either freestanding complete with matching pedestal, or built into a marble or mahogany surround. Taps are pillar-style with handles rather than modern levers or mixer controls. Toilets have

wooden seats and high-level cisterns with pull-chains or are concealed within converted Edwardian commode chairs with hinged wickerwork seats.

Decoration tends towards the masculine with rich, deep colours, plenty of dark polished wood, heavy rugs on the floor and elaborate curtaining. *Faux* panelling, either throughout the room or just below a dado rail (chair rail), can be painted in, while wallpapers inspired by archive print collections can lend an authentic touch. Window treatments in faded, tea-stained linens, old chintzes, silks and damasks are hung on heavy wooden poles with decorative finials, or enhanced by pelmets finished with lavish fringes and tassels.

These bathrooms have a warm and lived-in feel. Ornaments, photographs and books reflecting the owner's interests are arranged on every possible surface and, together with glass-fronted prints and paintings hung on every wall, would look equally at home in a study or dressing room. Furniture features prominently. A large mahogany chest of drawers, topped with a dressing-table mirror and perhaps a set of silver-backed brushes, provides storage for linen or clothes. Space permitting, there might also be a wardrobe, a linen press or an upholstered ottoman.

Accessories such as a gleaming brass bath rack, a shaving brush and bowl, a collection of glass bottles for scent, bath oils and aftershaves, and monogrammed linen hand towels and bath sheets hung on a chunky chrome heated towel rail continue the old-fashioned theme. Comfort, above all else, was the ultimate aim of the Edwardian bathroom and, thanks to modern heating and plumbing, today's reproductions far exceed those original expectations.

In deliberately not conforming to any particular style, shabby chic has become a style all of its own. Fixtures in these bathrooms are unmatched and unfitted but every piece is unusual and beautiful in its own right.

An antique blue-and-white bowl (near right) has been converted to a basin and sunk into a work surface, and is filled by means of two taps similar only in style and finish. The pipework has not been chased into the wall but is clearly visible.

The eye is drawn to the splendid bath, the vast open fireplace and the array of decorative objects in this characterful bathroom (centre right) and the general air of dilapidation merely enhances the atmosphere. The scale model of a toilet, complete with minuscule toilet-paper holder, provides an eccentric focal point, while an elegant, if tattered, armchair invites rest and relaxation.

In the pale blue bathroom (far right), an old-fashioned enamel sink is backed by a slab of grey-veined marble and flanked by cupboards painted with an appropriately distressed finish.

SHABBY CHIC

An expression which has only recently entered the home decorator's vocabulary, 'shabby chic' describes that peculiar mix of style and dilapidation which, in the right hands, can be a truly magical formula for decorating success. It takes a practised eye, a confident touch and, preferably, a crumbling French *château* or Italian *palazzo* to achieve its full glory, but there are elements which are adaptable to bathrooms on a more modest scale.

The shabby-chic bathroom is the absolute antithesis of the fitted bathroom. No elements are built in, nothing matches, pipework and plumbing are flaunted rather than disguised and fittings are either old or, at the very least, unusual. The focus is often one particular element – a magnificent cast-iron bath, a splendid wardrobe or a beautiful mirror – beside which everything else in the room pales into insignificance.

Fittings have an individual touch. They may be new but seem curious and original, as if they have been picked up at random from auctions or antique shops. This is not the look for those who have just invested in a brand-new bathroom suite; it is more appropriate for those who have inherited a bathroom and need to replace one or two items but cannot find anything that matches the existing scheme. Variety here is definitely the spice of life, and differences should be exploited rather than concealed.

Unusual pieces of furniture or decorative items are employed in unexpected ways. A china bowl, sunk into a washstand, makes an eye-catching basin. An antique jug might be used to hold toothbrushes and toothpaste. A panel of old tiles, set into the wall, could make a

characterful splashback above the bath. Objects are used and valued for their intrinsic beauty rather than their conformity to an overall decorative scheme.

When it comes to decoration, the theme is the same: nothing is conspicuously new. Walls are either left in their natural state or subtly colour-washed and irregularities in the plasterwork are left untouched rather than disguised. Woodwork can be left unpainted or rubbed down to allow the grain of the wood or the layers of paint underneath to show through. Rather than conventional blinds or curtains, window treatments might include an old velvet throw or an oriental hanging loosely draped from a pole or tacked to the window frame and swagged to one side. Using the original shutters, if your house still has them, or placing a Victorian decoupage screen in front of the window might prove an apt alternative. Upholstery is visibly ancient, with worn tapestries or washed-out chintzes covering a chair or

chaise longue. A magnificent but tattered Persian rug may take pride of place on the floor, but the boards underneath show their age and imperfections. A gilt-framed mirror is propped rather than hung above the basin while an unframed old master hangs above the bath.

The overall effect is one of gracefully faded grandeur and elegance, with every item in the room telling an intriguing and nostalgic story. But do not be deceived: the taps may not match but they produce gallons of hot water just as effectively as their brand-new counterparts and the old-fashioned radiator pumps out heat. Shabby chic definitely does not mean spartan chic.

MODERN

Most new bathrooms are modern as opposed to antique in style, but the truly modern bathroom goes one step further. Here are state-of-the-art fittings, encased in sleek, sophisticated materials such as chrome, stainless steel, sand-blasted or acid-etched glass. The emphasis is on design with a capital 'D' and the effects are invariably dramatic.

Modern bathrooms tend to be monochromatic, with clean lines and sharp contrasts. Walls are white, either painted or tiled, or may be sheathed in panels of glass or steel. The floor may be lined in studded rubber or crisply chequered linoleum in black and white or a combination of bold primary colours. Windows are uncluttered by curtains but could be shaded by metallic slatted blinds or custom-designed glass panels.

Bathroom fittings are striking to look at but always supremely functional. Many modern furniture designers have turned their hand to bathroom design, reinterpreting the standard shapes of basins, baths and taps in dramatic and highly individual ways. Some of these pieces are unique, designed to order; others are more accessible and can be found at good bathroom showrooms.

Alternatively, standard fittings can be given a contemporary feel by clever use of the materials around them. Side panels of brushed steel and up-to-the-minute mixer taps with high-tech controls would transform the most basic bath, while a standard under-counter basin could be sunk into a glass worktop for a streamlined effect. Inset low-voltage lighting adds drama to any room and even the smallest details, such as chrome cupboard door handles, can contribute to the overall effect.

STATE OF THE ART

Contemporary bathrooms make full use of high-tech materials and state-of-the-art lighting. They push back the boundaries and experiment with new techniques and combinations.

Polished stainless steel and sand-blasted glass are the key elements of this ultra-modern bathroom (left). The bath appears almost suspended above the floor due to its reflective stainless-steel plinth and to the sand-blasted glass side and end panels which are back-lit with fluorescent lighting. The polished stainless-steel panel above the bath creates another play on space, reflecting the wall-mounted taps and mixer spout.

Fluid curves counter the strong lines. There is a tubular towel rack (seen reflected in the panel) and the washstand is almost spherical with a sand-blasted glass top and a curved bowl. A bolster-style headrest adds a touch of luxury.

TALE OF THE UNEXPECTED

A fantastic bathroom may be supremely
luxurious, just plain enormous or
downright eccentric but it always
contains that element of the unexpected
– the 'gasp' factor. Stepping into this
bathroom (right) with its vista of the
garden is a case in point. Not only is the
bather virtually at one with nature –
note the extensive 'daylighting' set into
the timbered ceiling – but this is also the
most luxurious of personal health spas. A
huge whirlpool tub with cushioned mats
and pillows at either side, a massage
table and (safety regulations permitting)
a television screen allow for moments of
quiet relaxation, while the more
energetic can make use of the wall bars,
weights and exercise bicycle.

   The stone-and-white bathroom (far
right) is a more contemplative retreat.
Here objects of art and antiquity
surround the bathers as they recline in
the vast double bath with dual headrests
and mosaic surround. A decorative glass
panel on wheels can be used to screen
off the view through the ceiling-high
French windows and an alternative vista
is offered by the television screen
encased (together with a music system)
in the cupboard at right.

FANTASY

Fantasy bathrooms are literally the stuff of dreams for most of us but, with a little thought and a touch of self-indulgence, any bathroom can become a sybaritic retreat.

Fantasy bathrooms are spacious, comfortable and luxuriously decorated and equipped, with good heating, an abundant supply of hot water, a large bath, possibly fitted with a whirlpool, and deep-cushioned seating. They are rooms that indulge the mind as well as the body, and can double up as exercise rooms, health spas, media rooms or studies. In some countries, such as the United Kingdom, safety regulations preclude having hi-fi systems or televisions in bathrooms, but equipment outside the room can be connected to speakers within so the bather can relax to a favourite concerto. Similarly, a portable telephone or one with a long lead allows for conversations in the bath. Most average-sized bathrooms could incorporate a set of wall bars or an exercise bicycle, while a whirlpool bath need not take up any more space than an ordinary one.

DECORATION

A practical bathroom can still be a stylish one; in fact, decorating the bathroom often allows the imagination greater scope than the more public rooms of the house. Colour and pattern can be introduced in paint, fabric or tiles, or simply used to accent a monochrome scheme through accessories such as towels, soap dishes, pictures or plates. A favourite decorative object such as a piece of china or a special mirror is often an effective – and very personal – starting point.

Three rectangular windows, punched out
of the wall, allow the view from this
seaside bathroom (previous page, left)
to become part of the decoration. Wild
in winter and calm in summer, the drama
and movement of the seascape is
uncluttered by curtains, blinds or
architraves. The only adornment is the
trio of tiles which lend height and
interest to the windows and link with
the tiled basin surround. The walls and
vaulted ceiling are rough-plastered and
painted throughout in a deep
Mediterranean blue to echo and frame
the view outside.

A completely different 'all-over'
effect is achieved in this small
windowless bathroom (previous page,
right), lined with tongue-and-groove
boarding. A shelf at basin height divides
the boards used below from the slightly
narrower ones above, a device which
increases the feeling of height in the
room. The walls, cupboards and mirror
surround are all painted the same shade
of blue, which unifies the scheme and
allows features such as the moulded
mirror to stand out.

WALLS AND CEILINGS

The earliest Victorian and Edwardian bathrooms were either wonderfully grand, marble-walled affairs or smaller, more modest rooms bedecked with flowery wallpaper and gathered curtains. For today's bathrooms, however, the array of choices is vast and choosing the right finish can be more than a little daunting.

Start with an analysis of the room itself. The bathroom, for all its sybaritic connotations, is essentially a functional room and it is important that you take this into account when planning your decorative scheme. For example, wallpaper might be an appropriate choice for a spacious, well-ventilated room with windows, but a less practical option for a small, windowless shower-cum-toilet that is likely to generate a lot of condensation.

Damp causes problems, particularly in old houses, and it is therefore vital to protect vulnerable areas of the bathroom. Even if you do not intend to tile the whole room, consider the areas around the bath, basin and shower and remember that a shower head placed over the bath will require a much more extensive splashback than a bath with conventional taps. Alternative solutions to tiling include glass, mirror or clear Perspex (Plexiglas) screens.

Give yourself a realistic budget. Bathrooms are expensive rooms to fit and often there is little left over for decoration. If costs have to be cut, look at other ways to achieve the effect you want. Enliven plain tiles by using a coloured grout or by laying them diagonally; paint existing tiles a more appealing colour; paste inexpensive prints straight onto the wall with wallpaper paste instead of spending money on frames, and don't dismiss the idea of

WAYS WITH WALLS

Tiny mosaic tiles are used in this distinctive bathroom (far left, above) to create a decorative and practical wall finish around the basin and bath. Based on a cream-coloured ground, the pattern incorporates the charcoal grey of the cupboards and mirror frame. Note how the design depends not only on the colour but the positioning of the tiles to create a fluid, freehand effect.

At the opposite extreme, this shower room (left) uses tiles and colour on a grand scale. Large squares in a palette of earthy tones line the walls, the chequerboard effect enhanced by dark grey grouting. Pipework for the shower is concealed, with just the controls, the shower head and soap dish visible.

Tongue-and-groove panelling creates an alternative and effective form of splashback and bath surround in this simple, uncluttered bathroom (far left, below). The boards rise to chest height to protect the walls from spray from the hand-held shower. Painted pale aqua blue, using an oil-based, water-resistant paint, they give way to plain white above. Wooden hooks provide storage for towels and other necessities.

a plain white bathroom out of hand – sometimes less is more. Finally, take the size of the room into account. Turning a tiny bathroom into a palatial marble-lined 'spa' might be within your budget whereas creating the same effect in a larger room would prove extremely costly.

Paint is a wonderfully versatile medium and can play both a practical and a highly decorative role in the bathroom. Water-based paints are traditionally used on walls and ceilings alike; the latest ranges of heritage paints have added another dimension to the standard colour charts, and are ideal for decorating rooms with a period feel. Oil-based paints include gloss and eggshell, the former producing a very high gloss finish, the latter a more subtle, silky sheen. Both are suitable for woodwork and are wipeable, which is always an advantage in family bathrooms. For rooms with poor ventilation which might be especially prone to unsightly damp and mould, some manufacturers are now producing special fungicidal bathroom paints.

Applying a specialist paint finish is a relatively easy way to give walls added colour and interest. The simplest forms are the techniques of sponging, ragging and stippling; more complicated are effects such as marbling or wood-graining. Traditionally, the coloured glaze is applied onto an eggshell ground, using sponges, cloth or special brushes, but the latest innovations on the market are 'instant' paint-effect kits with rollers, which create similar results. Seal with matt varnish for a very practical, hard-wearing finish.

For a paint-free alternative, seal bare plaster with varnish, adding a dash of colour if desired, to exploit rather than conceal any imperfections in the wall.

MARINE THEMES

A treasured shell collection has been put to good use in this bathroom on a seashore theme (left). Against a background of glazed aquamarine walls, with a natural-looking, almost 'rubbed' paint effect, shells and starfish motifs are ranged above the mirror and tiled bath surround. Painted white and applied at random, they also appear on the tiles themselves, making a striking decorative feature out of a plain white, inexpensively tiled wall.

The oval mirror is framed with shells of different shapes and sizes, some set inside-out to vary the effect and to reveal the delicate colour variations of the shells' undersides. Reflected in the glass, a wooden shelf displays the overflow of the collection.

Shells and starfish are popular themes for the bathroom and, in the absence of the real thing, look out for fabrics, wallpapers and tiles with seaside motifs; stencil walls and ceilings with a variety of marine life; hang framed shell or fish prints on the walls, and choose towels and other accessories with a seashore theme.

LABOUR OF LOVE

The free-form wall design of this shower cubicle (left) was painstakingly created from fragments of tiles. You may baulk at the idea of buying perfectly good tiles only to break them into pieces, but here the final result is totally unique and eye-catching. The original shapes and colours of the tiles can be seen in the unbroken squares around the shower tray – white, black, brown and light blue – but the finished design owes nothing to straight lines or right angles. The fluid curves and scrolls are abstract and elegant and create a dramatic feature out of functional necessity.

Wallpaper is not usually recommended for bathrooms because damp and condensation can cause it to peel away. However, given a spacious room with plenty of ventilation, wallpaper is certainly an option to consider and it works particularly well in traditional-style bathrooms. Vinyl wallpapers are specially designed for bathroom use and, though formerly rather heavy and 'plasticky', some are now almost indistinguishable from ordinary papers and come in a good selection of colours and designs. Wallpaper borders can be pasted around the top of the walls at cornice level to finish a painted wall, or placed at dado-rail (chair-rail) height to divide, for example, a painted area below from wallpaper above. Use up the remainder of the roll to create imaginative 'frames' around mirrors or prints, or to add depth and interest to plain, unmoulded cupboard doors.

Tiling is an art form in itself and is a practical and decorative way of creating a waterproof surface around showers, basins and baths. Tiles come in a variety of materials including ceramic (machine- or hand-made), terracotta, marble, granite and slate, and in every imaginable colour and design. Vary the theme by using small mosaic tiles to build up a pattern or motif, or by using contrasting borders or insets.

A BATHER'S-EYE VIEW

Mirrored panels play a dual role in the bathroom. First, a mirror of some shape or size is invariably necessary for shaving, applying make-up and so on; second, thanks to mirror's reflective quality and play on light, it acts as a 'space enlarger', making even the smallest bathroom appear more spacious. A mirror can be an attractive and practical option for a dingy bath or basin alcove.

Panelling walls in wood or metal has added advantages: the panels can be used to conceal any unsightly pipework and to visually unify an awkwardly shaped room. Edwardian bathrooms often featured dark polished mahogany panels to dado- or to picture-rail (chair- or plate-rail) height, and the same technique can be reinterpreted today. Tongue-and-groove, which can be either painted or stained, is an inexpensive option;

alternatives include panels of stripped pine, limed oak, painted wood, or stainless steel for a streamlined look.

Ceilings are a neglected area when it comes to decoration and are usually painted unobtrusive white or cream. However, the bathroom ceiling does come into view when you are lying back in the bath and repays a little time and effort. Consider taking your chosen paint finish up and over the ceiling for a cosy, cocooning effect. Alternatively, create a real 'sky' by sponging soft clouds in white against a pale blue backdrop, or stencilling gold stars over a deep blue ground. If your budget allows, commission a painted mural or consult one of the specialist vinyl suppliers who use computer-aided design to create intricate patterns for floors: the same techniques can equally well be applied to ceilings.

AIMING HIGH

Ceilings are the Cinderellas of the
decorating world, almost always
overlooked when planning the
decoration of a room and invariably
painted in muted, plain colours. Here,
however, the ceiling echoes the brilliant
yellow of the cast-iron bathtub and is
very much part of the vibrant decorative
scheme (right). Partnered by pink walls
and reflected in the mirrored mosaic
detail in the tiles, the colour is warm and
bright and acts visually to lower the
ceiling, counterbalancing the tall,
narrow proportions of the room.
Accessories such as the towels and bath
mat play on the colourful theme,
ensuring a sun-filled room even on the
dreariest of winter days.

FLOORS

Bathroom flooring must be practical but it need not necessarily be cold or clinical. Just as with walls and ceilings, the starting point must be to assess the future use of the bathroom. If it is to be used by children or old people, the floor must not become slippery when wet. If it is en suite to a bedroom and therefore only for the use of one or two people, comfort might come higher up the list of priorities. Or if it is likely to be subjected to a lot of 'traffic' and wear and tear, durability and ease of cleaning will be of paramount importance. When making a choice, estimate both for the cost of buying and for the cost of laying the floor; sometimes the cheaper floor-coverings can be more expensive to fit, and vice versa.

Top of the list for comfort is carpet. Ordinary carpet is not usually recommended for bathrooms as it can become smelly and rot if continually subject to damp. However, in cases where comfort is more important than practicality, and where splashes and spillage can be contained to a minimum, this is a risk worth taking. A useful alternative is bathroom-quality carpet, which is rubber-backed and made of cotton or synthetic materials that are more resistant to a damp atmosphere.

Natural floor-coverings such as seagrass, jute, sisal and coir are also vulnerable to damp but most varieties are rubber-backed and, with care, can be used. Some natural materials are rather scratchy and therefore unsuitable for bare feet, so test them for feel as well as appearance. Good-quality bath mats, particularly if used over old-fashioned cork boards, can help considerably towards keeping any floor-covering dry.

Vinyl and linoleum are traditional bathroom floorings which have recently come back into favour and are available in an excellent variety of colours and patterns. Both are relatively cheap to buy and to lay (depending on the state of the original floor) and extremely easy to maintain. Contract-quality vinyls are completely non-slip and would be appropriate in bathrooms with open showers. Cork tiles, another traditional option, are similarly easy to clean, appealing to look at and comfortable on the feet. They do, however, need to be properly laid and sealed in order to function well. A more

NATURAL CHOICES

Natural materials make good choices for bathroom floor-coverings. Traditional terracotta tiles lend warmth and character to this all-white bathroom (left). They provide a firm base for the roll-top bath with its cast-iron legs and are proof against any accidental splashes or spray from the hand-held shower. The drain hole shown in the foreground makes cleaning less of a chore; water can be sluiced under the bath and storage units, then wiped up with a mop.

Seagrass matting is rubber-backed and can be laid with or without underlay. A smooth base is important and a layer of hardboard underneath to cover uneven floorboards is often a prerequisite. The natural textures and tones of seagrass complement the decoration of this colour-coordinated bathroom (right) with its polished plaster bath and basin surrounds and translucent cotton curtains. A cotton bath mat protects the matting beside the bath while the pair of stainless-steel basins are set well back to minimize spillage. Chunky soaps and a collection of wooden boxes continue the natural theme while the sculpture makes a striking focal point in the corner of the room.

THE BARE ESSENTIALS

Sometimes in our haste to select a floor-
covering, we neglect the obvious choice
– the existing floorboards. To make a
satisfactory floor, particularly in a
bathroom where bare feet are the order
of the day, the boards have to be in
reasonable condition. Replace any rotten
boards and re-fix loose ones before
sanding and sealing for a smooth and
lasting finish.

   In this old-fashioned bathroom (right)
the floorboards have been given a
decorative twist with a black-and-white
painted chequerboard design. While the
grain of the wood is still clearly evident,
the effect is a play on the classic vinyl
bathroom floor and works well with the
old-fashioned roll-top bath and wrought-
iron washstand. By contrast, the wooden
panelling and Shaker-style pegs have
been given a pale limed finish.

modern look can be achieved with rubberized studded flooring which is available in a variety of textures and colours. Though totally waterproof and practical, it can be awkward to clean if the studs are too prominent.

Marble, ceramic and terracotta tiles are all highly appropriate for bathrooms in that they are water-resistant. If very highly glazed, they may be slippery when wet, but non-glazed, non-slip and textured tiles are all available. A tiled floor can be cold on the feet and care should be taken when planning the heating of the bathroom to counter this; underfloor heating is one possible solution. When laying new tiles on floors (or walls), try to ensure that grouting is flush with the surface of the tiles; insufficient or chipped grouting creates the perfect haven for dirt and germs.

A useful detail for any bathroom with a tiled or vinyl floor that needs regular cleaning is a drain hole. This need not take centre stage but can be discreetly concealed in a corner, and even if it is not possible to slope the floor towards it, it makes washing a great deal easier, as well as taking care of any accidental spillage from the bath, basin or shower.

Finally, many houses have wooden floorboards which, if in reasonable condition, can be suitable as a bathroom floor. The boards need to be sanded down and then polished or painted – stencilling is a particularly decorative option – before being sealed. Add colourful cotton rugs for extra comfort in front of the basin or the bath. In the absence of old floorboards, consider laying a new wooden floor. Warm and comfortable on the feet, wood can be stained to any shade and is certainly one of the most durable and timeless materials.

The floor in this light, airy bathroom (above) was given the simplest possible treatment. The original boards were painted in plain white gloss, echoing the white stencilled designs on the turquoise walls, and topped with colourful cotton rugs. The floor catches the light that streams in through the window and bounces off the mirrored panel on the wardrobe.

LIGHT AND SHADE

Privacy is important in the bathroom, but there are alternatives to the ubiquitous net curtain. The windows in this all-white bathroom (right) are screened by simple white cotton Roman blinds which provide privacy while allowing sunlight to stream into the room. Their completely plain, unfussy design does not detract from the ornate detail of the tiles, which are the chief decorative focus of the room.

Internal shutters such as the ones in this bathroom (centre right) allow the bather to see yet not be seen. Light filters through the openwork pattern, casting ever-changing shadows on the walls. Recalling the latticework screens of the Moroccan *hamman*, the shutters lend a tantalizing air of mysticism to this otherwise functional modern bathroom.

An ugly view from a bathroom window can be successfully screened from sight by the use of a decorative glass panel (far right). Opaque glass alternates with lustrous blue to create a striking feature out of a formerly unprepossessing window. Good artificial lighting and the mirrored alcove help to compensate for the lack of natural light.

WINDOWS

Bathroom window treatments depend as much on what is outside the window as on the interior scheme. Urban houses may look out onto blank walls or neighbours' windows, both of which it might be preferable to screen off. A country bathroom, on the other hand, might open onto a marvellous vista with no other house in sight, and in this case privacy would not be a major consideration.

Ensuring privacy often means designing one form of screening for the day and one for the night. A voile curtain is effective in daylight but, at night, with the light behind

it, the bather is completely visible from outside. Conventional window treatments such as blinds or curtains are one solution; another, particularly if the view is poor, is a fixed screen of some sort – a wooden lattice, perhaps, or a decorative opaque- or coloured-glass panel.

Often used at night or early in the morning, the bathroom is always equipped with artificial light – many bathrooms are completely windowless. Hence, window treatments need not be constrained by the desire to maximize daylight. Use it and enjoy it if it is there but do not be afraid to screen it, either by a fixed panel as described above or perhaps by draping a curtain across the window or hanging a blind trimmed with a deep fringe.

Blinds are particularly practical for bathrooms, as they can be rolled up and kept well out of the way of damp floors and work surfaces. Roller blinds, either plain or made up in the laminated fabric of your choice, are one of the most basic forms. Roman blinds are equally simple, hanging flat against the window when down and pulling up into neat 'accordion' pleats. Pull-up or gathered blinds give a more decorative effect, and can be finished with a contrasting frill or pleated edging.

Even the simplest curtains can add great style to a bathroom. Gathered muslin, looped over a pole and held back at either side of the window with large bows, can add a touch of softness to the most functional of rooms; calico and ticking are inexpensive alternatives, while sprigged floral patterns add old-fashioned charm. It is also worth remembering that the original function of curtains was to exclude draughts and, in an house without the benefit of double glazing, thickly lined and interlined curtains might make the difference between a cosy bath and a chilly one.

Though the chrome finish of the details such as the towel ring and taps gives this bathroom (above) a sense of unity, the main decorative focus is the large circular mirror, complete with a useful magnifying mirror on a swing arm.

A few carefully chosen accessories can help create a restful and relaxing environment. This folding stool (right, above) provides a place to sit but is light enough to be easily moved to gain access to the cupboards behind, while towels are kept within easy reach on the chrome rail above. While some would consider a set of bathroom scales a necessity rather than a decorative accessory, this particular model also looks stylish.

ACCESSORIES

Bathroom accessories range from the purely practical to the purely decorative and run the whole gamut in between. In few other rooms do functional elements contribute so much to the decoration, with even mundane items such as soaps, towels and bath mats playing an important role.

When choosing your bathroom accessories, space and storage are two criteria to be considered. Space, or the lack of it, will limit choices as to what can be displayed and how. Some bathrooms barely have room for the minimum daily requirements, others can be used to display favourite collections of china or pictures. Make the most of the space available: a shelf at picture-rail (plate-rail) height is a decorative way to display objects while keeping them clear of water and out of the children's reach; a wall cabinet makes a perfect high-level base for a hand-painted plate, a china jug or an arrangement of dried flowers; a boxed-in toilet cistern becomes a useful shelf for soaps and bottles of scent and bath oil.

Objects in daily use need to be accessible, hence the use of open shelves, bath racks, towel rails and toilet-roll holders. Positioning needs to be practical: towels should be easy to reach from both shower and bath, if possible. Alternatively, double up and have two towel rails. There might be space at one end of the bath to keep shampoo, extra soap, bath oils and loofahs, as well as plants or decorative china.

Start with essentials. Bath towels, hand towels, face cloths, robes, a stool or chair and a bath mat can all be colour-coordinated with your scheme, but do not forget

the more mundane items such as the toilet-roll holder, toilet brush, towel rail or ring, hooks for bathrobes, a shelf or cabinet for medicines, toothbrushes and so on. Bathroom cabinets come in a selection of woods as well as chrome, brass, nickel, gold plate or plastic (white and coloured). A mirror, either framed or unframed, is another essential, and can be cut to size. Bevel the edges of an unframed mirror for a smarter finish.

Next, consider 'extras' which might both ease the running of your bathroom and contribute to its overall look: a bath rack, available in a variety of metal finishes

USEFUL EXTRAS

Accessories should be tailored to your requirements. In this bathroom (right, above) the accessories are more than purely decorative objects: note the folding table positioned so that the bather can still enjoy a drink while relaxing in the tub, the wooden floor mat by the basin – a warmer option for bare feet than chilly ceramic tiles – and the laundry basket with wheels allowing for easy manoeuvrability.

Chrome accessories work particularly well with bold colours. Here, the laundry basket, bath rack and table are all finished in chrome, while the soap dish, toothbrush holder, mirror and towels are in bright primary hues, taking their cue from the smartly patterned yellow-and-white tiled floor.

For bath-time bookworms, a chrome bath rack (right, below) is the ultimate luxury, keeping reading material well out of harm's way and still providing plenty of space for face cloths and soaps.

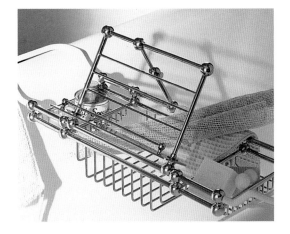

and woods; soap holders, either fixed to the wall or in the form of attractive china dishes or large shells; a shower rack; a laundry basket.

Even the smallest object can lend character or colour. Soaps and bath oils look decorative if artfully arranged. Toilet paper can be stored in a wicker basket or a large porcelain bowl. Toothbrushes can be kept in fine china, coloured glass or brightly patterned plastic cups. And nothing gives a bathroom greater character than a collection of favourite objects: a montage of photographs, clipped under glass; old certificates; inexpensive paintings and prints; shells, starfish, pebbles – anything goes.

LET THERE BE LIGHT

Bathrooms often require a combination of general and task lighting, the former casting a diffused glow over the whole room, the latter targeting certain areas. In this bathroom (right) the inset bathroom spotlights provide the general light while the row of vertical lamps

above the basin cast the task lighting needed for shaving or applying make-up.

The natural light that streams through the window of this cloakroom (above) is supplemented by the task lighting cast by the wall-mounted lamp. The wrought-iron sconce complements the ornate shell-shaped basin and swan's-head tap.

5 2 ■

Mirror is an essential requirement in every bathroom and its reflective qualities can be used to enhance the room's lighting, as illustrated by the two bathrooms shown at right. The mirrored panel above the basin (right) visually doubles the effect of the three exposed light bulbs and their smart chrome fixings, bouncing the light back into the room. White tiles on the walls and the floor and accessories in crisp red-and-white add to the overall feeling of brightness. In the all-white room (far right), a pair of powerful inset spotlights provide task lighting above the basin but are also sufficient to light the whole room, including the shower area at the far end, thanks to the mirror which extends right across the alcove. A skylight provides additional light by day.

LIGHTING

Nothing is worse than a dingy bathroom and, given that this is a room that is most likely to be used in the early morning and late at night, a dark, gloomy atmosphere can only be avoided by well-planned, effective artificial lighting.

The main areas to target are the basin, where activities such as shaving can be disastrous without adequate light, and, to a lesser extent, the bath – particularly if you enjoy a leisurely soak with a good book. Depending on the size and shape of the room, choose between ceiling lights and wall lights or use a combination of the two.

Hanging lights can be decorative but are often impractical in a bathroom, especially if ceilings are low. Water and electricity are a dangerous combination and for reasons of safety and space it is better to opt for inset spotlights which fit flush to the ceiling. These do require adequate space between the ceiling and the floor (or roof) above, however, so check that your ceiling is suitable before you buy. Special bathroom spotlights, where the bulb is sealed into the unit to protect against splashes, are available for areas such as shower cubicles or low-ceilinged bath alcoves.

Don't forget that lighting also has a decorative role to play. Theatrical spotlights inset around the basin mirror make a feature of that area as well as providing an excellent source of light. Alternatively, for a different effect, an attractive, old-fashioned mirror can be enhanced by a pair of traditional lamps with coloured shades, set on wall-mounted sconces.

FITTINGS

Whatever the style and decoration of your bathroom, there are certain elements that are constants in every scheme: the bath, basin, toilet, shower, bidet and storage units. You may not require all of them but making the right choices is vital. Most bathroom fittings, if properly installed and cared for, will last many years and a mistake will be expensive and time-consuming to put right. Arming yourself with a few facts before you buy will help you to choose what is right for you and your home.

ON TAPS

Taps, together with plug, chain and 'waste' (the technical term for the plug hole and overflow) are often expensive 'extras' additional to the cost of baths and basins and it is important to choose designs that are appropriate and function well with your choice of fittings. The taps are wall-mounted in this streamlined modern bathroom (previous page, left), with a single swivel-arm mixer spout feeding into each of the twin stainless-steel basins. All plumbing is concealed behind the wall and in the units below the custom-made glass work surface. There is ample storage space both within these cupboards and in the rectangular niches in the wall, to leave the basins and work surface completely clear and uncluttered. Uplighters set into the top of the cupboards cast a translucent glow upwards through the glass.

Wall-mounted above the bath (previous page, right), one set of taps controls the flow of water to both the bath and the shower. The bold, square design of the taps is matched by the chunky spout and chrome grip handle. The shower has a hose long enough to be used for hair-washing in the bath as well as conventional showering.

BATHS

Traditionally made of enamel-lined cast iron, today's baths also come in steel, acrylic and new composite synthetic materials. Price may be a deciding factor in determining your choice but bear in mind that a cheap bath may not offer the best value for money in the long run.

Cast iron is still popular for traditional bath designs, and is strong, hygienic and exceptionally durable. Steel is a cheaper and lighter alternative; it, too, wears well but, like cast iron, has the disadvantage of being cold to the touch.

Moulded acrylic baths are warmer and come in a variety of colours but are not nearly as strong as metal baths and are more liable to scratch. Reinforced with fibreglass and mounted on a steel frame, they are light and easy to install. Look for a bath with a relatively thick layer of acrylic and a firm, well-designed casing; it is unnerving to step into a bath that 'gives' with your weight. Check especially around the curves of the bath where the acrylic may be thinnest and where the bath will be under most strain. Proper installation is also important to ensure that the bath is correctly supported and to safeguard against leakage.

TAKE THE PLUNGE

Most of us opt for metal or synthetic baths, but there are alternatives. Taking its cue from oriental soaking tubs, this bath (left) is made of wood. Extra deep, it can be used as a plunge pool for a refreshing dip after exercise or a sauna, or the bather can relax and float, in semi-suspension, in warm water up to the neck. The slatted seat is an optional extra and the chrome spout was specially designed to reach from the wall over the rim of the bath. Also available in more conventional materials, compact, deep baths are useful for small spaces.

REST AND RELAXATION

This curvaceous oval bath (left) is carved from a single piece of marble. As there are no taps or waste attachments to dictate which way to lie, the bather can either look outwards through the window at right (not visible) or gaze inwards at the surrounding monochrome space. Cool, restful and uncluttered, the room is devoid of any architectural or decorative details, cocooning the bather and allowing his mind as well as his body to be rested and refreshed.

The bath is filled by means of a floor-standing mixer spout which curves elegantly over the rim of the bath and is controlled by means of taps semi-concealed in the wall behind.

BACK TO BASICS

This stainless-steel bath (right) illustrates the concept of the metal bath at its most literal level. Devoid of panelling or enamel, the metal reveals its streamlined, reflective qualities to the full, making a striking feature in this marble-lined bathroom. The gleaming surface is easy to keep clean and, though cold to the touch initially, warms up quickly and is more heat-retentive than conventional cast iron.

The bath was designed to fit precisely into the alcove and the shower spray and taps have been wall-mounted accordingly. The high-level porthole window echoes the metallic theme and accessories are neatly contained in a net hung on the wall and in a glass storage jar.

HIGH AND LOW

As well as being panelled, baths can be raised on legs or, alternatively, sunk into the floor. A platform, running along two sides of this bathroom (right), creates a built-in surround for the spacious sunken cast-iron tub. A conventional bath in the same position would have cut into the deep sash window; given that there was sufficient space below floor level, this arrangement provided the ideal solution.

The ornamental ball-and-claw legs of a traditional cast-iron tub can be painted to match the body of the bath as shown here (far right) or given a contrasting colour. This Edwardian-style tub looks just as much at home in this sleek, spare setting as it would in a period room, its curved lines offset by the terracotta floor, white tiles and floor-to-ceiling glazed doors. The shower area is defined simply by a recessed floor and, on warm days, is literally open to the elements.

Relatively new to the market are baths made from composite synthetic materials developed and designed specifically for bath manufacture. Thicker and more rigid than acrylic, these materials are easily moulded, long-lasting and repairable. Baths made from synthetic composites keep the heat in well – six times longer than acrylic and twelve times longer than cast-iron baths – and are resistant to knocks and scratches. Their disadvantage is that they are comparatively expensive.

Baths can either be freestanding, as in the traditional cast-iron roll-top tub with ornamental legs, or panelled. Standard baths are usually panelled but matching side and end panels are generally not included in the price of the bath. Most baths are fitted into corners but if you decide to centre the bath against a wall, giving access from both sides, do not forget to budget for an additional side panel.

Bath sizes do vary, so it might be worth stretching out in a few different ones in the showroom before you buy.

Deciding factors should also include: lower sides if the bath is to be used by children but higher sides for the elderly so that they do not have to bend down very far if leaning on the side for support; a non-slip, flat base if there is to be a shower over the bath; a handle on one or both sides if required; tap holes positioned close enough together or far enough apart for the taps of your choice; the width of the bath (the larger the bath the more hot water it will require and if your supply is limited a narrower or contoured bath is a more economical option), and the possibility of fitting extra 'luxuries' such as whirlpool spas with jets of water which are particularly relaxing after hard exercise, as well as helpful in alleviating muscle stiffness or pain.

Before jettisoning your old cast-iron bath, consider restoration. Re-enamelling is not a long-term solution but the process of polishing the existing enamel to smooth out roughness or stains is very effective and can bring an old bath back to remarkable new life.

SHOWERS

Whether to bathe or to shower may still be the subject of debate but most modern bathrooms can, with a little planning, offer both options. The days when a feeble trickle of lukewarm water passed off as a shower are long gone and booster pumps and powerful shower heads have done much to restore the shower's image. On average, a shower uses one-fifth of the water of a bath and is a much quicker – and, some say, more hygienic – way to get clean.

Showers either draw on the hot and cold water tanks of the house, mixing the water to the required temperature, or are supplied direct from the rising cold-water mains, heating the water as required by means of a wall-mounted electric or gas-fired heater. If the first option appeals, it is essential that you consult a plumber first. Problems can occur if taps are turned on or toilets are flushed while the shower is on, causing the cold water supply to be diverted and making the shower suddenly too hot. The flow of water from the tank to the shower head is another factor to bear in mind as this will determine the pressure of water. A booster pump may be required. A shower supplied from the cold-water mains may be a less expensive and disruptive option, but for safety reasons, the gas- or electric-fired heater should be fitted by a professional.

Most modern showers are thermostatically controlled, avoiding sudden, potentially dangerous surges of too-hot water. Shower heads vary enormously; some have adjustable sprays allowing for both invigorating jets and a relaxing soft rinse. Fixed shower heads are neat and compact but detachable handsets are flexible and can be used at low level to wash hair or rinse out the shower.

If the shower is to be positioned over the bath, some sort of waterproof screen will be necessary. Panels of clear safety glass or toughened plastic, either fixed or hinged, are effective; a shower curtain is a relatively cheap alternative and is easy to install. The walls around the bath will also need to be splashproof up to shower height.

Shower trays for self-contained shower units come in various forms of vitreous china, acrylic, composite synthetic materials and enamelled steel. Sizes vary and rectangular and triangular forms are also available; if you are intending to tile the walls around it, check that the join between tray and tile can be properly sealed to prevent leakage.

Shower doors can be hinged like conventional doors, or can pivot, slide or fold back; these latter options can be useful in cramped bathrooms where there might be little room for a shower door that opens outwards.

TILE STYLE

Whether your shower is contained within a cubicle, positioned over a bath or 'open-plan', the walls around it need to be splashproof. A practical and relatively inexpensive option is to tile the area to shower height, ensuring that the grouting is waterproof. Plain white tiles line this shower (far left), including the recessed niches carved out of the wall for soap and shaving kit. The shower itself is a particularly compact model with all pipework concealed neatly behind the tiled wall.

The shower area in this bathroom (centre left) is open-plan, and walls and floor alike are tiled with terracotta squares. Triangular marble slabs provide shelf space and the shower fitting combines a slide rail and a hose for complete flexibility.

The curved casing of this enclosed shower (left) is designed to retain as much water as possible, the position of the shower head (not visible) directing the spray away from the deliberately narrow opening. Lined inside with white mosaic tiles and painted outside to match the walls, it makes an unusual feature in this attic bathroom.

GLASS WORKS

Positioning the shower over the bath
necessitates a waterproof screen as well
as surround. Standard shower curtains
are available ready-made in washable
and wipeable materials. Use plastic or
rust-proof hooks and fixings.

The two bathrooms shown here
illustrate the use of fixed or hinged
panels. The screen of glass blocks (right)
provides a semi-opaque divider, allowing
the bold tiling behind the bath to show
through and retaining the fall of water
at the shower end of the bath.

By contrast, the bath (centre right) is
completely contained behind a four-
panel glass-and-chrome screen, creating
in effect an extra-large shower cubicle.
The two central sections fold back and
the clear glazing allows light from the
window into the room.

TOILETS AND BIDETS

Most toilets and bidets are made from vitreous china, a form of clay which is fired at a very high temperature and glazed to create a durable and hygienic surface. There are numerous different designs to choose from, some looking to the past, others more streamlined and modern. More important than the cosmetic differences, however, are the different styles of plumbing and operation. Low-level toilets, where cistern and pan are connected by a short length of pipe, are one of the most common forms. Close-coupled toilets do away with the connecting pipe altogether, with cistern and pan incorporated into one construction. Back-to-wall models contain all outlet pipework within the shape of the toilet, while the cistern is hidden behind panelling for a neat and streamlined look. Wall-hung toilets are similarly compact but are mounted on concealed brackets, leaving the floor space below completely clear. High-level cisterns, set high on the wall above the toilet and worked by means of a pull-chain, look particularly good in traditional-style bathrooms.

Toilets usually operate on the 'wash down' principle, whereby waste is carried away by water flushed around the rim of the bowl. Also available are quiet and efficient syphonic flushes which draw down the water rather than pouring it in. Conventional waste pipes are bulky, some 10cm (4in) in diameter, and can be a problem to fit, especially in a small space. A useful solution is to choose a toilet fitted with a macerator which shreds waste on flushing and pumps it through a small bore pipe, about 2.5cm (1in) in diameter. This pipe, unlike normal waste pipes which rely on gravity to bear matter away, can run horizontally and therefore allows the installation of a toilet almost anywhere in the house.

Bidets can be either floor-standing or wall-hung and operate on two different principles: either the bidet fills in the same way as a basin (over the rim, from conventional or mixer taps), or it fills from beneath the rim and often includes a spray option. Consult an expert before buying a bidet or toilet to ensure that your chosen model is suitable for your house and conforms to local water regulations.

Plumbing guidelines usually recommend that the bidet is sited as near as possible to the toilet and the two sit side by side in this cool, all-white bathroom (above). Positioning toilet, bidet and, if possible, bath and basin in a line is most cost-effective, allowing for one straight run of water pipes. Here, matching fixtures, together with co-ordinating taps, mixer spouts and shower fittings, give the room a strong sense of unity. Spray from the shower attachment would fall within the confines of the capacious corner bath, so there is little need for a shower screen, especially as walls and floor are tiled throughout. Downlighters wash the walls with light and efficient ventilation has been installed to compensate for the lack of windows.

The basin area is invariably a focal point in a bathroom and, complete with mirror, good lighting and accessories, can be made to look decorative as well as functional. Cantilevered out from the marble-tiled worktop and splashback, the curvaceous lines of this basin (right) are still visible. Everyday items are stored in the cupboard below and there is space instead for a striking vase. A heated ladder-style towel rack means that warm towels are conveniently at hand.

Double pedestal basins are a feature in this mirrored bathroom (centre right); their generous proportions and linear design look neat and streamlined and together they fit snugly across the width of the room. The mirrored recess provides ample space for bottles and hairbrushes, supplemented by wall-hung accessories such as toothbrush holders, mirrors and towel rails.

By contrast, two basins have been built into a specially designed unit in this bathroom (far right), incorporating work space above and a towel rail below. The shape and construction of the unit perfectly complements the circular stainless-steel basins and the quirky curves of the taps and mixer spouts.

BASINS

Most basins, together with toilets and bidets, are made of vitreous china. They come in a vast array of sizes and designs and can be white or coloured, but do be wary about choosing darker tones for these bathroom fixtures: they show up any hard-water scale and soap deposits much more clearly than white or pastel colours.

Basins can either be supported on pedestals and secured against the wall, or be wall-hung. The former allows pipework to be concealed and is often the more decorative option, as the design of the pedestal usually complements the other fittings in the suite. The pedestal also provides a stronger base if, for example, the basin is going to be used for washing clothes. Wall-hung basins free up space below and can look neat and streamlined,

particularly if pipework is concealed in a half-pedestal. They also leave the floor uncluttered for ease of cleaning. A third option is a counter-top basin, which can be sunk into or under a work surface and can be combined with built-in storage underneath. If space is limited and the design of the basin permits, mounting taps on the wall above will free up more of the basin shelf for toiletries.

Some counter-top basins have a pronounced rim designed to sit over the work surface, ensuring a watertight seal. Others are specially designed with no rim at all and are intended to sit under the work surface; in this situation, it is vital that the work surface extends far enough over the edge of the basin to prevent leaks but not so far that there is an overhang which will harbour dirt and germs.

BEFORE YOU BUY:

- Go to bathroom showrooms and try out fittings for size as well as style.
- If starting from scratch, choose fittings that complement each other; basins, toilets and bidets come in matching suites and you will need to select an appropriate bath.
- If you are trying to coordinate old fittings, beware the different shades of 'white' available. They range from pale grey through to almost-cream and finding a perfect match can be difficult.
- White bathroom fittings are timeless classics; darker colours tend to date quickly and have the added disadvantage of making soap stains even more obvious.
- Don't forget to budget for essential 'extras' such as taps and plugs for basins and baths, and levers and seats for toilets.
- Ensure that a shower is suitable for your home before you buy. The position of the water tanks, the water pressure and the existing plumbing will all affect your choice.
- Work out your storage requirements at the outset rather than as an afterthought; they may have a bearing on the fittings you choose.

door and a built-in light fitting and shaver socket, wall-hung units provide useful over-basin storage for toiletries and other everyday items. Floor-standing cupboards are usually designed for use with a specific basin, either one with a decorative upstand or surround in the traditional Edwardian style, or a counter-top basin which can be sunk into a work surface. Also available are standard bathroom shelves in glass, wood or plastic; some have holes designed for toothbrushes, others have small decorative rails to contain the items on display.

Every bathroom is different but some often under-utilized areas include the space below the basin, the wall space above the bath, the area around the hot-water tank (provided it is easily accessible) and around the toilet cistern. Under-basin cupboards (see above) are one space-saving option but a simple and decorative way of creating extra storage here is to hang a gathered frill around the basin. This can be attached to the basin itself by means of Velcro or tacked on to a wooden frame, but either way will cost little in terms of time and money. Wall-hung shelves, corner cupboards and Shaker-style pegs are all ways of utilizing space over the bath in an attractive and practical fashion, while boxing-in the toilet cistern creates an instant shelf. If your hot-water tank is located in the bathroom it may be feasible to install slatted shelves around it, creating the ideal airing/storage cupboard for linen and laundry.

Don't neglect the idea of comfort in the bathroom. A heated towel rail, either run by electricity or connected to the hot-water system, will provide warm, dry towels as well as a modicum of heating, while an armchair, upholstered in soft towelling, or a cushioned window seat provides somewhere to relax.

STORAGE

Storage is a necessary element in most bathrooms and it is a fact of life that however much space is available you will always have too much clutter to fill it. Depending on the size and style of your bathroom, towels, toiletries and other items can either be concealed behind cupboard doors or curtains or left visible on open shelves. A practical combination of the two, with less decorative items such as cleaning fluids and medicines hidden well out of sight and the reach of small children, often proves ideal.

Ready-made storage units include wall-hung cabinets and floor-standing cupboards. Often fitted with a mirrored

A PLACE FOR EVERYTHING

The choice of storage is usually dictated by the style and fittings of the bathroom. Recessed into the marble-tiled wall, this mirrored cabinet (left) blends easily with its contemporary surroundings. Inset lighting enhances the coppery tones of the interior as well as illuminating the basin, while the mirrored door conceals the items inside and also serves to reflect daylight into the room. The narrow gap between the basin and the window allows just enough room for a towel rail.

In this attic room (far left, above), the exposed beams set the tone for the chunky travertine worktop and natural linen curtains, tied with tapes, which conceal extensive storage space below. The arrangement of pictures and mirror echoes the slope of the roof, and a high-level towel rack makes use of the often redundant wall space above the bath.

Under-basin storage is given a completely new meaning with this custom-designed cylindrical cabinet (far left, below). Tapering down from the elegantly curved basin, the doors open to reveal a smart black interior with a chrome and glass shelf.

STORAGE SOLUTIONS

As well as fitting conventional cupboards, assess the potential of any under-used areas such as above the bath or around the basin. A sturdy shelf at cornice level like the one in this all-white bathroom (above right) creates a perfect display area for accessories as well as a neat framework for mirrored panels below.

This basin (below right), set into a simple, mosaic-tiled surround, incorporates an open shelf for towels. The remaining space beneath is filled with wicker baskets with handles which can easily be pulled out and used for storing clean linen or dirty laundry.

Sometimes the simplest measures can serve to increase storage space. Positioning the bath out from the wall rather than up against it (far right) freed up space under the windows to right and left for basins set into cupboards. Their unusual curved design allows easy access to both shelves and bath taps.

SMALL
BATHROOMS

With a little planning and careful measuring, a bathroom can be created out of a remarkably compact space. Whether it involves new use of an attic or other previously redundant area or whether it is a case of carving the space out of an existing room, it is often surprising just how little is needed to create that invaluable extra bathroom. Specially designed fittings, devices such as under-basin cupboards and clever use of mirror and lighting can all make the most of the smallest space.

ON REFLECTION

Mirror plays both a decorative and a functional role in small bathrooms, acting to make the room look larger and as an effective, waterproof splashback.

In this attic bathroom (previous page, left) a triangular mirrored panel makes a feature of the dividing wall between shelves and basins. Conventional vertical mirrors above the basins were impossible to fit due to the sloping ceiling, and the panel plays a practical role, visually extending the chunky pine work surface. Note how effective the simple, modular shelving becomes when filled with an array of well-chosen and imaginatively displayed accessories.

Lining opposite sides of a room with mirror creates reflections 'ad infinitum'. The entire basin corner in this bathroom (previous page, right) has been mirrored, allowing plenty of 'viewing' space as well as bouncing light back from the mirror on the opposite wall and from the window.

SAVING SPACE

As space is at a premium when planning a small bathroom, be ruthless about what you need. List out the essentials: do you need a bath and a shower or could you survive with just one or the other? Is a bidet absolutely vital? Can you make do with a small corner basin rather than a full-size one? Plot out the fittings on a piece of graph paper (see page 12) and take into account the space required between them, particularly if the room is to be used by more than one person.

The small bathroom is a fact of modern life and there are numerous space-saving fittings and fixtures on the market. Compact plunge baths compensate for lack of

DECORATIVE DETAIL

Even the smallest bathroom can be given character and charm with decorative objects and accessories, but it can require imagination and ingenuity to display them. In this tiny bathroom (far left), space is limited and the toilet is positioned right up against the bath. With little room for conventional shelving, the toilet cistern provides a display area for a brass sailing ship. There are other space-saving measures at work here: the large, framed mirror has the effect of making the bath alcove appear larger, and the slatted wooden blind is a more appropriate window treatment for a small room than a festooned curtain.

Sky-blue panelling, running horizontally to resemble the hull of a boat, provides a high-level shelf for a collection of starfish (left). Often under-utilized, the picture-rail (plate-rail) area of the wall provides a safe haven for bathroom ornaments, well out of splashing range, and here the angled points of the starfish lend a deceptive feeling of height to the room and draw the eye up towards the decorative arch of the window. White porcelain bottles are neatly graded by size on a decorative hanging shelf and the starfish motif reappears in white above the basin.

■ 7 3

ATTIC LIFE

Attic conversions do not usually require planning permission, though you should consult an expert if you plan to make changes to the exterior, such as fitting new windows. If the attic space is to include a bathroom, take advice from an experienced plumber before you begin.

This bathroom (right) has been carved out of the roof space, and the ceiling on one side slopes steeply to the floor. Blocking off the lowest section with a false wall (see cross-section) allowed the toilet cistern and pipework to be hidden and also left space for storage. The bath fits across the room, one end almost touching the sloping ceiling but, with taps fitted on one of the long sides rather than the end, the bather can stretch out in comfort. The door opens outwards but a sliding door could be fitted if space is at a premium.

Two dormer windows flood this attic bathroom (far right) with daylight and the all-white scheme makes the space look bright and airy rather than cramped. All-over splashproof tiling negates any need for a shower cubicle and the shower, fitting neatly under the peak of the roof, is open-plan with the rest of the room. An extractor fan fitted into the sloping ceiling provides extra ventilation.

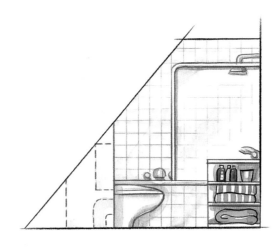 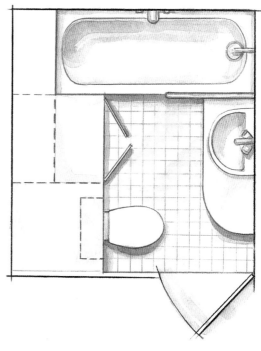

length by extra depth, allowing the bather to enjoy a relaxing soak despite restrictions of space. A corner bath can be useful, fitting more easily into certain rooms than a conventional rectangular bath. Taps can be wall-mounted or fitted to one side of the bath, allowing the bather a little extra room to stretch out.

Installing a shower over the bath is one space-saving measure, but self-contained, freestanding shower units take up less space than you might think and can be fitted either within the bathroom or elsewhere in the house.

Supplied with four panels and sometimes a roof as well to keep in steam and reduce condensation, they are completely watertight and do not rely on existing walls for support. Provided that plumbing and ventilation requirements can be met, they can be fitted into spaces such as under-stair cupboards or hallways as well as into bedrooms or one-room apartments.

Wall-hung basins are ideal for smaller bathrooms. Available in all shapes and sizes, including tiny corner models for hand-washing, they free up valuable floor

THINK SMALL

- Keep fittings to a minimum and consider space-savers such as wall-hung basins and 'back-to-wall' toilets.
- Design access to the bathroom to take up as little room space as possible: hang the door to open outwards, or fit a sliding door or two half-doors.
- Maximize storage to minimize clutter, using wasted empty space such as the area under the basin.
- Keep to a one- or two-colour scheme, continuing it through from walls and tiles to towels and accessories.
- Long, lined curtains can be bulky. Substitute unlined voile or muslin, or a Roman or roller blind.
- Visually 'open out' the space with mirrored panels and/or framed mirrors.
- Utilize areas such as boxed-in cisterns and picture-rails (plate-rails) to display decorative accessories.
- Accent your decorative scheme with well-planned lighting inset into the ceiling and/or set above the basin.
- Scale up rather than down: large pictures or objects make a room look more spacious, while costly materials such as marble, polished wood and brass are more affordable in small quantities and add a touch of luxury.

space. Alternatively, counter-top basins set into cupboards allow for valuable extra storage space beneath and on the worktop itself. Streamlined modern mixer taps are compact alternatives to traditional taps and leave more room on the basin shelf for soaps, bottles, toothbrushes and so on.

'Back-to-wall' toilets and bidets, in which pipework is hidden within the unit, have a neat finish, while wall-hung versions free up floor space and are particularly compact, especially if the cistern is boxed in or hidden behind a panelled wall. A standard toilet requires an area of about 140cm x 70cm (55in x 28in) for comfortable use but new slimline cisterns can reduce this. If the room is high enough, an old-fashioned high-level cistern fixed to the wall above the toilet is a good space-saving alternative, as the toilet pan can sit against the wall beneath it rather than projecting forward from the cistern, as it does in more modern designs.

One of the main obstacles to installing a new bathroom, whether large or small, is often the plumbing for the toilet. As discussed in the previous chapter, toilet

CURVES AND CONTOURS

Unusually shaped rooms call for unusually shaped baths. If you think you have insufficient space for a tub it is worth investigating the variations on the standard rectangular theme. Curved and contoured baths mean fewer hard angles, allowing for easier passage in a restricted space; corner baths can provide a full-length tub in rooms where a normal rectangle might not fit; small, square plunge baths take up minimal space, as well as conveniently doubling up as shower areas.

In this triangular bathroom (right), a contoured bath has been fitted into the narrowest angle of the room, with pipework for both shower and taps neatly concealed. The mosaic-tiled floor is stepped up around the bath, accentuating its curves and creating a splashproof surround. A clear glass panel screens the shower. Despite the size and shape of the room, there is still space left over for double basins, wall-hung to leave the floor clear, and a row of spacious cupboards above. The streamlined mixer taps are a compact option for small basins, leaving more space to either side for soap, toothbrushes, and so on.

waste pipes are bulky and sometimes awkward to connect, especially in small spaces; consult an architect or plumber first. One possible solution is a toilet fitted with a macerator (waste shredder). These require only a narrow pipe, which can be run horizontally rather than on a gradient and fits more easily behind walls. If the bathroom is close to or en suite to the bedroom, ask to hear the macerator in action before buying; they can be disconcertingly noisy, especially in the middle of the night.

Awkward corners

If your bathroom is an unconventional shape, use all the space available to the full. An L-shaped room might provide the perfect location for a shower cubicle to be tucked away in the shorter branch of the 'L'. A square room, on the

other hand, would lend itself better to a small bath with a shower head over it, screened with a curtain or panel. An awkwardly steep, sloping ceiling in an attic room can be turned to your advantage: screen off the lowest area with a false wall and use it for storage or to conceal pipework and cistern for the toilet and bidet; the higher-ceilinged level is then free for a bath and/or shower. Rethink the access to the room: a full-size door can take up valuable space if it opens inwards and two half-doors or a sliding door might be more appropriate. Sometimes simply rehanging the door to open outwards can make all the difference. Utilize any recesses or other nooks and crannies: the most unlikely spaces can be used for storage, either for everyday items or for decorative accessories that will lend your bathroom character and charm.

Decoration

Decoration can play an important part in the small bathroom. A monochrome or near-monochrome colour scheme makes for an unfussy, uncluttered look, especially if carried through to towels and other accessories. A small room can be ill-proportioned; draw an imaginary line around the walls at dado- or chair-rail height and paint them a darker shade below and a lighter shade above to give a feeling of height. Conversely, darkening the ceiling will draw down an over-high room.

Finally, do not be afraid to scale up. A large picture or a bold sculpture can give a cramped room an unexpected feeling of space, whereas smaller items may simply accentuate the lack of it. Use mirrored panels or framed mirrors to visually enlarge a room and install good lighting to brighten the whole scheme.

ANGLES AND DIAGONALS

Space is very restricted in this sunny yellow, top-lit bathroom (left) but there is still room for a full-sized bath and basin. Even with the bathroom mapped out on graph paper, the owners might have thought twice before placing the bath and basin so close together but, thanks to the unusual angles of the bath, there is just enough space both to use the basin and to pass between it and the bath to reach the toilet. The toilet itself is a neat, compact 'back-to-wall' design, with the cistern and pipework hidden behind the tiled wall. Panels of mirror above the basin and triangular shelf and at the far end of the bath 'open out' the space, while the tiling has been imaginatively designed: not only does the smart black-and-white border add a dramatic note but the minuscule floor space has been tiled diagonally, echoing the angles of the room and creating a deceptive feeling of space. The black bath handle and black-and-white towel radiator pick up the theme of the border and even towels and soap are fully colour-coordinated.

■ 77

INDEX

Page numbers in italics refer to illustrations

PUBLISHER'S ACKNOWLEDGMENTS

Conran Octopus would like to thank the following photographers and organizations for their permission to reproduce the photographs in this book:

1-3 photograph: Simon Kenny (designer: Danny Venlet)/Belle; 4-5 Jerome Darblay; 6 Deidi von Schaewen; 8-9 Alexander van Berge; 9 Bernard Toillon/S.I.P./Elizabeth Whiting & Associates; 10 Hoetze Eisma/V.T. Wonen; 13 Hoetze Eisma/V.T. Wonen; 14-15 Russell Brooks/Australian House & Garden Design; 16 Marianne Haas/Elle Decoration/Scoop; 17 Verne Fotografie; 18 Rodney Hyett/Australian House & Garden Design; 19 photograph: Roland Beaufre (chateau Smith Haut-Lafitte)/Agence Top; 20 photographer: Alexandre Bailhache (stylist: Catherine Ardouin)/Marie Claire Maison; 21 Spike Powell/Judi Goodwin/ Elizabeth Whiting & Associates; 22 Richard Davies (architect: John Pawson); 23 Chris Drake/Homes and Gardens/Robert Harding Syndication; 24-25 Deidi von Schwaen; 25 Elizabeth Whiting & Associates; 26 James Mortimer/The Interior Archive; 27 Tim Beddow (designers: Craig Hamilton & Tina Joyce); 28-29 'Colourwash'; 28 left: Fritz von der Schulenburg/The Interior Archive; 30 Rodney Hyett/ Australian House & Garden Design; 31 left Tim Beddow; 31 right: Hoetze Eisma; 32-33 Tim Goffe courtesy of House & Garden; 34-35 Verne Fotografie; 35 Jean Pierre Godeaut; 36-37 Jacques Dirand; 37 Tim Goffe/Conran Octopus; 38 above: Trevor Richards/Homes & Gardens/Robert Harding Syndication; 38 below: Simon Wheeler; 39 Paul Ryan/International Interiors; 40 photograph: Peter Rad (designer: Nicola McGaan)/Belle; 41 Hoetze Eisma; 42 right: Nadia Mackenzie/Elizabeth Whiting & Associates; 42 left: Weidenfeld Nicolson Archive; 43 photograph: Pascal Chevallier (designer: MichelKlein)/Agence

Top; 44 Abitare; 45 Marianne Haas/Elle Decoration/Scoop; 46-47 Hotze Eisma; 47 right: photograph: Gilles de Chabaneix (stylist: Rozensztroch)/Marie Claire Maison; 48 right: Jacques Dirand (designer: Gordon Watson); 48 left: photograph: Nicolas Tosi (stylist: Marion Bayle)/Marie Claire Maison; 49 Henry Bourne/Elle Decoration; 50 left: David Parmiter; 50 right: V.T. Wonen; 51 below: Polly Wreford/Country Homes & Interiors/Robert Harding Syndication; 51 above: Hoetze Eisma/V.T. Wonen; 52 left: photograph: Nicolas Tosi (stylist: Julie Borgeaud)/Marie Claire Maison; 52 right: Paul Warchol; 53 right: photograph: Neil Lorimer (architect: Andrew Norbury)/Belle; 53 left Wulf Brackrock; 54-55 Dennis Gilbert (designer: Rick Mather); right: John Hall; 56 Jan Baldwin; 57 Claudio Silvestrin; 58 Richard Bryant/Arcaid; 59 right: Reiner Blunck (designer: Geoffrey Pie); 59 left: James Mortimer/The Interior Archive; 60 left: photograph: Neil Lorimer (architect: Andrew Norbury)/Belle; 60-61 Hoetze Eisma/V.T. Wonen; 61 right: Fritz von der Schulenburg/Country Homes & Interiors/Robert Harding Picture Syndication; 62 Alexander van Berge; 63 right: Russell Brook/Australian House & Garden Design; 63 left: Gilles de Chabaneix/Elle Decoration/Scoop; 64 left: photograph: Simon Kenny (designer: Chris Hosking)/Belle; 64 right: Marianne Majerus (designer: Barbara Weiss); 65 John Hall; 66 below: Marzia Chierichetti - Fabrizio Bergamo/Elle Decor Italy; 66 above: Marianne Haas/Elle Decoration/Scoop; 67 Paul Warchol; 68 below left: Bernard Touillon/S.I.P./Elizabeth Whiting & Associates; 68 top left: Jan Baldwin/Homes & Gardens/Robert Harding Picture Syndication; 68-69 Guillaume De Laubier/Elle Decoration/Scoop; 70-71 Hotze Eisma; 71 John Hall; 72 Simon Brown; 73 Jerome Darblay; 75 Jacques Dirand (designer: Compain); 76 Richard Davies/Future Systems; 78 Schoner Wohnen/Camera Press

AUTHOR'S ACKNOWLEDGMENTS

I would like to extend my warmest thanks to the team at Conran Octopus for their help and encouragement, which made this project both enjoyable and remarkably stress-free. I would also like to thank my husband and my children, who still find it highly amusing that anyone could actually write a whole book about bathrooms.